PRAISE FOR *THE NEW CRUSADES*

"*The New Crusades* is an intellectually rigorous history of global affairs, but it is also a series of moving narratives about what it is like to be human, Muslim, and betrayed."

—SARAH KENDZIOR, author of *The View from Flyover Country*

"This text offers the most nuanced and subtle treatment on the subject to date. Khaled Beydoun has the mind of a scholar, the soul of a freedom fighter, and the pen of a poet."

—MARC LAMONT HILL, coauthor of *Seen and Unseen*

"Beydoun harmonizes his breadth of legal expertise with his rich personal insights and experience, piecing together a foundational text on the faces of global Islamophobia plaguing Muslims near and far."

—IMAM DR. OMAR SULEIMAN, Yaqeen Institute for Islamic Research

"Beydoun courageously places himself in the thick of a global struggle as a Muslim, as a scholar, and most importantly as a thinker who writes beyond borders."

—ROKHAYA DIALLO, journalist

"An accessible and compelling read for the general public."

—JOHN L. ESPOSITO, Georgetown University

"*The New Crusades* brilliantly describes China's war on Islam. It also examines the hypocrisy of some of the powers that be, standing alongside Ukrainians rightfully, but silent on China's active genocide of Uyghurs."

—RUSHAN ABBAS, Campaign for Uyghurs

"Beydoun deftly weaves together social science, law, and compelling narratives to reveal how Islamophobia shapes the lives of Muslims the world over."

—SHIRIN SINNAR, Stanford Law School

Named in remembrance of

the onetime *Antioch Review* editor

and longtime Bay Area resident,

the Lawrence Grauman, Jr. Fund

supports books that address

a wide range of human rights,

free speech, and social justice issues.

The publisher and the University of California Press Foundation gratefully acknowledge the generous support of the Lawrence Grauman, Jr. Fund.

THE NEW CRUSADES

Islamophobia and the Global War on Muslims

||||||||||||||||||||||||||||||||||||||||||||||||||||||||||||||||||||||||||||||||||||||||||

KHALED A. BEYDOUN

Foreword by Kimberlé Crenshaw

UNIVERSITY OF CALIFORNIA PRESS

University of California Press
Oakland, California

Library of Congress Cataloging-in-Publication Data

Names: Beydoun, Khaled A., 1978– author. | Crenshaw, Kimberlé, writer of foreword.
Title: The new crusades : Islamophobia and the global war on Muslims / Khaled A.
    Beydoun ; foreword by Kimberlé Crenshaw.
Description: Oakland, California : University of California Press, [2023] |
    Includes bibliographical references and index.
Identifiers: LCCN 2022036126 (print) | LCCN 2022036127 (ebook) |
    ISBN 9780520356306 (hardback) | ISBN 9780520976061 (ebook)
Subjects: LCSH: Islamophobia. | Muslims—Non-Islamic countries.
Classification: LCC BP52.5 .B49 2023 (print) | LCC BP52.5 (ebook) |
    DDC 305.6/97—dc23/eng/20220825
LC record available at https://lccn.loc.gov/2022036126
LC ebook record available at https://lccn.loc.gov/2022036127

32 31 30 29 28 27 26 25 24 23
10 9 8 7 6 5 4 3 2 1

This book is about people.
Not myths.

Contents

Foreword

I MET KHALED BEYDOUN in August 2001 during the UCLA
School of Law's special orientation program for Critical Race
Studies students. Khaled came to UCLA Law to enroll in our
program, the first and only one of its kind. Fresh out of college and hailing from Detroit, Khaled caught my attention,
and I have not lost sight of him since.

I had taught the nation's first Critical Race Theory class at
UCLA about a decade earlier. By 2001, the course had blossomed into a full concentration with the onboarding of several colleagues of color with expertise in race matters and
the law. Twenty years ago, long before the massive reckoning around race and injustice that would take place in the
spring of 2020 and galvanize millions of people all over the
world to take to the streets in protest, Critical Race Theory
was an expanding body of knowledge reflecting the legal
dimensions of racialization that impact many racially marginalized groups. A core observation that stretched across

several projects attached to CRT was the notion that race and racism were not biologically-based concepts but socially constructed, partly by law. The effort to Think, Teach, and Act through a CRT prism on racial power that transcended the narrow understanding of racism as merely prejudicial treatment based solely on skin color opened a world of possibilities to explore the dynamics of Islamophobia. Our program and its wider footprint were growing, but the reach of critical race thinking to Islamophobia was at that time only a possibility, a door left open by our anti-essentialist understanding of racism. Any subordinated group could be subject to racism; we knew this much. The particulars of these other racisms—how they function, what they are called, whether the analog to colorblindness could be ameliorative—were questions that a practitioner and theorist might consider.

Khaled was destined to turn this theoretical possibility into a reality. The 9/11 terror attacks and the War on Terror coincided with Khaled's entry into law school, changing him and the entire world. Contemporary politics forged Khaled's journey to becoming a leading critical race theorist in the fast and furious slide into Islamophobic discourse and policy in 2001. In some ways, a sudden break with the religious chauvinism and cultural othering that characterized the pre-9/11 world was afoot. In other ways, the slide was continuous with the *othering* codes that described Muslims as suspect and unassimilable. As these dynamics unfolded, Khaled adapted CRT's analytic tools and interpretive prisms as tools in his journey to becoming one of the leading thinkers in naming, analyzing, and contesting Islamophobia.

The student I came to know initially in my "Race, Representation and the Law" seminar was on a mission to fill intellectual voids and connect analytical dots with his unique blend of a Detroit fighting spirit and a broadening worldview. Khaled found himself directly immersed in the fire during the earliest stages of the War on Terror, experiencing a unique analog of being criminalized for *doing anything while Black*. Both Arab and Muslim, Khaled studied and learned the law during those bleak formative years of the War on Terror from 2001 to 2004. *His experience* was formative in the ways that living in a discordant state of existence always is; the promises of formal equality under the law say one thing, but the exceptions allowed by a panoply of justifications for second-class treatment created something entirely different. Khaled was a student in several of my courses, and I intimately witnessed that for him, Critical Race Theory and the law, Islamophobia, and Intersectionality were not merely academic exercises or abstract ideas. They were tools—potent, practical tools—that he wielded as an activist and as an intellectual. As his professor and mentor, and later on, his colleague and friend, I witnessed Khaled evolve as a trailblazer in the Critical Race Theory and Islamophobia fields, fusing disciplines and connecting discourses to elevate dimensions of Orientalism and Islamophobia that were grounded and institutionalized in and by law.

Let me share a story. Days after the Bush administration declared war on Iraq, Khaled appeared in class noticeably rattled. He had a keffiyeh on his bag and a look of concern on his face. Khaled had relocated to Los Angeles for school but came from a city where Iraqis flocked in waves as refugees. He'd grown up alongside victims of wars new and old. And so when Edward Said, the prolific Palestinian intellectual, was set to speak on campus, Khaled lobbied not only for me to allow him to miss class to attend the lecture but to require the entire class to attend. He was a strategist, an activist, and an intellectual, introducing his classmates to a trailblazing voice during a moment of unprecedented urgency and alarm. Not satisfied with the simple goal of mastering legal concepts or rules, he strove to create tools that could educate others and impact change. I was fortunate that Khaled urged our class to attend that lecture, which would be one of Edward Said's last. It was a gift to be on the receiving end of a masterful address and mobilization given by Said and Khaled, respectively. Edward Said died that same year, and it was clear how much the passing of such a heroic intellectual and truth-teller deeply affected Khaled. And at the same time, it was clear that Said's influence was like water to a seed, one uniquely situated to yield new fruit. So, I encouraged Khaled to write—to expand his observations, experiences, theorizations, and cautions about the world that the War on Terror had made and unmade, all under the imprimatur of law. He did so and has not stopped, as the trenchant narratives you will read in the coming pages reveal.

My confidence in Khaled, however, extended beyond the academic voids he could fill. After his graduation, I reached out to him as an organizer in the battle to preserve affirmative action in Michigan. Khaled's ability to speak from within and to serve as an effective interface between communities was crucial in galvanizing Muslim and Arab communities to find common cause with their Black and Brown neighbors. While the coalitions to preserve affirmative action could not overcome the coordinated efforts of well-resourced and highly organized factions bent on destroying it, the brainstorming, debating, and organizing that we pursued in partnership with the African American Policy Forum (AAPF) would deepen our understanding of the parallel and overlapping dimensions of Islamophobia. Khaled became a regular participant at AAPF's annual social justice writers retreat, where he drew connections between the new frontier of American imperialism abroad and domestic campaigns of so-called counterterrorism and long-standing systems of racism against Black people and sexism against women. Those retreats offered freestyle intellectual engagement, and Khaled's organic observations from those informal debates and observations would later appear in his books and articles. "Muslims are being racially constructed as terrorists," he observed during one of our retreats, noting how "the War on Terror was a global imperial project." These discussions often featured ideas that would later form the thesis of his subsequent publications, including his critically acclaimed first book, *American Islamophobia: Understanding the Roots and Rise of Fear.* The importance of internationalism embodied in *The New*

Crusades was similarly a central topic that participants discussed at length under the sweltering sun in Jamaica. In all of this, I learned that Khaled was a fighter, unafraid to stand his ground and fully commit to the battle at hand. By then, it was a foregone conclusion that his ideas had to be heard in a world that marked Muslims as the enemy. And while there were many ways for Khaled to amplify his voice, a career in legal academia offered a unique platform to uncover the multiple ways that Islamophobia—under construction by law—could be understood as natural and even essential. This kind of aggression in the name of self-defense is not new to the US or elsewhere worldwide. Still, Khaled has adapted this dynamic to the particulars of the War on Terror to create usable knowledge in the pursuit of freedom.

In this respect, Khaled stands apart because he deftly connects American racial justice crises with parallel global concerns. The son of a single mother, Khaled and his family fled war to land in one of the poorest, and most segregated cities in the United States. He experienced firsthand how American imperialism abroad delivered him into the belly of the beast, where systematic forms of discrimination faced by poor, Black, and Brown people are taken as natural facts of life. Khaled is Muslim, Egyptian, a Detroiter, and a son raised by a single mother during an era of citywide school shuttering, the crack epidemic, the undoing of affirmative action, and the dawn of the War on Terror. While the latter has made the most vital imprint on his writing and public voice, the other dimensions of life that shape his perspective are evident in the soul and spirit of his work. Acknowledging the salience of Intersectionality and structural inequality in his writing and worldview, he is deeply concerned about those living on the margins and the individuals often overlooked by commentators. As he notes, "This narrative of global Islamophobia is at the delta of crusades old and new." Most fundamentally, this book centers on the voices of the very victims caught in the crucible of state-sponsored and prevalent Islamophobia. In the words of Palestinian poet Mahmoud Darwish, those perilous middles are where Muslims are forced to live and strive to "live free, or die like the trees, standing up."

The New Crusades conveys that spirit of empathy; it sets Khaled's writing apart. Moreover, his commitment—his mission—is to make his work accessible to everyone. As a result, he has emerged as a leading public intellectual on matters tied to Islamophobia and Critical Race Theory. As a scholar, his work on theorizing Islamophobia and its relationship with the law has been groundbreaking, and in many ways he has played a significant role in refining the term "Islamophobia." His ability to shift from academic to public scholar to activist makes Khaled's work indispensable.

The New Crusades is an intersectional milestone. It lucidly illustrates how converging systems of subordination, power, and violence related to Islamophobia are experienced across the globe. For example, Uyghur Muslim women locked away in Chinese prison camps must endure the intersecting fury of torture and sexual violence rooted in a genocidal project that rips them from their children. Their "Islamophobic intersection," if you will, is dramatically unlike that of a French Algerian male in Paris, whose masculinity is marked with the suspicion of terrorism in a liberal state that criminalizes headscarves worn by his mother or sister—dimensions of the global Muslim experience that Khaled understands well, and brings to life in this book. Race, gender, location, the form of government in a host nation, and so much more determine the circumstances that Muslims occupy in countries across the globe unified by a War on Terror that spreads Islamophobia beyond borders and across intersections. Khaled elevates the voices and experiences of the victims of Islamophobia; he reveals the stunning heterogeneity of how Islamophobia is imposed and experienced. Repeatedly, his eye turns toward the furthest margins and to the most vulnerable intersections that many of his contemporaries neglect: the Somali widow blinded by a relentless sun and forced to live between CIA surveillance and local terror groups, the young Rohingya widow swept from the ethnic cleansing in Myanmar to poverty in Chicago, or the dynamic Uyghur activist in Turkey who champions the cause of his people although each word he utters, every post he publishes, may endanger his family members in China. Khaled fuses these disparate stories of Islamophobia into a compelling and cogent whole. *The New Crusades* is a text about humanity that maps the furthest margins of Islamophobia while centering the voices of the most ignored victims of intersecting fronts of global subordination. This must-read book is a masterful embodiment of the ways in which critical race thinking and Intersectionality are moving toward an overdue reckoning with Islamophobia.

INTRODUCTION

Two Tuesdays

SOMETIMES, YOU CAN SENSE that something terrible has taken place. You just know it. The ringing and vibration of your phone doesn't let up. It rings and rings, and after you silence it, it shakes and shakes. In these moments, turning it off seems the best option. But doing so would disconnect you entirely. So it rings then shakes, shakes and rings. Until those familiar sounds form a spellbinding shrill that shouts what the weight of the mood silently whispers to you.

You don't want to hear it. But you can't help it and can't ignore it. The force is relentless, and that feeling stretches itself in every direction. It fills every corner of the room and everything within it and within you. Its urgency, amplified by the nonstop shaking and buzzing of that black device that you watch from a short distance, summons you toward it. That black mirror, which keeps you connected to people and places far beyond while simultaneously trapping you inside its four corners, becomes the messenger of news you don't want to receive. News you've heard before, which stalks you and stalks you at every turn of life.

That *feeling* lords over you before you know what event or incident triggered it. It orders you, simultaneously, to run toward it and heed its message and to avoid it at any and all costs. This existential paradox fixes upon you for moments that feel like forever. Stopping life as you know it and reminding you, although you have hardly forgotten, that *your life* is defined more by these enigmatic moments than those passing, prolonged stretches that parade as routine life in the spaces between.

These are new world warnings. The stalking shadows of our brave new world that digitally blur distances geographic, real, and surreal. A world where the devices we faithfully carry in our palms are at once mechanisms of ongoing surveillance and machines of doomsday warnings.

At 11:43 a.m. on August 4, 2020, the nonstop shrill of that phone finally won me over. I walked over to it and then opened up a Pandora's box of messages from friends and family: "Beirut has been bombed!" and "Did you make sure Aboudy and his kids are OK?" Seconds later, I opened files of videos and images that, with gruesome color and lucid horror, confirmed the texts. The visuals verified that the city that was home to so many family and friends, and that I called home during a stretch of my childhood, had been targeted by what seemed to be a foreign airstrike. Or, as some reported, a terror attack.[1]

I continued to scroll through my phone, watching a bleak roll of images and videos sent by family and friends, mixed with real-time posts strangers shared on social media. This is a dystopian custom in our bleak new world—tragedy, and all of its morbid detail, is instantly disseminated and explicitly conveyed on our small mobile screens even as it is still unfolding. The reels rush in, in real time, without stopping. And oftentimes, without filter or forewarning.

Time froze. And I stood there fixed along with it, absorbing surreal scenes of streets I knew so well, in a city seated deep in my heart. A place where our apartment building on Verdun Street was submerged by the gray smoke from the explosions and the ghosts of faded memories. A place where only twelve months earlier, my mother and I walked to family visits, to restaurants, and took evening strolls to maintain strength in her aging legs, only miles from the port where the explosions detonated and brought Beirut back down to its war-torn knees. Explosions that, in that apocalyptic aftermath that Beirut knew so well from wars past, revealed that more than 200 people were killed, 300,000 people were left homeless, and more than 100,000 homes were destroyed.[2] For "a nation pitied" for its modern misfortunes with war and the internal rifts that sink it even deeper, the Beirut blasts revealed that terror is an enterprise not tied to any one faith or nonfaith.[3] While news outlets and pundits pushed us to blame the catastrophe on the familiar list of Muslim networks, in line with War on Terror impulses, the truth revealed that global crusade's fundamental lie: that terrorism is a uniquely Islamic enterprise. Sometimes, terror is a consequence of corruption, negligence, and as this book illustrates, religious and even secular ideology. More than often, terror is the outcome of old empires and their modern successors, chiefly the United States—my country—which occupies the citadel of neocolonial wars on terror and the new crusades they have spawned.

Flashbacks of memories, recent and those rooted in my childhood, juxtaposed with the reel of horrors I absorbed from my cell phone screen.

Sometimes, you just get *that* feeling. That eerie feeling in the pit of your stomach that looms on the other side of those text messages that you have yet to open, or those incessant phone calls a voice inside orders you to avoid, is what you already know. Not *knowing* in terms of collecting all of the facts and appreciating what has actually taken place, but that deeper, metaphysical *knowing*—a knowing not spurred by detail or evidence, but memory and trauma. Trauma and memory, the two legs of that shadowy feeling that rips through your gut and stirs the fear and anxiety that grip your head and hold your heart.

I felt that feeling for the first time on the morning of September 11, 2001, the day that spawned the War on Terror and that feeling it permanently seeded within me. From that Tuesday onward, and the countless days in between, that feeling has swelled in line with the twenty-year-old "war" and evolved into a forlorn companion I have come to know as well as I know myself. In fact, that feeling has become part of who I am—as a Muslim, an American, a scholar, a public intellectual, a son—every dimension of an identity contoured by it since that tragic Tuesday in September more than two decades ago.

That feeling, which at first felt foreign but evolved into familiar companion, is hardly mine alone. Rather, it is one that lives within and walks alongside 2 billion Muslims all over the world. It, on Tuesdays and days before and beyond it, rumbles and pulsates like that mobile device on my dining table signaling the occurrence of another disaster in a city that raised my father and houses so many family members and friends. It stalks us, from afar, then comes menacingly close when disaster strikes. This was a disaster I felt in my core before hearing word of it. That feeling I experienced for the first time that dark Tuesday morning on September 11, 2001, loomed over me and over those tragedy-stricken Beirut streets again on the Tuesday morning of August 4, 2020.

Two Tuesdays. Two mornings on opposite sides of the world, on distinct sides of a War on Terror, which stand as permanent signposts of an evolving sense of difference spawned by it. Two Tuesdays, that for me serve as bleak bookends of a narrative about Islamophobia that was no longer isolated to one country or one population alone, but had become a global phenomenon. A phenomenon that ripped across manmade borders and the divides of time, one morbidly fused together by technology while pushed forward, violently, by new empires spearheading new crusades against Muslims in Lebanon, the United States, and the world over.

The world was not the same place on August 4, 2020, that it had been on September 11, 2001. In fact, it was irreversibly and unmistakably different. But so was I.

I was no longer an anonymous Muslim American student sitting on the sidelines as disaster unfolded in New York City and Washington, DC, and Pennsylvania. I was now a law scholar and public intellectual recognized for his work on law, critical race theory, the War on Terror, and more profoundly, Islamophobia. My first book, *American Islamophobia: Understanding the Roots and Rise of Fear,* connected global audiences with my academic work and helped me launch a term I helped shape into a trenchant tool wielded by students and activists, scholars and non-scholars. The War on Terror changed the world, but it also indelibly altered my trajectory and shaped who I am. Despite my best efforts to pursue other paths, the weight of this *war* and the new world order it ushered in pulled me in, and I was helplessly submerged by it.

I could not stand on the sidelines even if I wanted to. People looked to me to make sense of senseless disasters that fell upon Arabs and Muslims. Members of my faith community, in particular, sought me out to make rational and intellectual sense of that very *feeling* that shook through them when crises rattled cities like Boston or Beirut, New Delhi or New York, and to predict what those events that implicated or impacted Muslims spelled for them and their loved ones.

The feeling that moved through me on that Tuesday in September twenty-one years ago, and countless days after that, is that unseen front of Islamophobia experienced by every Muslim. However, Islamophobia as a subject of academic study is, as it stands, bereft of that feeling and the firsthand experiences of Muslims on the ground. The human condition of Muslims, and the countless intersections they occupied in the world remade by the War on Terror, was absent from academic literatures. In turn, Muslims were essentialized as terrorists or targets, faceless culprits of violence or voiceless victims of state aggression, flattened on the pages of academic treatises and newspapers without the rich color of firsthand testimony we experienced off of them.

Islamophobia can be rationally theorized and configured into a system of popular and state-sponsored bigotry, and this is the approach I took in my first book. Scholars interrogating Islamophobia on the domestic front, including sociologist Erik Love, root American Islamophobia in its host nation's history and contemporary systems of racism.[4] This position is echoed and expanded by law scholar Sahar Aziz, who pays close attention to American constitutional principles—most notably the religious freedom safeguarded by the First Amendment—to challenge Islamophobia in the United States.[5] Both Love and Aziz build on a rich literature that conceives of Islamophobia as an emanation of American racism, with the War on Terror "racializing" Muslims as the "terrorist other."[6]

The work of these scholars and many others has expanded the discourse on Islamophobia's relationship to racism, particularly American racism. But as the War on Terror spun distinct myths in different countries and the world spun along with it, an understanding of Islamophobia untethered from the American experience, its distinct history, and unique configurations of race and racism has become essential. Islamophobia is now more than ever a global phenomenon, and the War on Terror has evolved into an imperial project that advances it across longitudes and latitudes.

Media scholar Deepa Kumar makes this very case in her important book *Islamophobia and the Politics of Empire*.[7] Building on her expertise in the realm of journalism, Kumar interrogates Islamophobia as a transnational menace that predates 9/11 and the ensuing War on Terror. The book sounds the alarm that Islamophobia is not uniquely American, despite the hegemon's leading role in facilitating its global expansion and entrenchment over the past two decades. Kumar's framing of Islamophobia as an imperial campaign is vital to the spirit and scope of this book, which documents the most nefarious crusades of imperial

Islamophobia.[8] While tying Islamophobia to racism, broadly and globally construed, Kumar's imperial framing highlights the importance of gender, or what political scientists and myself have theorized as "gendered Islamophobia."[9] She observes that "Orientalism had strong gendered dimensions, and the era also saw the development of colonial feminism, that is, feminism being weaponized to serve empire."[10] Like its epistemological mother, Islamophobia is strategic with its deployment of "imperial feminism," and as governments across the globe spearhead Islamophobic crusades in the form of hijab bans and the regulation of Muslim women's bodies, disregarding Islamophobia's gendered dimensions would veil its most menacing tentacles.[11] Following the intellectual direction of pioneering Muslim feminists like Fatema Mernissi, *The New Crusades* seeks to unveil how societal and state-sponsored Islamophobia is often first concerned with policing female bodies: "The so-called modesty of [Muslim] women is in fact a war tactic."[12] To further particularize the imperial anatomy and aims of Islamophobia as a global project, international law scholar E. Tendayi Achiume notes in her landmark treatise "Migration as Decolonization" that "the present era is defined by *neocolonial* imperialism, even if formal colonial imperialism has been outlawed."[13] This novel era of neocolonialism is spearheaded by the United States, and its War on Terror stands as the principal instrument in intensifying Islamophobia as it expands its global footprint.

The scholarly canon on Islamophobia is expanding, and thinking about it in line with empire reveals an even deeper, venerable trove of knowledge. However, the existential episodes that Muslims endure, and the feelings spawned by Islamophobia as it creeps in and toward us, is *feeling* and by its very nature often *irrational*. It cannot be reduced to neat technical terms or meticulously crafted definitions intended for scholarly citation. While academic discussion of Islamophobia is vital to our ability to understand it, and indeed to fighting it, it must be coupled with the voices of those on the ground who endure it. This is the liminal space seldom explored, which is why I, as a public scholar, chose to write this book, and it is where the coming pages will take you.

Islamophobia is, to borrow the words of Jean-Paul Sartre, "what we feel, what we live, [and] what we are."[14] That state of being that sits in the pit of our stomach and then steers our fears toward the worst possible ends is what being Muslim in the world fundamentally means. It is that unmistakable feeling that rears its menacing head when disaster strikes, then struts alongside you while you try to pick up the pieces and stave off indictment, or worse, demonization, by keeping your head down, concealing your faith, or apologizing for evil acts to which you bear no connection. Islamophobia is a subject of serious academic study, and I am entrenched in it. But it is also existential drama, and for millions around the world, the source of unfathomable trauma, pushing me to give voice to victims silenced by circumstance.

Before friends and families began to pick up the pieces of shattered glass and debris in Beirut on Tuesday, rumors about the possible culprits circulated. These rumors, particularly for those wed to the War on Terror, were refracted through an Islamophobic prism. Was it Hezbollah or a transnational Islamist terror group tied to the Islamic State of Iraq and Syria (ISIS), as some suggested? Or were the explosions the work of Israel or a diabolical conspiracy staged by Iran to push the embattled nation of my father toward war with Israel, as others speculated?[15] Islam was, then and always, a central character in the theater of terror, even when it was not Islam or Muslims at fault, or an act of terrorism at all.

What seemed to matter mattered little, and it mattered even less as that irrational feeling inside of me transported me back to the streets of Beirut. Back to the days of my childhood, living across from Goodies market, blocks from Beirut's Corniche, during the blackest days of the civil war that decimated the streets and *abducted* formative years of my childhood.[16] A period in my life when the daily trek home from school passed through a mise-en-scène of misery and mangled bodies, shattered buildings with more shattered beings living within them.

The vivid images I viewed on the glass screen of my phone that Tuesday were identical to those I took in from the back seat of a car as a child, only distinguished by that feeling that set in thirteen years after my childhood days in Beirut. That feeling that I did not know as a child from 1986 to 1988, but one that after 9/11, I recognized as readily as I knew the faces of my own niece and nephew.

The culprits of the Beirut explosion were not Muslim terrorists or "Islamists," but the slow-plotting terror of government kleptocracy, corruption, and neglect.[17] Terror of a less conspicuous sort, enabled by former empires and abetted by foreign banks.

But again, those irrational episodes of fearing the worst, then bracing for it, is what characterizes the Muslim experience in a world remade by the War on Terror. A world where Islamophobia is far more than just an enterprise of intellectual examination or a racial project to be diagnosed and then dismantled—but even deeper in the marrow, an existential state of being that dwells in the core of nearly 2 billion people across the globe. A feeling sowed and spread by an "imperial" campaign, as it has been incisively branded by Kumar, that feeds the distinct crusades persecuting Muslims across the world.[18]

This book begins and then builds from that feeling. It seeks to remove it from its hiding place and give voice, flesh, and bone to how Muslims across the globe respond to disasters that unfold in their respective towns and cities, provinces and nations. My first book, *American Islamophobia*, examined Islamophobia as it has unfolded in the United States and offered a platform for engaging with people all over the world about how they experience anti-Muslim animus, bias, and violence. During the intervening years, my research and advocacy, travels and relationships moved me to examine Islamophobia as a global phenomenon.

Listening to the testimony of Muslims from places that I knew very well, like Egypt or Canada, while learning about ongoing crises in places that were beyond my familiarity, like Myanmar and China, compelled me to write this book. Their stories, which I collected by way of questionnaires and interviews, in-person discussions and virtual conversations, are the very lifeline of this project.[19] I met many people through formal channels, and others through the organic passages of activism, personal travel, and kindred travail, both online and in off-the-grid spaces in Istanbul, Cape Town, and cities and villages beyond and between.

As a Muslim American scholar known for his work on Islamophobia, I occupy that rare space between its rational and irrational axes. I have spent nearly a decade theorizing about the very meaning of Islamophobia and have published numerous academic articles on the subject, its relationship to the law, and intersecting areas of concern. Yet my faith and identity apart from my scholarly profile keep me tethered to the irrationality of it all when disaster strikes and during the turbulent aftermath that the War on Terror prolongs and even threatens to make permanent. I am, at once, the *subject* and *object* of the War on Terror, and that unenviable status carves a pathway into the intimate spaces of similarly situated peoples, all over the world, who stand at different points but feel what I feel.

In his memoir *Out of Place,* Edward Said characterized this liminal space as a source of "strength" and "possibility."[20] In the journey of writing this book, this *liminality* transformed into a wide portal that enabled me to connect with Muslims in places near and far. I spoke to them as both a scholar of Islamophobia and a fellow Muslim, our shared liminality giving me access to their stories and shoring up the trust that only empathy can build. They knew me, and through affinity and familiarity, a bridge toward knowing them was constructed. This bridge has led me to places distant and distinct, and even more importantly, contexts in which Muslims suffer invisibly, ignored by cameras.

Kindred lines of faith and common political experiences overcame linguistic barriers, and technology dissolved geographic distance. When the coronavirus pandemic crept in and closed down the world in the spring of 2020, virtual connectivity was strengthened, and ironically, enabled me to meet with people who were difficult to reach, and in some instances would have otherwise been unreachable. I forged relationships on social media platforms, where I was recognized for my work and advocacy, and technology formed a bridge when the world locked down travel.

Their individual accounts are undeniable, but it was the collective tapestry of feelings that compelled me to tell this story of global Islamophobia and to write *The New Crusades*.

The word "crusades" evokes images and ideas that overpower its technical definition. This is especially the case when the subject is religion, and specifically, the religion of Islam: the adversary that European Christian forces fought against to reclaim the Holy Land during the eleventh, twelfth, and thirteenth centuries. Tying Islamophobia to imperialism and unveiling it as a global phenomenon requires a return to its formative roots, the Crusades, when "notions of race and of Muslims as inferior beings could come to the fore in a context where European nations were in a position to actually challenge and eventually dominate once-powerful Muslim empires."[21] The orientation of Islam as the sworn enemy of the West, and Muslims as the irredeemable bloc wed to dismantling "Western civilization," is seeded in the overpowering imagery and ideology of these eleventh- through thirteenth-century battles. The Crusades painted those in the Christian West as sanctified heroes and the Muslim factions as warmongering interlopers in a Manichean struggle between good and evil. As law scholar Leti Volpp observed in the wake of the 9/11 terror attacks, the tropes tied to the Crusades were powerfully "redeployed" to repaint Muslims—nearly a thousand years later—as the inimical and ominous rivals of Christendom and Western civilization.[22]

This book seeks to reclaim the name of those earlier campaigns, to demystify the longstanding stereotypes surrounding them, and to examine how those stereotypes are manufactured and deployed globally against Muslims today. Furthermore, *The New Crusades* satirically challenges the trope that the global War on Terror is a religious standoff between Christian (and today, Judeo-Christian) values and Islam, and more broadly, a spiritual war between good and evil—a platitude echoed by politicians and pundits in Europe, Asia, and places beyond and in between.[23] This longstanding binary, which maps Christianity as good and Islam as evil, was modernized by Samuel P. Huntington's *Clash of Civilizations,* which oriented Islam and its adherents as a threat to the West.[24] A new world worldview that gave a popular face and political force to the belief that the War on Terror is a contemporary extension of the original Crusades.

The new set of crusades that target Muslim populations across the world, facilitated and fueled by the American campaign that came into being after the 9/11 terror attacks, are not pointedly religious battles between *occidental* Christendom and *oriental* Islam, but political and cultural wars.[25] They are waged against Muslims in nations where Islam has been cast as unassimilable with that nation's societal values, oriented as inimical to political quests for racial purity, or profiled as threatening to national security.

This book presents this narrative of global Islamophobia at the delta of crusades old and new, homing in on the center of their stages of violence and examining the margins even more closely. Most fundamentally, this books centers on the voices of the victims locked between the violent crucibles of state-sponsored and popular Islamophobia—those perilous middles where Muslims are forced to live, and in the words of Palestinian poet Mahmoud Darwish, strive to "live free, or die like the trees, standing up."[26]

In addition to primary sources, this book draws on foundational scholarly literature from within the law, social sciences, humanities, media studies, and beyond. With regard to cases where access to data is sparse and suppressed by authoritarian regimes like China, the stealth work of journalists and direct testimony of individuals in the diaspora brought firsthand accounts of stories hidden by digital authoritarianism and postmodern firewalls.

Given that I am no bystander in this grand narrative of global Islamophobia, but very much a subject implicated by it and its effects, I could not avoid weaving in personal experiences, which practically wrote themselves while I was piecing together the diverse and disparate passages of *The New Crusades*. My personal accounts often blur with the stories of the very individuals that color the pages of this book, a testament to the links this project forged across the panoply of divides sowed by the War on Terror and the distance natural to our world.

Balancing the subjective with the objective, the dressed-up evidence juxtaposed with the stripped-down feelings of real people, is what drives the spirit of this book. This investigation of liminal spaces embodies what Islamophobia is. Beyond academic discourse and political punditry, Islamophobia's genuine contours reside in the "out of place" margins, where the feelings of real people must be made understandable to, and accessible to, the rest of the world.[27]

The New Crusades offers a view of global Islamophobia that harmonizes facts and feelings. I seek to invite the reader into this liminal gray zone that offers a view of what Muslims think, endure, and most saliently, *feel* when facing the many fronts of Islamophobia. For Muslims globally, that feeling has a delicate relationship with facts, which are often set aside by a War on Terror baseline that indicts Islam, their faith, as predictive of subversion or violence, foreign allegiance and terrorism.

On the one hand, this presumption, which occupies the very marrow of how I define Islamophobia, drives how governments and societies discriminate against Muslims. But on the other, it pressures how Muslims consciously and subconsciously respond to the waves of Islamophobia that stalk them after every disaster and crisis.

The American War on Terror cemented this dictate, and during the two decades after the 9/11 terror attacks, it strategically expanded and exported connected crusades into nations across the globe. This dictate, which held Muslim identity as presumptive of terror suspicion, was the principal product of this global project, which countries across the globe adopted—and then adapted—to fit their domestic political ambitions.[28] Since its inception, the War on Terror has gradually metastasized into a network of crusades against Muslims in nations in Europe and Asia, Africa and the Americas. In a short time, it has birthed new campaigns of persecution in some nations, while emboldening existing cultural and political wars in other countries. As I articulated in my legal research,

> Beyond genuine national security threats, countries across the world capitalized on the conflation of Islam with terrorism to serve discrete national interests. This American War on Terror furnished nations with license, and more importantly, a policing template and language to profile and persecute their Muslim minority populations. American Islamophobia, buoyed by swift state action including the War in Afghanistan and the USA PATRIOT Act, manifested in a surge of vigilante violence against Muslims and "Muslim-looking" groups and had global impact.[29]

To echo Kumar, *Islamophobia is empire.*[30] Fueled by the War on Terror and its fundamental baseline, which ties Muslim identity to terrorism, a new kind of empire, advanced by a network of governments with distinct anti-Muslim crusades, has taken shape.

These new crusades are fluid, and in some cases are becoming more ominous for Muslims by the day. New campaigns take form as others expand and intensify before our very eyes. Make no mistake—this book does not aim to provide a detailed, rote analysis of every case of global Islamophobia. Nor does it seek to provide an exhaustive rundown of what anti-Muslim violence and discrimination look like in every nation across the globe. Libraries are stacked with studies and the internet replete with expert analyses that meet that demand.

This book is at once an intellectual and a spiritual project. It meshes the perspectives of Muslims, and most notably Muslims victimized by Islamophobia in places across the world, with my perspective as a Muslim public intellectual and my expertise as a law scholar. It was conceived at a middle ground where I sought to join the formal hand of academic production with the outstretched grasps of real people. As I wrote, I was motivated by the spirit of joining hands with others around the world, and blazing a space where their voices would be heard and their flesh would be extended the dignity otherwise denied them.

This book is organized in line with that spirit. Chapter 1 maps the margins of the journey that birthed this book, starting in Wajir, Kenya, on a mission trip aiding Somali nomads stricken with blindness. There, seemingly off the grid in a nondescript corner of the Horn of Africa, my path converged with that of agents of the American War on Terror enlisted in the mission of advancing empire in the name of preventing terrorism.

Chapter 2 examines the development of the War on Terror and that campaign's disintegration from an American-led effort into a network of connected systems of subordination enforced against Muslims across the globe. It proceeds with a presentation of my framework for understanding Islamophobia.

Chapter 3 centers on India, a global epicenter of Islamophobia today. The nation is governed by a regime zealously committed to Hindu supremacy, a regime that has spawned myriad horrors for the nation's massive Muslim population and, beyond its border, the besieged Muslim communities in occupied Kashmir. In India and the neighboring territories vulnerable to the Narendra Modi regime's imperial vision of Hindutva—Hindu supremacy—Muslims are a foreign caste to be removed by any means from Indian soil.

Chapter 4 moves east from the Indian subcontinent to China and Myanmar, sites of horrific ethnic cleansing against two indigenous Muslim populations. I examine the American War on Terror's facilitation of the persecution of Uyghur Muslims in China's disputed northwest territory, Xinjiang. In 2014, that mass persecution devolved into a full-scale elimination program encompassing mass detention, torture, and the criminalization of Islam through law and violence. I then delve into the ethnic cleansing of Rohingya Muslims in Myanmar, which like its Chinese counterpart is a campaign steered by the government to remove a people from land the state desperately covets.

Chapter 5 analyzes the origins and modern-day emergence of Islamophobia in France, which has spawned perhaps the most recognizable form of structural Islamophobia—the Hijab Ban of 2004.[31] This chapter examines the accompanying systems of policing and punishment that target Muslims in France and territories—Quebec and Belgium—that are heavily influenced by its anti-Muslim bigotry, and most notably, its campaign to ban the headscarf.

Chapter 6 focuses on a sphere of global Islamophobia that until the terror attacks in Christchurch, New Zealand, on March 15, 2019, was underexamined. On that fateful Friday, fifty-one Muslims were slain by a white supremacist terrorist who traveled to New Zealand from Australia. It uncovers the perilous connection between the development of white supremacy in these two settler colonial states and the recent uptick in political and popular Islamophobia in both. The chapter closes with a rebuke of the media penchant for only finding Muslims newsworthy when villains, not when victims. By paying tribute to the victims of the New Zealand terror attack, the final section of the chapter counters that tentacle of Islamophobia that is intertwined with white supremacy and drives media coverage.

A world marred by Islamophobia has inspired new fronts of resistance and leadership that are central to the spirit of *The New Crusades*. Celebrating the most compelling figures that challenge global Islamophobia forms the core of chapter 6. In the aftermath of the Christchurch terror attacks, New Zealand Prime Minister Jacinda Ardern issued a refreshing and timely challenge to the Islamophobic populism spreading across the world, a populism spearheaded by strongmen like Narendra Modi and Donald Trump.[32] In the world of sport, two Muslim athletes, Mohamed Salah and Khabib Nurmagomedov, have competed against Islamophobia and claimed victories in the minds and hearts of billions of fans. Finally, the chapter returns to the United States and follows the footsteps of the Black Lives Matter (BLM) Movement to learn from its transformative currents, which are reshaping America and the world.

In the midst of the coronavirus pandemic, while drafting the final pages of this book, I found myself in the belly of the place where the War on Terror was conceived. On this particular Tuesday in September, much like the world that it fundamentally remade, Washington, DC, looked dramatically different than it had during my previous visit a few months earlier. On that late-summer day, as masked strangers walked past me, those months felt like years; a pandemic and a new wave of Black Lives Matter protests had given the capital and its sparsely populated streets a lasting makeover. However, despite a new look that included a wholly barricaded White House and the words "Black Lives Matter" ubiquitously emblazoned on the city's walls and pavement, this was still the *belly* of the beast and the source that seeded that feeling in my core on a different Tuesday in September, nearly two decades earlier.

For most tourists drawn to Washington, the majesty of the capital and its ornate string of memorials and monuments, gallant statues and government structures are sights that inspire awe. For most Americans, particularly those privileged with the nation's greatest gift, whiteness, these structures are symbols that communicate belonging. As I walked down H Street, away from the barricade separating me from the White House, I stopped and reflected. I wondered what it felt like to be a Moor passing the Colosseum at the apex of the Roman Empire. And on this side of history, how life looked for a Uyghur Muslim living in a land where the threat of being thrown into a concentration camp stalked their every step.

I reflected on the trail left by the past and the present's indefinite path as I walked outside the margins of the most powerful building on earth. A building that mothered the War on Terror two decades ago, and continues to feed the new crusades that unfold in places far from its ivory columns and pearly gates, a world away from where I stood that Tuesday in September.

I thought, until I did not have to think anymore. My reflections were interrupted by that familiar feeling in my stomach, the one I know better than my best friend, the one I have battled more fiercely than any other foe. That feeling that was wholly foreign when I first met it, but that twenty years later was as familiar as the pain I felt after the loss of my father, or my hunger on the longest days of fasting during the holy month of Ramadan.[33]

It was not there with me, *it was me*. Rumbling inside my core, like it did when Beirut was shaken at its core, as I made my way to the intersection of 14th and H Streets. This time it commanded not to reach toward my phone or scroll through the news, but to walk in the other direction, away from the memorials and the monuments and the memories they evoked in me, and that feeling that moved with me that I wished I could shake.

I gave in, like I always did, and darted left, turning away from the structures that summoned tourists and fabricated terrorists. Structures that exported democracy in the sordid shape of drones that shot down young men who looked like me on the opposite side of the world. Only blocks away stood hallmarks of freedom that inspired patriotism in the Americans I envied from my place on the margins. Structures that for me and other Muslims who set foot in this city or have felt its might from afar are every bit as menacing as they are majestic.

I kept walking, away from the memories and monuments and memorials that gradually blurred into a distant gray cloud. I walked away, and toward a power that pulled me closer to it and away from fear. As I approached the corner of 14th and L, a passage from the Islamic poet and thinker Rumi strummed through my mind. My stride grew stronger. I walked closer and closer to that undeniable power, a force that rivaled the fear, the forlornness, and across the field of feelings in between. It spoke to me through scripture, music, and other muses, like Rumi, who wrote as if writing to me in that very moment: "Although the road is never ending, take a step and keep walking, do not look fearfully into the distance. On this path let the heart be your guide for the body is hesitant and full of fear."[34]

I could no longer see the monuments or the memorials, or the amorphous gray shape they formed. I just saw words, scrolling across my mind like lyrics, moving my feet in the right direction and forcing my hand to write. I felt a renewed urgency to write, and write these words and the thousands that follow, which I pray—and have faith—will come together to form a testament to a truth that those monuments and memorials conspire to conceal.

Washington, DC
Tuesday, September 1, 2020

CHAPTER ONE

FOREVER TURNED AROUND

BETWEEN THE GLASS AND ME

It is not the eyes that are blind, but the hearts.
QUR'AN, 22:46

Mohamed stood motionless as his schoolmates wandered around him. He bore the name of the Prophet, both a blessing and a burden for any Muslim boy his age. But he carried a burden far heavier than his exalted name. A weight so thick that it sank his black feet deeper into the cracked red earth that held him, firmly, in place.

Mohamed was locked in the cracks of that earth before he was born. He could not see the world beyond his young brown eyes and those earthly crevices that confined him. Mohamed's crusade was a simple one: to remain alive. It was a struggle that began and ended with avoiding that fall into those gaps carved deep in the earth below his feet—cracks that had swallowed so many others before him. This daily jihad, an everyday struggle, was an ungodly one for a radiant boy with a holy name.[1]

We locked eyes one last time. Only minutes earlier, we had prayed and played atop that barren plot that poorly masqueraded as a schoolyard for Mohamed and his schoolmates. I sat in the back seat of the black jeep, peering out of the window in his direction. His bright yellow shirt set him apart from the other students, as did an expression that settled somewhere between despair and defeat. I remembered a line from *The Kite Runner* as I looked at Mohamed and his classmates: "There are a lot of children in Afghanistan, but little childhood."² Khalid Hosseini's reflections about Afghanistan could have easily been written with Wajir, and the Somali child between the glass and me, in mind.

From behind the glass, I saw the cruel future that awaited Mohamed. For a moment, I envisioned a rail-thin man with an undersized yellow shirt standing in that very spot where, seconds ago, a young boy stood. My mind transformed that boy into the emaciated figure that Mohamed would become twenty years from today if that cruel sun above, and the earthly traps conspiring along with it below, had their way with him.

Perhaps it was a momentary hallucination from that damned sun that pierced the pale shelter of the glass dividing me and Mohamed. Or a divine message from a stronger power that sat above us. Maybe it was both. The blinding sun blurred earthly forces with the metaphysical, and in that moment, they merged indistinguishably in my mind.

Then, as quickly as he had appeared, tomorrow's ghost disappeared, and little Mohamed was there again. My anxiety subsided, and I smiled at him. He smiled back, revealing cracked and yellowed teeth that matched his shirt's hue. As I sat in the car, I wondered what he was thinking about as he started toward me and the group of Americans and Canadians I was traveling with. Perhaps he wanted to trade places with me, or one of us in the group. Maybe he contemplated what the world that we came from looked like. Maybe he fantasized about jumping into the empty seat in the jeep and driving far from the soil that confined him, and never turning back. Or perhaps Mohamed had too much to leave behind, in the form of a loving mother and family members who brought solace to the cruelty of his world.

I continued to imagine what he was thinking about as I looked in his direction. Then the jeep's engine signaled our imminent departure, ending our silent exchange. In the spirit of his lofty name, the little boy was passing on *a message*. A message delivered without uttering a single word and without written testament, articulated lucidly and wholly with his eyes.

I received it as I sat in that car, and more poignantly in the days after.

We drove off, and Mohamed returned to a reality marred by the routine raids of wild hyenas and Al-Shabaab terrorists, the leering stalk of famine and the blinding poverty rooted in the bright red soil.[3] Mohamed had seen far too much, far too soon. But his reel of horrors was very likely only beginning. He would see darker days, until that final sunset came and he could see no more. He stood there, and I looked back as the jeep pushed forward until little Mohamed faded from sight. I would never see him again.

There are many children in Wajir, but little childhood. Mohamed was a child in age, but stripped of its hallmark innocence by the spite of circumstance. He was thrust into the cruelest corner of life at birth, blind of the innocence and ease and joys of childhood that radiate on children in Europe or America.

The sun sets, for one final time, on everybody. And for those tasked with life's heaviest struggles, its most daunting jihads, that final sunset descends like a ravenous vulture from on high, preying on their will to live before they are even granted an opportunity to make sense of a world that appears so senseless.

BLIND FAITH

"He was defeated long before he died," James Baldwin said of his brother in *The Fire Next Time.*[4]

Mohamed, who was no more than ten years old, met defeat at a far younger age than the elder Baldwin brother from Harlem. It stripped his innocence from him before he became a teenager and aborted any hopes or dreams the young boy might have had before they took form.

The son of Somali nomads living in the badlands of northeastern Kenya, Mohamed's ancestors stopped there in the early 1900s, long before modern borders were drawn and new nations were created, when the only boundaries that mattered were the very lines and cracks in the sand that would trap Mohamed.[5]

It was a remote plot in the world that I knew nothing about until I boarded a plane four days earlier. It was the only place Mohamed knew, having been born into a world so blistering that it hated his very sight. And short of some divine revelation from above, the only place he will ever know before he leaves it and joins his maker.

Ours was an unlikely meeting. I was in the remote Kenyan town of Wajir to help restore the vision of Somali Muslims blinded by cataracts, settlers who are the parents and grandparents of the schoolchildren we visited at the Elmi Primary School, where I met Mohamed and heeded his message.

The majority of these refugees were older, well into their sixties and beyond. Their eyesight had been stripped by the merciless sun under which they sold vegetables and fruits in order to feed their families. It harvested cracks in their eyes as they worked, day in and day out, between those unrelenting desert crevices that bound them and the ungodly power above that blinded them.

One of these elders was Kalsoum, a noble woman who was well into her sixties and could not see out of either eye. I met her for the first time in the hospital courtyard, then accompanied her for the corrective surgery that she had traveled a long distance to undergo. We formed a bond during our time together in the small surgery room; I was in awe of this woman, who wanted nothing more than to *see* her sons and daughters again.

The doctor's blade was as sharp as the Kenyan sun that blinded her. Kalsoum laid under it, motionless, as the doctor penetrated her cornea with its edge. I was more afraid than she was, it seemed, writhing as the doctor sank the blade deep into her eye while I stood near her side. I didn't want to see.

I alternated between closing my eyes and sneaking peeks at her face as her hands twitched with each movement of the blade. I gripped her hand as I stared at her brow, seeing my mother's face in this woman roughly her age. Her lips whispered a faint prayer, *al-Fatiha*, summoning courage from a higher place as the blade sank deeper.[6] She was blind, but faith, and the unrelenting strength that only it can provide, gave meaning to the trials she endured. A new kind of *blind faith*, I thought, redefined by a resilient elderly woman lying in front of me.

Looking into eyes that only saw blackness, a blackness that Kalsoum was forced to live with for much of her adulthood, I was reminded of the Egyptian feminist Nawaal El Saadawi's words: "Life is very hard. The only people who really live are those harder than life itself."[7] Her face affirmed that Kalsoum was one of those rare survivors, as did her hardened palms. I could feel the arid and rough earth in her hands, cracked and hardened by the same sun that blinded her.

Kalsoum tightened her grip on my hand. The doctor paused, then released a deep breath. That faint gesture lightened the heaviness in the room. With his forceps, he removed the black cataract. Kalsoum moved, released her hand from mine, and then proclaimed the divine custom, *Allahu Akbar*, which spoke hope into a room swallowed by desperation and poverty.

Those two words, which I knew so well, were music to my ears. Lyrics that spilled like a song from a mother's mouth, into the ear of a new son who stood by her, with her hand in his own. And "whoever says that all music is prohibited, let him also claim that the songs of birds are prohibited," the Islamic scholar Imam Al-Ghazali recited. Those that make that rigid claim likely never heard the song of small prayers from blind mothers bringing light to a room so utterly consumed by darkness. They never witnessed a blind woman wed so tightly to her faith sing the Most High's name the very moment her vision was restored.

These were new songs written between the walls of makeshift hospitals, under an oppressive sun that tuned out the music of life as it stripped lives of their eyesight. A corner of the Horn of Africa where Europeans unsaw the natives as real people, and recorded laws and the history that followed to strip them of dignity, followed by American successors with new marching orders. But there is music in unmaking the dehumanizing word of empire, and Kalsoum's sublime prayer sang with lyrical rebellion. "This is exactly how the music called jazz began," wrote James Baldwin, "and out of the same necessity: not only to redeem a history unwritten and despised, but to checkmate the European [and American] notion of the world. For until this hour, when we speak of history, we are speaking only of how Europe [and America] saw—and sees—the world." But there is a very great deal in the world which Europe does not, or cannot, see.[8] When Kalsoum finally spoke, and sang Allah's name, I knew that she could see.

I could still feel Kalsoum's calloused hand as I walked out of the operating room and into the hospital courtyard. There, lines of refugees waited patiently for their turn to lie down under the knife and hope that "Allah restores the sight" stolen by that ungodly sun.[9] Belief in Him was all they had, and all they relied on when their coffers went bare and their eyes went blind. And that, for Kalsoum, was enough.

It was February 24, 2020. Winter back home, but hotter than July in Kenya. I looked up and saw little Mohamed's face in the visage of another young boy sitting against the hospital wall. He looked back, at a man who looked *out of place* but precisely where he belonged. I saw in his face the very image I tried to unsee in that operating room: Mohamed, whose only fate was working under the same sun that stole Kalsoum's vision, tomorrow finding himself in that very bed. Old and wrinkled, his body broken and eyes blinded by slaving under the same sun that terrorized Kalsoum for decades.

That vision stayed with me for days. It haunted me in my sleep and stalked my thoughts while awake. In only three days' time, I fully saw the crucible of existence in Wajir for what it was, and understood that the arc of one's life would be determined by that unseen battle between a cruel sun and a benevolent God. This was, I discovered, how the predominantly Somali population of the town saw it—a people who placed their faith in Him as the sun summoned them to work every morning under its devilish command.

PRAYER AND PREY

The call for the morning prayer—the first of the day's five—rang before the sun, that ungodly sun, dawned and took its place. A call to pray that reminded me, and the proud people waiting for their turn to see again in that hospital courtyard in the middle of nowhere, that He was more powerful than it.

> Allahu Akbar,
> Allahu Akbar
> 'Ašhadu 'an lā 'ilāha 'illā -llāh
> 'Ašhadu 'an lā 'ilāha 'illā -llāh
> 'Ašhadu 'anna Muḥammadan rasūlu -llāh
> 'Ašhadu 'anna Muḥammadan rasūlu -llāh
> Hayya 'ala-s-Salah. Hayya 'ala-s-Salah.
> Hayya 'ala-l-Falah. Hayya 'ala-l-Falah.
> Allahu Akbar! Allahu Akbar!
> La ilaha illa Allah.

The *adhan*, the call to prayer, filled the dark sky, summoning us to the nearby mosque. It was not one of those opulent mosques with golden domes and gallant minarets reaching toward the heavens, the type of prayer houses you see in oil-rich Arab nations. This was a modest structure, a "makeshift mosque," as a companion commented, built into the gate that wrapped around the Wajir Palace Hotel.

I prostrated alongside my Canadian and Kenyan colleagues, who quickly became friends and called me "brother." We prayed, collected our shoes from outside the entrance, and returned to the hotel for dinner. As we approached, I saw two white-headed vultures claim their position in a tree near our table. The birds looked like guards, monitoring the grounds from above as we walked below. It was impossible not to feel menaced by them, particularly since they sat so close to the table where we would eat—and they, if they saw an opening, would join us. Their presence was heavy and weighed down my appetite.

"Where are you all from?" The question darted in from the table on our right, spoken with that familiar Midwestern accent that took me back home. The man who posed the question sat across from a woman whose eyes turned to our table—a table with twelve Muslims from five different countries seated around it.

"We're from different places," answered a Canadian member of our group. Still on guard, I cautiously observed and volunteered no morsel of information. However, my colleague continued, "We came to help blind refugees get cataract removal surgery." That answer, which I naively thought would end the discussion, only heightened their curiosity. Their ravenous appetite for information expanded the more that we spoke and grew stronger as the exchange continued.

"Are you with a group or a mosque?" the man asked. The director of the project identified himself and the organization, United Muslim Relief, which piqued the interest of the two even further. "So who . . . ," he began to ask, when I finally interjected my own question: "What brings you two to Wajir?"

The tables were now turned, and the eyes of twelve Muslims turned toward the two interlopers. We delivered question after question, which revealed that the two individuals were far more comfortable interrogating us than the reverse. This was how surveillance worked back home, in American cities and towns with concentrated Muslim populations. War on Terror surveillance, whether at home or far from it, was the same beast and left the same footprint. Wajir, Kenya, like Los Angeles or Detroit, was another theater of the War on Terror's "field of fight," where the new "world war" pursued terrorist boogey-men and -women near and far.[10]

A week before my arrival in Wajir, the town had been menaced by another set of intruders. The terror group Al-Shabaab had ripped through the city from nearby Somalia, stopping at the school that Mohamed attended and the hospital where Kalsoum reclaimed her vision.[11]

This was not their first visit to Wajir, but in fact the most recent in a string of violent tirades through the town. Locals, who feared being robbed, attacked, or killed by young militant men with similar origins, were forced into their homes. Al-Shabaab's raids usually ended with destruction or death, and more often than not, both.[12]

Months earlier, an Al-Shabaab terrorist had murdered one of the teachers at the Elmi Primary School. During our visit the principal shared, in meticulous detail, how the terrorists kidnapped and killed his colleague. Her crime: she was a Christian teaching Muslim youth, like little Mohamed, how to read and write.

Before that, the terror group bombed a food store, killing three people. This was a shop that Kalsoum regularly bought food from before she returned home after a grueling workday. Al-Shabaab ripped into the town and then vanished after scavenging bodies already stripped of so much by that cruel sun above. Then they disappeared as quickly as they came.

The border between Somalia and Kenya is porous, and Al-Shabaab mobs run through it regularly, seeking revenge on Kenya for sending troops into Somalia in an effort to stifle the terror group's domestic and regional advances. Their frequent victims, however, are the Somali population in Wajir—stateless people like little Mohamed and Kalsoum, and the hundreds of thousands of Somalis living in makeshift huts and villages spread across Wajir. This is an element Al-Shabaab often refers to as "traitors" for fleeing Somalia and settling in Kenya. Wajir is also a place where the terror group looks to enlist fresh recruits among the children playing in schoolyards and squares. Fresh meat, like Mohamed, remade into monsters that slaughter.

Armed security warned us about the possibility of their return, which locals knew could be on any day and at any moment. The East African affiliate of Al-Qaeda descends upon young boys like Mohamed as potential recruits, and steals the wares of laborers like Kalsoum. This is yet another peril associated with life in Wajir, where it seems that Mother Nature and the devil himself conspire to make life for these exiles an inescapable hell—or a place where a fiery overseer lords it over everyone and makes it feel just as hot as hell. A place where drugged-up devils carrying machetes and machine guns shoot indiscriminately into crowds of people who look like members of their own families, and could very well be family. Devils that neither kindred religion nor protective gates can ward off.

We learned that months earlier, members of Al-Shabaab had shown up at the hotel where we were staying. The specter of their past attacks loomed heavy in the courtyard where we sat for dinner, and heavier in the minds of the two strangers who probed how we, a group of Muslim humanitarians, found our way to Wajir—a corner of the world in Kenya more associated with terrorism than tourism.

In their eyes, we were the strangers. Strangers in a land where 99 percent of the inhabitants are Muslim, like myself and the twelve bodies around our table.[13] That view was absurd, but in a world gripped by a global War on Terror that assigns immediate suspicion to our faith, Islam, it was hardly strange and not the least surprising. This is how Europe saw the world, and how the American imperial gaze currently sees it. The world, wherever and anywhere, was theirs, and neither the sovereignty of nations nor the walls of borders mattered when observed from their worldview. The haughtiness of the two intruders was jarring but reflected the imperial arrogance of the global crusade launched by the government that had deployed them here.

The man paused. He looked at his colleague across the table, then back in our direction. Darkness had fully set in, the cool moon having unseated the sun to reclaim its position in the Kenyan sky.

"We're here to combat radicalization," the man finally answered. I knew that word, that intricate yet amorphous word, all too well. I felt it in the pit of my stomach. It inspired police witch hunts down endless roads, giving local law enforcement the authority to steer anti-terrorism campaigns in the heart of Muslim communities.[14] These campaigns penetrated deep into the sacred halls of mosques, the homes of families, and the private in-boxes of teenagers.[15] This time, the fear of radicalization brought these two Americans from Washington to Wajir, chasing ghosts in a remote African town among old refugees blinded by an oppressive sun and young children hardened by an unforgiving earth.

I hated that word, "radicalization," because of what it meant in practice: what it meant for Muslims in the United States, what it meant for little Mohamed, and for Kalsoum. I hated that word for what it meant in a world where terror was no longer a crime, but a preemptive tool with which to punish innocents who had done nothing. Who had nothing.

"Radicalization" and the state effort to "counter" or "combat" it, in the US government's parlance, divided and destroyed communities. It turned family members against one another. It flipped imams into informants and criminalized Islam, the faith that brought us to Wajir to serve blind refugees, as a pathway toward extremism.

"We're with the State Department," the woman volunteered, affirming what my stomach had told me minutes earlier. Their assignment was clear: to "counter" and "prevent the spread of radicalization" among the local refugee population. Washington had elevated to its signature counterterror philosophy the theory that Muslims were predisposed to extremist behavior, and that terror networks could activate that potential through propaganda. Or even worse, that belief in Islam could prompt young boys like Mohamed to enlist in a terror network like Al-Shabaab, and years later, shoot up the very stores that mothers like Kalsoum frequent.

But every theory has its cracks. And the fissures in this one were larger than in others. "Radicalization theory" focused exclusively on Muslims, and like eugenics or the bell curve and grand racial or religious theories crafted before it, *saw* Islam as inherently violent. Islam itself, a religion so heterogeneous and deeply layered, was deemed prone to terrorism by a new theory that, like other bigoted philosophies, reduced the "essence" of entire peoples to vile stereotypes.[16] Muslims were flatly reduced to presumptive terrorists, and the War on Terror imposed that as the worldview of its agents and enforcers, spies and soldiers. This was their myopic view, wide-eyed with ignorance in the belly of a village ravaged by medical blindness.

The Americans did not see little Mohamed or Kalsoum or the refugee population of Wajir as victims of cruel circumstance, but as presumptive radicals. They were, despite the depth of their despair and the darkness of their sight, *always* terrorists in the making, always two steps from becoming full-fledged terror threats. The two agents did not see Wajir as a place of humanitarian crisis, but as a rugged training ground for terrorists. A soil where souls were snatched and made into "radicals" by terrorists who roamed the badlands like hyenas in search of fresh meat.

I could not unsee the look of defeat on little Mohamed's face as I viewed it from the back seat of the jeep. Nor could I lose sight of Kalsoum's wrinkled visage as the blade plunged into eyes that had stopped working long before the mother of ten retired from her place under the sun. One child who has seen too much, too soon; one elder who could see no more because of what her eyes had to absorb over countless years. Theirs are two faces I will not ever forget.

As for the two State Department agents seated across from me, their sight was marred by a vision of unrelenting war and empire, a blindness that no medical doctor could cure. Although they knew little about the local people and made less time to get to know them, these two American agents "believed that they could determine how Muslims think and behave. [That] their essential character could be understood from the texts of their civilization" and modern faux theories.[17]

This is what I saw during my three days in Wajir. Rough portraits of a people scarred by the elements and stalked by extremists and agents who did not recognize them as victims or people. But only as an enemy that could be "radicalized" in the blink of an eye, by a faith that gave them *inner vision. A faith* that lent meaning to lives of hardship and offered a portal of escape—five times each day—until that final sunset came.

Virtually everything that I saw signaled to me that Wajir was a world away from Washington. Its red earth clashed with the gray urban concrete of the District of Columbia, and the slowly plodding men and headscarved women had a distinctly different look and rhythm than the suits rushing about the American capital. Wajir was not Washington, until the latter descended on it in the form of the two agents seated next to us. In the words of Malcolm X, Plymouth Rock landed on them.

During the past two decades, the War on Terror has expanded into a truly global campaign, and Washington is now everywhere that Muslims live. Those years, and the foreseeable ones ahead, mark the tenure of a war that orients Islam as the source of terror threats, and in the words of an American president, the enemy of "civilization." George W. Bush affirmed, days after 9/11, that this new American crusade would be the "world's fight."[18] A fight that turned its guns on Islam and its adherents anywhere and everywhere.

This war, unlike its predecessors, has stretched beyond the bounds of what seemed conventional and constitutional.[19] It has spawned two bloody military campaigns in Afghanistan and Iraq and deployed agents to remote corners of the globe, like Wajir, to track down terrorists. Any spot in the world could be a theater in this new war, and every place—no matter how remote—a front for finding the next crop of terrorists.

The American War on Terror sees Muslims, the fastest growing religion in the world, with nearly 2 billion adherents, as presumptive terrorists.[20] This vision of Muslim identity has blinded the architects and agents of this war to the genuine contours of Muslim life in American neighborhoods and the unimaginable plight of refugees falling into the cracks in Kenya.

But more than two decades in, it is clear that the War on Terror is no longer just America's imperial project. It has morphed and metastasized into a global crusade—a crusade encompassing a circuit of interconnected campaigns unfolding within nation-states, in which governments weaponize the faux theory that Muslims are a demographic threat and that Islam inspires "extremism" and "radicalism." These governments launch their own campaigns in the name of the War on Terror, institutionalizing the baseline that expressions of Muslim identity are tied to terrorism. This has been written into laws across the world, legitimized by a war started and spearheaded by the world's greatest superpower.[21]

This baseline forms what is now widely known as Islamophobia, a term that spurs the unseeing of Muslims like Mohamed and Kalsoum for who they truly are, in exchange for the blanket cover of terror suspicion.

Neither age nor impoverishment, emaciated bodies that have worked too late in life and still-developing minds that have lost innocence too soon, mean more in this war than religion. Islam, a faith undressed of its rich meaning and normative complexity, has been cloaked with a blanket of suspicion that now envelops its adherents. Anywhere and everywhere.

That is what the War on Terror intended. It was, and remains, principally a war of ideas and optics, cracked vision and unseen threat. A war in which grandiose narratives of civilizational standoffs and grand theories of radical religions were deployed long before boots were on the ground in Baghdad or Kabul, or the silent footsteps of agents stalked schoolyards in Wajir or *banlieues* in Paris. A war that reduced a supremely diverse faith population of 2 billion people spread across six continents—Muslims who worshipped and looked and lived in dramatically distinct ways—into a single sinister caricature.

This is Islamophobia, a creation so diabolical that it blinds people to what stands before them, embedding vile myths and misrepresentations deep in their imaginations. It is the progeny of a blind mother, Orientalism, which divided the world into two clashing civilizations, "Islam and the West," eternally locked in a crusade that constructs the most vulnerable Muslims into villains and scorches the earth in the name of empire.

Islamophobia is more powerful than any military weapon. More deft than any drone. More menacing than any soldier. It is the War on Terror's most potent weapon, its slowly exploding atomic bomb, which sweeps across the globe as governments keen on unseeing the world as Washington sees it feed off its blind hunt for boogeymen that loom larger in their heads than in reality.

New crusades are rooted in old testaments of power and plunder, burned earth and marching empire. The War on Terror is no different, particularly the chapters of it unfolding right now in countries across the globe. Its proponents have revived historic rivalries and unearthed long-buried hatreds. These hatreds have been swiftly remade in the image of the War on Terror, in line with a vision that America has exported by way of military invasions, stealth propaganda campaigns, agents who prey upon the weak, and demagogues who masquerade as presidents and prime ministers.

I traveled in many of these countries and observed Washington's ever-present footprint in the policies of governments that saw their Muslim populations through the lens of the War on Terror and its prism of lies. These governments have adopted its rigid frames to carry out domestic crusades that further additional political objectives in their own lands. For governments in India and China, France and Myanmar, and regimes beyond and in between, Islamophobia has been wielded as a blunt weapon. A weapon so familiar, and so accessible, that it can be handled by anyone; not just politicians or pundits or soldiers, but anyone who has eyes that refuse to see for themselves, and hands willing to punish those the state, and the new crusade that has enlisted it, labels as terrorists.

As in every great crusade, everybody could be a fighter for *good* unless they were branded as the enemy. And everywhere Muslims lived was a battleground, whether a hotel courtyard in the Horn of Africa or a working-class neighborhood in the heart of India. For every little Mohamed I locked eyes with, there were tens of young Muslims I spoke to whose dreams had been deferred and futures denied by the shadow of Islamophobia looming over them. For every Kalsoum I held hands with as I closed my eyes, praying that hers would reopen to beloved faces not seen in years, there were scores of mothers and fathers I sat with who had been stripped of the vision of a better tomorrow for their children. These visions were stolen by policies enacted by populists keen on scapegoating Muslims as a means of revving up nativism and its ugly sibling, ethnic nationalism. These visions allow authoritarian regimes to push indigenous Muslims into "high-tech penal colonies" and Chinese concentration camps while peddling the threat of internment deep in their own neighborhoods.[22] Warning them, while toppled minarets foreshadow a looming holocaust, that practicing Islam could entrap them within that earthly crucible that no human should, or could, bear.

It became a common thought of mine, while speaking to these individuals, that being blind could make life more tolerable than seeing what they saw every day, what stalked them at every turn. I felt ashamed for having that thought, but learning about the depths Islamophobia has sunk to in China and the heights of violence it has risen to in India revealed dangers so existential, and conjured up fears so extreme, that I have no choice but to level the harshest possible indictment at the American War on Terror. It is a war far more gruesome than war as we know it, more ominous than dystopian novelists could imagine, one that has spiraled into crusades of mass internment and ethnic cleansing in parts of the world seen and unseen.

These are dangers that cannot be fully understood without the words of the people who face them directly, who live an existence where dodging persecution is a daily ritual that accompanies their five prayers or their fasts. I met these Muslims wherever I could, and they were keen on meeting me and sharing stories that few others care to hear. We spoke near their schools and in their living rooms, in neighborhoods that they have never left and cities where they live as exiles. When the pandemic arrived and everybody was quarantined and confined, I spoke to even more Muslims around the globe, conducting virtual interviews and meetings, communicating on social media platforms and phone apps, connecting on digital terrain where our virtual footprint likely summoned the scrutiny of agents from Washington and other new War on Terror capitals.

While the virus put much of the world on pause and sank everybody into paranoia, it spawned new strands of Islamophobia that kept the War on Terror in motion. From distant corners of the globe, I learned about the horrors of harvested Muslim organs and toddlers seated atop the corpses of their dead grandfathers, how Muslims in New Delhi were scapegoated for the outbreak of the coronavirus, and how French laws banned Islamic head and face coverings but mandated face masks.

An absurd world birthed absurd tales, particularly in relation to a crusade against Muslims that no pandemic or plague could quarantine. I learned from the voices of Muslims already confined by an Islamophobia that preceded, and will outlast, this or any pandemic. They spoke and I listened. They painted portraits with colors so vivid that they changed my outlook on matters I believed I knew well. They shared stories and sentiments that seeped into the pages of this book, and even more deeply, into the diary in my mind. They changed me, profoundly and permanently.

The world became even more absurd when Russia invaded Ukraine in late February 2022, several years after I began writing this book. What explains the world of difference between the Ukrainian struggle for freedom and the ongoing quests for self-determination in Muslim-majority lands? Why are Ukrainians "freedom fighters," while Muslims struggling for that very same dignity and independence in occupied Kashmir or the West Bank, Gaza or Yemen are dubbed "terrorists"? Theaters where a protracted war on terror renders anybody Arab, Brown, or Muslim as a putative terrorist, notwithstanding the righteousness of their struggle or the unhinged imperialism of their opponents. Shortly after the invasion, I wrote in the *Washington Post* that "the public's ideal of *freedom fighter* and *terrorist* is intensely racial, which enables the seeing of lay Ukrainians taking arms and throwing molotov cocktails as heroes and Muslims engaged in the very same acts, in pursuit of the same self-determination, as extremists."[23] Terrorism was made in the image of the dark and brooding Muslim, while the blonde-haired and blue-eyed archetypes out of Ukraine that saturated our television screens and social media timelines were shrouded with the innocence and valor of whiteness, the very face of racial domination that reigned over the nation that made the War on Terror, its new global crusade.

New heroes and old villains, traced in the racial order that white supremacy and Islamophobia made. The American War on Terror, spearheaded by an administration bent on exacting revenge on a single terror network, has devolved into something unrecognizable from its original form. It has spawned a monster that has mutated wherever it has landed, that has been shaped and then reshaped by the histories and marching orders of its local host.

Islamophobia varies across national and cultural lines but retains regardless of location the fundamental trait crafted by the architects of the War on Terror: the conviction that the threat of terror is inextricably linked to Islam, and Muslims anywhere and everywhere carry its threat wherever they roam. Both old and new crusades have reduced the Islamic essence to one of violence, unseeing Muslims as real people and unmaking them into standing myths of terrorists.

The jet ascended from the makeshift runway. I stared out of the window as if it were a movie screen, peering down at the cracked desert, seeing the faces of little Mohamed and Kalsoum in my mind's eye. The cracked earth looked more vast and more pronounced the higher the plane soared. I marveled at the strength of the Somali nomads blinded by that unholy sun. Those people, who I embraced and held, marked as enemies by gun-toting terrorists and agent-vultures menacing them between cracks and crevices that swallow weaker women and men.

I stared at those cracks as the plane ascended into the clouds. "If people come together, they can even mend a crack in the sky." I recited the Somali proverb in my head, lyrics composed by the ancestors of the nomads living below, as I flew over badlands that few beyond them knew existed, let alone had ever walked across.

I thought of little Mohamed and his schoolmates, who played in an unfenced yard between shoddy structures where no child could feel safe, let alone learn. The Elmi Primary School stood more as an emblem of the world's savage inequalities than an educational structure, and it made the dilapidated school buildings in my hometown of Detroit look opulent in comparison.

I thought of Kalsoum's wrinkled face, a face that bore the grooves and holes of the very land that stole her vision and of a will harder than the earth she toiled above. I thought of the other elders who followed Kalsoum's footsteps from hundreds of miles away, in hopes that they will see their sons and daughters, husbands and wives again before their final sunset comes.

I saw them, and this book is my attempt for you to see them as well. Their courage in the face of limitless cruelty demands that we see them for who they are, not what diabolical minds too cowardly to walk their earth compel us to see, and unsee, from distant silos.

The War on Terror is not invested in mending cracks, bringing people together, or restoring clairvoyance. Rather, it seeks to widen the cracks and deepen the crevices, to turn people against one another, to distort religious and civilizational divides and keep us all bound to war and blind to reality.

The War on Terror has put a violent new spin on the longstanding narrative that Muslims are a demographic threat wherever they live. The world, for Muslims everywhere, is spinning more and more furiously thanks to the hands of Islamophobia.

Hang on to the world as it spins around
Just don't let the spin get you down.[24]

The voice of soul legend Donny Hathaway was so deep, so moving, that I wished I could play it for Kalsoum and the others waiting for the day they had dreamt about, when their eyes could take in the heavens while their bodies remained bound to that cruel earth. The music whirled within me, dancing with the memory of Kalsoum's prayers and Mohamed's pretty brown eyes.

I envied that magic that musicians can unfurl with the power of their voice or instrument, that magic that can move the most down-trodden of hearts and summon wonder from eyes that have lost the ability to see beyond walls that bind and walls that blind.

"Take it from me," Donny sang, "someday we'll all be free." Donny sang, and I wrote. I wrote so that the world could hear the ballad of Kalsoum and heed the message from little Mohamed.

I wrote so unheard solos sung on tattered stages are seen and heard by people who would never know these settings exist, that these peo-ple exist.

I wrote because it felt like a divine order, stringing moments and memories and music together against orchestras of erasure, the silenc-ing of stories, and the marching band of new crusades.

My body was on that plane, heading away from Wajir. But my mem-ory and mind lingered there, so indelibly that I could see the plots of cracked land in the lines above and underneath the ink that spilled in between. "I start to think, and then I sink, into the paper, like I was ink."[25] Words linked together like lyrics in a song, a holy song, as the plane soared further away from Wajir but my spirit remained rooted in what I could never leave behind. I wished I could turn around, but winds and wings conspired otherwise.

Allahu Akbar—the words I knew so well were never sweeter than when they came out of the mouth of Kalsoum for the second time. A song so magical that my body shook and my heart pounded like two drum-mers were inside my chest.

I gripped her hand again in that hospital courtyard, embraced her with the same arms that I wrapped around my mother. She broke away, then her wrinkled hands held my face. I *felt* the earth that four days earlier I did not even know existed, and I will never forget how it touched me. For the first time, *forever turned around.*

She could see. And I saw her, for the first time, all over again. And then again, and again, as the plane rose higher into the sky, until the cracks faded from sight and blended into an evened earth so sublime that the heavens looked down with envy.

CHAPTER TWO

WAR AND TERROR

THE TERROR WITHIN

The terror within is far truer and far more powerful than
any of our labels: labels change, the terror is constant.
JAMES BALDWIN, *The Price of the Ticket*

John, a veteran of the Iraq War, spoke about what he saw
with meticulous detail and clarity.[1] I sat across from him at a
café in Lincoln Park, Michigan, a working-class city on the
outskirts of Detroit and in the heart of flyover country.[2]

In an indistinguishable strip mall buried between half-
barren strip malls, we talked about the future of our hometown, and in greater detail, our nation. We then walked
through crossing lanes of memories connecting my hometown and his, Lincoln Park, a fifteen-minute drive down
Southfield Freeway from my Detroit neighborhood, Warren-
dale. It was a short drive, but mapping the racially segregated
landscape that is metropolitan Detroit, Lincoln Park felt like
an entirely distant place. It was downriver but in many
respects felt like down south, where the sight of Confederate
flags and menacing stares from white men in pickup trucks
were common.

Like the scattered towns that surround it, Lincoln Park
once pumped generations of men into the assembly lines of
Ford Motor Company and General Motors. Those jobs
helped build Lincoln Park and other communities in metropolitan Detroit, providing people with the chance to buy
homes, make families, and come close to living out the

"American Dream." A dream so elusive, if not impossible, for most that legendary standup comedian George Carlin joked, "They call it the American Dream because you have to be asleep to believe it." John once believed it and *in it,* largely because his father and forefathers lived it. Or at least, had an opportunity to live something that resembled the American Dream. John's ancestors were immigrants too. They arrived from Ireland, with many pulled to the Greater Detroit area to work for the booming auto industry. On the assembly lines, they worked for their families and "worked toward whiteness," which they achieved while pursuing the American dream.[3]

That dream, however, was no more. John woke up every morning to a mounting nightmare, where auto assembly jobs had shrunk or were shipped abroad, and men like him were sent to fight in America's new crusades waged after 9/11. "Dark times," as Hannah Arendt called the intimate line between poverty and state control; times were bleak for John in Michigan, and even blacker stanzas awaited him in Iraq. Lincoln Park lost its identity as a link in the greater Detroit automobile assembly line and became another siloed community full of men with no futures, men shipped to foreign soil to fight other men with no futures. The luck of his Irish ancestors had run out, and John fell on hard times with only one door to walk through.

"I did not know what I was getting into," John recalled, as he stared down at his coffee cup. "But I knew that our country was attacked, and that I wanted to help defend it." John did not attend college, and he was thrust into parenthood before he himself was a fully formed adult. He was a fighter, and had always been. The tattoos that he wore testified to that, but the scars hidden beneath them were an even stronger witness to the fights he had endured, including some that got the best of him. In truth, I felt uncomfortable when I first sat down with him. He looked like somebody who would hate me on account of who I was, and what I looked like. Another disaffected white man who perhaps unleashed that disaffection on Muslims, Mexicans, or others he deemed un-American. But I wrestled with that discomfort as I sat there, across from him, committed to undoing my own stereotypes as he wrestled with his.

John's inability to articulate why he enlisted, and what he knew about the United States' complicated history with Saddam Hussein, reminded me of what Henry A. Giroux observed: "Since the terrorist attacks of 9/11, America has succumbed to a form of historical amnesia fed by a culture of fear, militarization and precarity."[4] Amnesia or ignorance, or perhaps a distinctly American blend of the two, colored John's struggle to identify a clear motive for enlisting in the army. But he did, as did so many young, poor, and working-class men whose only reason to fight a foreign war was, perhaps, the void of any reason to stay home.

John's father had earned an honest living at GM, and John wanted to follow in his dad's footsteps. He wanted to stay home, hold a normal job, attend the same Catholic church that set his childhood Sundays, and raise his children in Lincoln Park. But he ran into a dead end after dropping out of high school and when globalization sent most of the auto jobs at Ford and GM abroad, where labor was far cheaper. For his generation, the American Dream—and the vehicles needed to realize it—were being shipped abroad. The days of new sedans elegantly cruising down Southfield Road were replaced by "hillbilly elegies" scored to the tune of "declining home values" that "trap[ped] people" in white towns like Lincoln Park, towns that faded from working-class oases to opportunity deserts.[5]

John was trapped, with just one way out. He decided the military seemed a "good option." He was clearly a good man, someone who wanted to make a better future for his young daughters, and who, out of fidelity to his country, was motivated to exact revenge on the terrorists who crashed two planes into the World Trade Center. So John shipped out to a place he had never visited before enlisting in the armed forces, a place he had only seen in the Hollywood films and corporate news coverage that "make the Middle East" and that pushed him to fight for the country he loved so much.[6] The war would turn him into a shell of the man his family had known before he enlisted to fight in a foreign war. To fight for a nation that did not love him back.

John stuttered when he spoke. His hands shook nervously, tapping the metal table where we sat. The tapping made my coffee cup shake, matching my nerves. Reluctantly, he spilled memories of a war he was keen on forgetting. I was hesitant to explicitly inquire whether the war had altered him psychologically, but I had my suspicions. I had read about men and women who faced lifelong depression after making it back home, in one piece physically but disintegrating from within. And worse, veterans who took their own lives because they could take no more.[7]

John talked briefly about the friends he lost during the war, and the "dismembered bodies of Iraqis" he saw scattered on battlegrounds where children once played and elders once prayed. The terror was seated deep within him. I could tell that talking about death took John to places he did not want to revisit, and into a dark corner that would be difficult for him to escape. I didn't want to guide him down that spiral.

So I stopped. Instead, I turned the discussion to Michigan Wolverines and Detroit Lions football, our favorite MMA fighters, and the pandemic. When it was time to leave, the discomfort I had had was gone, and any preconceived notions of who John was—and wasn't—were retrenched. A mix of admiration and pity colored my new perspective of John, coupled with the feeling that a person most Muslims would count as their foe would ultimately become my friend. He was a white man from a part of the city I associated with racism because of past personal experiences. However, the wages of war had washed away the menace of his whiteness, and the despair that descended on him when he returned from war—with little to return to—drove me toward places I otherwise avoided.

I walked John to his truck and shook his hand, understanding that wars could turn the best of men into monsters. Monsters that destroyed the lives of innocents in the name of illusory virtues like "national honor" and "patriotism" and then, with the terror still lodged deep within, destroyed themselves when there was nobody else left standing.

The French philosopher and writer Jean-Paul Sartre wrote, "When the rich wage war it is the poor who die."[8] Some die on the field of battle, while the unluckiest among them, like John, return home shattered into pieces that cannot be glued together.

John plodded away from me. Barely alive but still there in physical form, the terror that he saw in Iraq and inflicted on innocent people now lodged deep within him. He was dead on the inside but walking among us.

Hussein lived less than ten miles from John, a short drive down Southfield Freeway in the very Detroit where I grew up and where my mother still makes her home. His neighborhood blossomed into what locals lovingly refer to as "Little Iraq."[9] It's a one-mile drag where Shia Muslim barber shops and bakeries, storefront mosques and restaurants proudly bear the names of Iraqi towns and villages that the proprietors left behind to build new lives in the Motor City.[10] These were not just businesses, but shrines they reconstructed along a central artery of an Arab American capital. After several wars in Iraq and endless bombs over Baghdad, a semblance of Iraq was built in the belly of west Detroit.

In this section of the city, refugees from Iraq landed in that rare Muslim community where Shia Islam—the religion's minority sect—was the majority.[11] A place where Iraqi storefront mosques sit along Warren Avenue and processions honoring Shia martyrs march down Greenfield Road.[12] A place where Shia Muslims like Hussein found sanctuary from the sectarian persecution inflicted by another Hussein, Saddam.

Saddam Hussein, with his mustachioed face, embodied Islamic threat during the decade before the War on Terror. Before Osama bin Laden, it was the secularist Hussein who provided the expanding American empire in the region with an easily identifiable Muslim enemy. Shia Muslims like Hussein in Detroit counted him as a villain for persecuting their people, and they celebrated when his statue fell in Baghdad on April 9, 2003, shortly after the US launched the war in Iraq.[13] There was celebrating again on Warren Avenue when that final fate befell the real Saddam on December 29, 2006.[14] I remember that evening vividly, the sound of gunshots ringing out just two nights before the fireworks and festivities of New Year's Eve. Gunshots were a common sound in our Detroit neighborhood, but on that night, they rang out with joy.

Hussein's new home is where the black flag of Ashura, which commemorates the day the Prophet Muhammad's grandson Hussein was martyred in the Battle of Karbala, sways as a living symbol of contemporary oppression and political identity.[15] A place to belong, finally, for a man and a Muslim diaspora flung far from home, a diaspora that endured war with Iran, war with America, and in the dark years ushered in by the War on Terror, a war with and within itself.

"I came here in 2008 because I was promised a job and had many friends who came here from Iraq," Hussein shared.[16] "My family is from Najaf, and I moved to Baghdad in 1998 so that I could study and earn more money."

Hussein, who switched from his native Iraqi Arabic dialect to English, spoke with long pauses between his sentences. It was clear that he was not quick to trust, an understandable trait for a Shia Iraqi who had lived under the cruel thumb of Saddam's rule for so long. That thumb left an impression on Hussein that remained prominent years after he had fled his homeland. Furthermore, that culture of mistrust blended with paranoia was pervasive in Arab Detroit, one of the most heavily surveilled cities in the US.

"I remember the American soldiers barging into our home [in Iraq], pointing their guns at me, my brothers, and parents, and I thought, 'Why are we being punished for something that happened on the other side of the world?'" Iraqi Shias like Hussein were trapped between the cruel persecution of Saddam and the violence of an American empire that marched into their homes armed to the teeth, illiterate to the distinctions between Sunni and Shia, let alone Arab from Iranian.

Hussein waved his arms when he recollected that story. It was as if he still saw those American soldiers right in front of him and was speaking directly to them, not to a fellow Arab raised in his neighborhood, which sits between the heart of Arab America and the heartbeat of Black America. A place that would claim its own plot of Detroit and carve out its own identity as Little Iraq.

This little slice of Iraq, inside the country that waged an illegal war on his native Iraq, was his new home. "My kids are safe here and can become whatever they want, Insh'Allah," Hussein shared, "and that's a blessing."[17] War brought him to this final destination, and a belief in Allah's design would, God willing, lead his children to better ones. The journey, for Hussein's children, would be distant from his haunting memories of a murderous dictator and the bloody war that succeeded him. Hussein desperately sought to rewrite that grand narrative of persecution that characterized the Shia Muslim ethos, "after the Prophet's" death and before the fall of Saddam, for his American children.[18]

John lived fifteen minutes from Hussein's home. Although just a short trek down the highway—the same drive that linked the segregated memories John and I shared—Lincoln Park was a radically different place from Little Iraq.

Like John and I, Hussein and John were connected in more ways than one. The same War on Terror that sent a working-class white man into a war that should never have been, pushed a Najaf native from the cradle of the Middle East into the belly of the Midwest. The war that ruined a man from within led another man to build a new life afar and to give life to Iraqi American children. It was absurd, but so was the war that spawned this existential duality. In metropolitan Detroit, the place that made me, yesterday's enemies are today's neighbors. Both are terrorized by nightmares of death and memories of hell that haunt them while asleep and shadow them in the din of day.

The terror within is always real. While the terror without is often manufactured, to marshal support for wars that deceive the masses at home and advance the interests of elites abroad. The marching orders of empire, history clearly reveals, never benefit the children thrown into its fires. "The poorest among us are the most disposable" is as quintessential an American slogan as any, and the indigent margins of Detroit and its outer enclaves represent that. John embodies those words more lucidly than anybody I've ever met, while Hussein represents the other side of that pallid coin.

John and Hussein are, in many ways, the same man. Men who adhere to distinct religions, born to different mothers, hailing from opposite sides of the earth, but both children thrown into a fire they did not make, then returned—broken shells of who they might have been—to the same place in the world. Once on opposite hemispheres, John and Hussein are today only separated by eight highway miles. Both are victims of a terror lodged deep within them, embedded by an illegal war made possible by an unholy crusade. A crusade that threatens to disintegrate their lives at any moment, long after one of them held that gun of "freedom" and the other stared down its American barrel.

One was the "patriot" defending national honor, the other branded a "terrorist" for no other reason than the land he came from. Both pawns, and indeed, both victims. John knew men who could no longer bear the terror they saw in Iraq and took their lives shortly after coming home. Hussein had family members and beloved friends who were slaughtered by fronts of American plunder with pithy names. Years later, he still contemplates why "God chose to take them and not me." That weighs on him, it was clear. But he has his new life, his family and children, and a community that counterbalances those unseen battles that still rage within him.

Hussein and John. Different sorts of victims left forever fractured, like the nation where an unjust American war was staged in the name of a fictive terror threat. A terror that broke away from the truth and broke women and men, on both sides, as it rolled onward. The last time John and Hussein were whole is when they were young men. Roughly two decades later, they are strangers who live in the same city, at opposite ends of a freeway. They were pitted against each other by a lie that drove an unjust war, orchestrated by a power that only knew real terror when it saw itself in the mirror. But in place of mirrors were mirages. Mirages of made-up monsters that unmade the poorest of women and men, in America and everywhere the lie was violently imposed.

"How can you have a war on terrorism when war itself is terrorism?" asked historian Howard Zinn, a question that pierced the façade of lies surrounding the War on Terror.[19]

Only nine days after the 9/11 terror attacks, the United States launched a war that would forever alter the world's course. A war that, like American imperial campaigns before it, relied on a foundational lie to justify the evil it was preparing to unleash on innocent Muslims abroad. On the domestic front, that lie was thrust upon unknowing men and women who were packed like sardines into planes, preparing to be thrown into a fire they did not start but blindly fell into. Their targets: men and women, children and elders who had nothing to do with the terror attacks of 9/11, whose only *crime* was adhering to a faith that the Bush administration would inextricably tie to terror.

The force of American history stood with George Bush as he prepared to address Congress on September 20, 2001. Its darkest passages, when presidents who spoke from that stage branded entire masses of people irredeemable savages, chattel, and three-fifths human, lurked like shadows behind him. Vile terms like "enemy aliens" and "enemy race" would resurface; terms used to place people in internment camps decades earlier would be wielded again.[20] That sordid history would meet this new millennium's chapter of American empire.

A series of heinous terror attacks on September 11, 2001, opened the passage for this new chapter of world history ironically dubbed "The War on Terror." The attacks that killed nearly three thousand people were the work of one terror network, Al-Qaeda, and were carried out by a mob of men led by a rich Saudi heir living in a cave on the other side of the world—an heir named Osama bin Laden.[21] A man inspired by the very fundamentalist interpretation of Islam that guided the kingdom of Saudi Arabia, the United States' primary ally in the region since 1933 and the nation that the majority of the 9/11 terrorists called home.

But the enemy of the new war was not Al-Qaeda or its corps of counterinsurgents.[22] Nor was it Wahhabi Islam, the inflexible brand of Sunni Islam that inspired the terror network and the rigid laws of the Saudi kingdom.[23] The enemy was certainly not Saudi Arabia, despite its prominent imprint on the 9/11 terror attacks and the transnational terror networks sprouting up across the world. Saudi Arabia's economic partnership with the United States was far too valuable to the latter's regional and imperial ambitions, despite the role American petrodollars played in spreading Wahhabi Islam across the world and into small villages like Wajir, which emboldened Al-Shabaab terrorists to wreak havoc on innocents.[24]

Any law school professor will tell her students that every case is dictated by the facts. But facts, in that irrational case of empire, were initially irrelevant and later crushed by the blind zeal for revenge. Revenge that unfolded on the streets and on our television screens and was followed by a neoconservative regime's design to marshal that zeal as fuel for the next phase of American empire.[25] In this phase, the enemy was not a terror outfit but the whole of Islam and its nearly 2 billion global adherents.

Mark Twain deftly wrote, "Get your facts first, then you can distort them as you please." The Bush administration took a page out of Twain's book and unleashed an aggressive propaganda blitz before any bullets were fired or any boots landed on foreign soil. The facts were the first victims of the War on Terror, and the disfiguration of the facts primed the terrain for a new crusade waged in the name of democracy but staged to broaden American empire.

What sets American racism apart is its efficiency, its workmanlike ability to rapidly manufacture the belief that an entire group of people is inherently evil or inferior, amoral and inassimilable. This is typically performed through the warped word of God and the wanton *want* of capital.

The law, a profession that I chose as my own, is the state's most potent wand in creating "races" to plunder so that a select few can prosper.[26] This is highlighted by the experience of indigenous Americans, members of a remarkably diverse network of nations who were branded godless "savages" before they met the genocidal might of Manifest Destiny and the burgling laws that paved its way.

The same formula was used in the earliest and middle passages of American slavery. Because indigenous peoples were thought to be too "unruly" to serve as slaves and white indentured servants became too costly, the American appetite for cheap labor turned to the westernmost regions of Africa for human capital. To justify African enslavement, legal gatekeepers invented "Blackness" as a category that branded all Africans as property to be sold and owned, a classification oriented against whiteness, its "superior opposite."[27]

As Cheryl Harris observes in her landmark article "Whiteness as Property," "The hyper-exploitation of Black labor was accomplished by treating Black people themselves as objects of property."[28] Whiteness, therefore, not only represented the pinnacles of citizenship and civilization, it was made synonymous with American as the nation forged its identity. However, its value superseded the bounds of the new nation and all earthly things within and beyond it. Whiteness was sanctified as divine, and its makers reconstructed religious institutions and recolored Jesus in line with that image.[29]

Overseeing the earth was not enough, so whiteness gave "itself a holy face" by "wrapping itself" in the form of a white-faced Jesus and entwining itself with a faith, Christianity, that would become its hallmark. Portraits of white Jesus and his fair-skinned companions sat high in government buildings, living rooms, and schoolhouses in America, and everywhere the budding empire would brush its color of influence.[30] Coupled with this holy whiteness was the sanctity of the dollar, and American capitalism provided a portal only available to European immigrants to shed their foreignness and be, like Christ, "simply white."[31]

Blackness was placed on the other end of the spectrum, thus assigning a permanent "badge of inferiority" to the skin of Africans.[32] The new category, invented by white men who owned slaves and lusted for more, held that Black people were placed on earth by God to serve them, the white masters. The Supreme Court ruled in favor of this view, counting Black people as "property" that held no rights.[33] Immediately upon crossing the Middle Passage and coming to America, Africans were "stamped from the beginning," converted into slaves, and sold to white men and women who curated the very laws and racial classifications that trapped them and their unborn descendants.[34]

Whiteness and Blackness, whiteness oriented against Blackness, the genesis of a new binary that followed the formula of old paradigms that pitted good against evil, crosses against crescents, and crusaders against Qur'ans. America's founding fathers constructed this racial binary and its sub-classifications "through both coercion and ideology, with legal actors as both conscious and unwitting participants," entwining law with white supremacy.[35] The law was at once a capitalistic carrot and an imperial stick that came down on nonwhites hard and fast.

Through law, American racism manufactured these existential binaries and then fluidly tweaked them in order to serve shifting interests. These binaries drove blanket characterizations of deeply complex and heterogeneous populations. Viewing Muslim peoples as an unbending monolith is hardly a modern invention, nor is it a hardened characterization christened after the War on Terror, the latest emanation of American racial and racist empire.[36] Rather, it is a primary device from the American racial toolkit, used against a broad host of peoples and the first Muslim populations—enslaved Africans—whose faith was stripped from them along with their humanity.[37]

The language of "national security" and "enemy aliens" that emerged into the parlance of the day during the War on Terror was also not new. These terms, and the hysteria that surrounded them, were first deployed to round up Japanese people on the American West Coast from 1942 through 1946. Nearly 120,000 people of Japanese descent were forcibly removed from their homes and placed in concentration camps after the Pearl Harbor attacks of December 7, 1941.[38]

They were cast, every single one of them, as "enemy aliens," despite the fact that the vast majority of them were bona fide citizens.[39] But citizenship did not protect them from the wartime racism drummed up by President Franklin Delano Roosevelt, or from the Supreme Court ruling that upheld his internment order three years later.[40] Nearly eight decades later, the Supreme Court would uphold a "Muslim ban" ordered by another president, using the same rationale of "protecting national security" to justify the mass internment of another nonwhite population.[41]

As these past annals of American racism rang in a new millennium, it was time for Muslims to feel the force of American terror.[42] Islam was a familiar foe from legal eras and political crusades past, but the 9/11 terror attacks and the geopolitical void left by the breakup of the Soviet Union created an opportunity for an empire that had yet to stretch itself thin.[43] The events leading up to the War on Terror, and ultimately the war itself, "displaced Communism as public enemy number one" and seized the opportunity to elevate the whole of Islam as the "enemy race," renewing plans for a new world order.[44] An order built on campaigns of war and disorder that legitimizes American military offensives in the name of defending civilization and democracy.

"On September the 11th, enemies of freedom committed an act of war against our country."[45] President Bush spoke these words, and many more loaded terms that peddled a new kind of war. But these words were written long before he uttered them.

As previous chapters of the American racial narrative illustrate, every act of terror levied against a targeted group is enabled by an accompanying dialectic, an ideology and a language subsequently made into law and then brutally enforced by the hands of the state. Manifest Destiny and its imperial aspirations were not limited to North America nor confined to the nineteenth century. Although American history books narrowly frame Manifest Destiny as a bygone crusade into the Wild West, it is anything but moot. Manifest Destiny is a living campaign, a dynamic and ambitious imperial project that taps into old strategies of demonizing entire populations while claiming to promote democracy and civilization, and then swiftly leveling them and taking everything that remains.

It was a new century, and a novel ideology would be employed by the Bush administration to justify its version of Manifest Destiny in the Muslim world. This ideology, and its carefully packaged language, was primed to be put into action. In 1993, eight years before those two airplanes crashed into the twin towers in New York City, Samuel

P. Huntington, a Harvard professor, wrote in *Foreign Policy* magazine: "The fundamental problem for the West is not Islamic fundamentalism. It is Islam, a different civilization whose people are convinced of the superiority of their culture and are obsessed with the inferiority of their power."[46]

That was it. The title, "The Clash of Civilizations?," was powerful. Undeniable. In fact, it was perfect. And the framing, which oriented the "West" as the citadel of civilization, and Islam—the *whole* of it—as its longstanding rival, fit the American orientation of classifying one race as "superior" and the other as "inferior."

Huntington said it himself: "To define themselves, people need an other." And he authored the script for the War on Terror, which found that ideal, ominous other in the entire religion of Islam.[47]

The Bush administration thrust the "clash of civilizations" paradigm and its pithy vocabulary into the War on Terror machine that it was ready to unleash on the home front and countries far beyond.[48] In the same vein that heterogeneous Native American tribes were flatly reduced to "barbarians" and a rich tapestry of African peoples were consolidated into Black "property," the War on Terror consolidated Muslims into the "enemy of civilization" and then flattened the extraordinary complexity of Islam into a monolith that inspired "terrorism."

Nuance of any sort was disavowed in favor of inflexible binaries. There were "citizens" and there were "terrorists," a duality the state capitalized on to elevate itself above the rights of the polity and the very charter, the Constitution, that extended those civil liberties and defined state power.[49]

There existed "civilization" and an irredeemably violent creed bent on destroying it. This civilizational paradigm emerged in the ideological engine that drove the War on Terror, summoning Americans living on the nation's margins, like John, to be sent to a foreign land as fodder for a baseless fight. Fodder in the name of "freedom" that marches like empire, and from the vantage point of the millions of Muslims who have died in its name, "democracy" that strikes like terror. And fodder that would be left for dead in Iraq, or a slowly dying veteran who would become my friend.

I met John again in July in another strip mall. This time, one where boarded-up stores and "going out of business" signs dressed up naked storefronts. I parked in a lot where there were only a handful of cars. John's truck was one of them, and he leaned against it and waved at me as I got out of my SUV. Actually, it was my mother's SUV, a Chevy Equinox. My car was still back in Fayetteville, Arkansas, the place I had left during the beginning stages of the pandemic so that I could shelter in place near my family in Michigan.

The make of the car mattered. We were in Detroit, after all, the Motor City. I drove a foreign car, but now I was back in a city where the manufacturer and make of your car tell half of your story. The bigger story, the tale of the economic downturn exacerbated by the pandemic, was narrated by an empty parking lot, evacuated businesses, and the military veteran I drove down Southfield Freeway to meet with, and rounds of long phone calls.

It was the thick of the lockdown, and John wore a face mask that signaled to me that I should do the same. I walked toward him, handed him Sarah Kendzior's *The View from Flyover Country,* a book I had promised to loan him when we last spoke.[50] It resonated deeply with me, and John's struggles gave face to several of the stories in that brilliant book.

We then talked, at length, about the struggles of life under lockdown, the season outlook for the Detroit Lions, how much we missed live sports, and how things would shake out after the pandemic. He looked upbeat despite the day's novel challenges, and shared how the nearly $4,000 he received from unemployment every month "made things a lot easier." I was happy to see John in good spirits, especially during a pandemic that had sunk stronger men into inescapable holes.

"That isn't very Republican of you, welcoming handouts!" I joked, which caused a laugh from John that, minutes later, I realized I had never heard before. It was good to see him, and even better to see him upbeat. He clearly felt whole, or as close to that as anybody could be after enduring a life-changing war.

Yet the pandemic we faced provided a stark reminder that everything, from depression to bliss, happiness to heartache, is in fact *temporary*. In the end, everything is. The distinction between transience and permanence was perhaps just as thin as the difference between normality and the absurd state in which we found ourselves in that Lincoln Park parking lot, or the state in which John found himself fifteen years earlier, in an abandoned square in Baghdad asking, "What the hell am I doing here?"

During the War on Terror, nothing felt normal for John, me, and Hussein back in Little Iraq. *Normal,* during this protracted war and the new pandemic that plagued us all, meant nothing. But we all had to learn how to move forward and grasp those last bastions of normality that reminded us that life was worth living. That it *is* worth living.

"We gotta meet up for some Middle Eastern food when things get back to normal, I love that stuff," he finished, and I nodded. "I know this amazing Yemeni restaurant, Sheba on Michigan Avenue, let's make it happen," I replied, looking to lure my friend from Lincoln Park to the other side of the tracks, where Arabs and Muslims saturate the streets.

"Never had Yemeni before. I'm game," John responded. "Authentic, traditional Arab food," I boasted, "Haven't lived until you tried it." "Well, my friend, you haven't lived until you've had a child. Anyway, when are you going to settle down and start a family?" he shot back at me with a wide smile. "You sound just like my mother, man. Are you sure you're not Arab?" We shot jokes at each other like two old friends.

We each let out a hearty laugh. In the middle of an empty parking lot, in the heart of flyover country, looking for rays of normality in a bleak space where war and terror, a novel virus and mental illness closed in on us and those fleeting moments of happiness, those fragile passes of normality. We fought back, a white war veteran and a Muslim author, in a united front where our distinct races and religions found kinship in our delicate mortality.

Getting to know one another, we both realized, melted the tension and just as quickly demystified the stereotypes that I had of him and that he had of me.

It was time to go. We bumped fists, a new handshake for a new world, and then went our separate ways. Closed restaurants alongside vacant stores evacuated by a bomb dropped by Mother Nature, with only one place open for business: an Army recruitment center, in the heart of a different kind of battleground, where the unemployment rate soared faster than the number of confirmed coronavirus cases.

A car pulled up in front of the recruitment center as I got into my mother's Chevy. A young white man—he looked not a day older than twenty—got out of his car and walked toward the center.

This was the world we lived in, where the demand for war was only outpaced by the supply of those willing to be fed into its ravenous belly. Fresh meat, fresh fodder for an imperial appetite without limits. There were few jobs for a man his age. The cost of college had skyrocketed and the prospects of making a living wage without an undergraduate degree had plummeted, particularly in a pandemic-stricken world that hardly "ended the War on Terror" or the "9/11 era," and especially for Muslims and working-class men like John and that young boy, ready to feed himself to the war and its wolves in Washington.[51] The War on Terror, called the "forever war" by some, had no end in sight, and there was not a vaccine that could end it.[52]

The young man stared the world that the War on Terror had made square in the eye. College was too costly, the pandemic accelerated mass layoffs, and the burdens of the world were growing heavier. War is what remains, so he walked toward it, into the only door left open for him. Peddled dreams waited with lofty promises of valor and victory, and a sales pitch about democracy and terrorism that matched the imagery of his favorite video games and Hollywood blockbusters.

He walked toward it alongside a mother who dreamt about far more for her son. A mother who wished that her job, or jobs, could pay the exorbitant tuition at the University of Michigan or Michigan State University—public colleges with tuitions that are prohibitive for poor students. Perhaps she wished that the jobs that NAFTA sent off on a one-way ticket to Mexico and other nations where other poor people are exploited were still in Michigan for people like her son.

The mother walking slowly alongside her son does not know John, the man who stood in front of me moments ago. But she knows many men like him across the metropolitan Detroit area, good men that the war in Iraq swallowed in whole or in part. She was helpless against the conjoined, violent pull of that future and the emptiness of the present. But so was I from my view in that abandoned parking lot.

I wish I could have walked alongside that young man and guided him toward a more intimate view of that future. I wish I could have introduced him to John, to show him a picture of the future he should not sign up for. John, broken, and only held together by an obligation to the two children he brought into a world that defeated him when he enlisted. Held together by fleeting smiles and transient moments of laughter that fueled him to move forward and live onward, with only enough gas in his tank to get to where he was going next. The only currency John had left was the white skin that wrapped his broken body.

John drove off and the young man walked in. Even when the world stopped, the War on Terror marched forward. And the terror it seeded, deep within John, Hussein, and the victims it claimed and will claim tomorrow, is constant.

The war on terror, the war and the terror, the terror and the war. The battle between the two is continuous and constant for all men and women, parents and children trapped between the war's violent lines and vile lies.

It is not reasonable that those who gamble with men's lives should not pay with their own.[53]

A GLOBAL CRUSADE

> Every empire tells itself and the world that it is unlike all other empires, and its mission is not to plunder and control but to educate and liberate.
> EDWARD SAID, July 20, 2003

I was a second-year law student at UCLA when I learned that Edward Said, the Palestinian American intellectual whose words lifted my intellect and pushed me to write, would be coming to campus. The news of his visit sent me over the moon, and I sank myself into his autobiography, *Out of Place,* dreaming about my opportunity to ask him a question.

However, my excitement quickly dissipated when I realized there was an obstacle: Said's lecture conflicted with my favorite class, "Race in Cinema," taught by a professor, Kimberlé Crenshaw, who would become my greatest mentor. What a dilemma! I did not want to miss class, my favorite at the time and one of the most memorable courses of my time in law school. On the other hand, I could not miss seeing Said speak, particularly at a moment when his work meant so much— perhaps more than ever—to me. I certainly did not want to choose between learning from the two intellectual giants who crafted Orientalism and coined "intersectionality."[54]

Stuck in that enviable yet difficult intersection, I set off to resolve the scheduling conflict. I built up the courage to ask Professor Crenshaw if the entire class could attend Said's lecture on February 20, 2003; his remarks were aligned with the spirit of the class and would resonate with the mood of the moment—a moment in which the War on Terror, still in its infancy, would change me and the world fundamentally. Remarks that, I learned seven months later, when Said passed away, would be one of his final public addresses.

"That's a great idea, Khaled," Professor Crenshaw smiled, agreeing to my plan. The dilemma was no more and the stage was set to listen to and learn from Said, one of the twentieth century's fiercest and most trenchant intellectuals. A week later, our class of fifteen students made the short cross-campus walk to Royce Hall, where the man who gave the world *Orientalism* would try to make sense of the War on Terror and the new world order Washington had plunged us into.

The world itself was at a crucial impasse. Everybody could feel it in the air, particularly the world's Muslims, who found themselves on the *wrong* side of the civilizational divide marked by the neoconservative Bush administration, the hawks that steered it from Washington, and the limitless school of vultures deployed around the world. The War on Terror, about sixteen months into its existence, had swiftly remade the structures of American government, unleashing strident legislation that enabled almost unchecked surveillance of Muslim citizens and residents on the home front and beyond.[55] As Henry A. Giroux reaffirmed in a chilling article on the modern state of surveillance mainstreamed by the American War on Terror, state "surveillance is not simply pervasive, it has become normalized. [George] Orwell could not have imagined . . . the intrusive capabilities of the new high-powered digital technologies of surveillance" that surround us, and define our modern existence.[56] Muslim Americans like myself were under intense scrutiny. Our religious expression and political views, our entire beings relentlessly examined and categorized. Were we "moderate" Muslims acting in line with the dictates of the state?[57] Or "bad" Muslims voicing our concern over the strident surveillance and sweeping dragnets imposed on Muslims at home and abroad?[58]

Almost instantly after the 9/11 attacks, the US launched a bloody war in Afghanistan.[59] There was a bloodier one on the horizon. Less than two years later, a second war would be launched in Iraq—a nation said, despite lack of evidence, to be hiding "weapons of mass destruction" and "harboring Al-Qaeda terrorists." A nation that, in the days that followed, would be sunk into a bloody sectarian war spurred by an illegal American crusade that left millions dead, and by subsequent proxy "conflicts within Islam" that continue to claim the lives of innocents.[60]

Back at UCLA, we took our seats in the cavernous hall with the ornate ceiling and illuminated stage. On stage was no other than Edward Said, the Palestinian exile whose body, made frail by leukemia, could hardly harness his strapping intellect. For the next two hours, we listened as he walked us through an analysis of a world spiraling into war after war, a world fractured by centuries of Orientalist imperialism that dawned a new age of Islamophobic crusading.

The experience felt surreal. Here I sat, alongside a professor who had pioneered new tools for analyzing how American racism was most destructive at its most neglected "margins" and vulnerable intersections.[61] And just a few rows away was the intellectual auteur who had laid the groundwork for understanding the roots and rise of Islamophobia in the United States and countries far from its shores.

That day felt like a call to action. I believe it was the day I first truly comprehended why Muslims were being cast as America's new principal enemy, the foremost societal menace in that revolving door of racial groups that had to be pummeled to protect national security, or civilization, or Christianity—neatly crafted proxies for whiteness and the political and economic wealth it aimed to maintain and monopolize. It was the day when I decided to fully commit myself and my career to combating the war machine that fed the violence ravaging Muslims near and far. I had not yet heard the word "Islamophobia," but I understood what it meant, and I understood that its scale was global.

I wanted to act, to make an impact, I realized that day. That call subsumed me. I would not accept being a bystander as wars were waged on Muslims abroad and at home. There I was, sitting between my greatest intellectual heroes, thinkers who typified, so incisively and sublimely, how the highest form of intellect are those ideas that are mobilized into transformative action. Had it not been for Kimberlé Crenshaw and Edward Said, I would not have become who I am today. My work only exists because of *Orientalism* and *intersectionality*, and every page I have ever written was inspired by being nurtured in between these two discourses and the giants who penned them.

The foundational War on Terror myth was anything but novel. In two hours' time, Edward Said synthesized his magnum opus, *Orientalism*, into a master class tied to the War on Terror and events that were unfolding at the time. A sage on that stage, Said demystified how Islam was flattened by scholarly discourses old and new, and how ideas shaped in ivory towers oriented Muslims as the enemy—ballads that preceded the bullets fired by snipers in Iraq, or the battalions in Afghanistan that bludgeoned innocent families and then branded them as "collateral damage." In ways that only he could, Said tailored *Orientalism*'s definitive ideas to break down how the Bush administration deftly suspended civil liberties in the name of national security and persuaded a frightening majority of the American polity that Muslims, regardless of their legal status, were "impossible Americans"—a fifth pillar cast out of the caste of meaningful citizenship.[62] With even greater diabolical deftness, the Bush regime carried forward a baseless war against a nation entirely disconnected from the 9/11 terror attacks: Iraq.

Iraq was not Al-Qaeda, but in the minds of most Americans, the distinction was irrelevant. Arabs were Muslims, Muslims were Arabs, *and the two conflated identities were tied to terrorism*.[63] This was the

Orientalist logic that Said dedicated his life to interrogating and undoing, a logic that reemerged more violently during the War on Terror, with deadlier global ramifications.

New wars, in essence, are only contemporary extensions of preexisting campaigns. This was particularly the case with Islam, a target of American empire and aggression from the 1970s through the 1990s,[64] well before it, and its global population of adherents, graduated to the pinnacle of racialized threat. In 1994, seven years before the War on Terror, Said made perfect sense of a world marred by it. In *Representations of the Intellectual,* a collection of masterful speeches Said delivered in London, he stated, "Dealing with the Islamic world—all one billion [plus] people in it, with dozens of different societies, half a dozen major languages including Arabic, Turkish, Iranian, [and English], all spread out over about a third of the globe—American or British academic intellectuals speak reductively . . . irresponsibly of something called 'Islam.'" These European and American voices, which Said labeled "Orientalists," flattened Islam into a singular system, a solitary whole stripped of any complexity or heterogeneity.

Said pushed forward, explaining how a cabal of formative Orientalists hijacked the very definition of Islam, ascribing to it a meaning that clashed with its essential being: "By using this single word they seem to regard Islam as a simple object about which grand generalizations spanning a millennium and a half of Muslim history can be made, and about which judgments concerning the compatibility between Islam and democracy, Islam and human rights, Islam and progress are quite unabashedly advanced."[65] Or in cogent War-on-Terror speak, *Islam against civilization* and everything that the civilized world valued, prized, and stood for. George W. Bush aptly summarized Samuel Huntington for the layman, proclaiming, "They hate our freedoms."[66] In both old and new crusades, "they" were Muslims. Those who adhered to the faith, domestically and abroad, were "they" unless and until they proved their allegiance to the United States and its new war.[67]

On that stage in UCLA's Royce Hall, Said crystallized how Muslims were reshaped and redefined into a vile shell of who they truly were, first by European and then by American institutions, which mutated the faith and its global following for the purpose of imperial conquest, war, and the pilfered spoils of each.

Islam was more than just a religion, and more often, in the minds of Orientalists, *not a religion*.[68] Rather, old- and especially new-guard Orientalists framed it as a competing political system—a totalitarian system made in the mirror image of the West, or what Said labeled the "Occident."[69] Islam, therefore, was a rival "civilization" mangled by Western hands to facilitate their imperial ambitions and justify the violence they inflicted on masses of Muslims who—far from the shores of Europe—were painted as imminent threats. The imminence was not physical or even geographic, but tied to memory and lucid in the imagination; namely, the memory of those old and original Crusades, always present in the collective psyche of Europe, and later, the United States.

Orientalism disfigured Islam into an utterly unrecognizable form and replaced its bona fide dimensions with a thin caricature. Orientalism was Orwellian, and as the author poignantly observed in the disturbingly prescient 1984, "We do not merely destroy our enemies; we change them."[70]

The new War on Terror discourse was intellectually emaciated and obsolete, but as revitalized and repackaged by the likes of Samuel P. Huntington, it provided an undeniably powerful paradigm and potent language for a world in which the images of falling towers and bearded terrorists were seared deep in the imagination. Huntington's "clash of civilizations," to no surprise, "utterly stormed Washington" and curated the framing of the War on Terror.[71]

American history has proven, through formative passages of puritanical ethnic cleansing and eugenics-driven racial apartheid, that discourses need not be true or even intelligible. Discourses of imperialism and dehumanization just have to be resonant, palatable to crowds bent on vengeance, then remade into law.

Where Said theorized how the "Occident" defined itself as the opposite of the "Orient," the War on Terror pits the "civilized" West against the "uncivilized" Muslim world.[72] If Europe laid the foundation for that civilization, the United States—the West's modern citadel—carried its torch forward in the minds of the Bush administration and its interlocutors. For them, the United States, and its War on Terror, is the Occidental beacon of light. But for Muslims, collectively cast as the enemy, they stand together as a tower of massive fright. A tower from which American snipers *thrill-kill* Muslims, then equip nations around the globe with ideological ammunition and pellets of propaganda to join their ungodly crusade.[73]

Everything was the same. Everything except the labels, the laws, and the casing that concealed the same lies. Said's master discourse, *Orientalism*, laid the intellectual foundation for understanding the hate that Washington crafted into the War on Terror, which it then globalized and exported. It was shipped off like a new line of Chevy trucks—manufactured at first by American hands on Detroit assembly lines, but then handed off to others to manufacture more inexpensively for the benefit of the brain trust at home.

A year after the 9/11 terror attacks, Leti Volpp, law professor at the University of California in Berkeley, published the influential legal treatise "The Citizen and the Terrorist" in the *UCLA Law Review*. The article drew an essential conclusion—and an even more essential *connection*—to Said's Orientalism and its potent role in driving the War on Terror's foundational and ferocious tropes.

Volpp observed that the War on Terror, through its propaganda and war-making machines, was potently remaking and "redeploy[ing] longstanding Orientalist tropes."[74] These four words—compact but cogent, efficient yet immensely instructive—tied the vicious rise of Islamophobia to the potent bank of misrepresentations of Muslims that were embedded in the imaginations of governments, institutions, and people long before the 9/11 terror attacks took place. In short, as I have written before and echoed countless times, *Orientalism is the mother of Islamophobia,* and its dense memory of intentional distortions, meticulous lies, and "mythical abstractions" accelerated the War on Terror and expedited its spread on the domestic and global fronts.[75] Americans did not have to look far to source their disdain for Islam and its adherents—American legal and political history was saturated with damning stereotypes and destructive narratives.

James Baldwin, the founding father of America's hidden soul, adroitly observed that "history is not the past. It is the present. We carry our history with us. We are our history."[76] Perhaps nothing represents this more than the War on Terror and its epistemological lifeline, which draws on the vile history of Orientalism to vilify, and then victimize, Muslims through state-sponsored Islamophobia and its accompanying tentacles of private propaganda and jingoism. Orientalism, and its deceitful history of fabrications and tropes, is an "invented past" that leaves Muslims in that deadly intersection of sub-humanity and threat, which its progeny, Islamophobia, seeks to perpetuate to drive new crusades, every bit as deceitful and violent, against Muslims around the world.

Furthermore, Volpp's observation illustrated how the Bush administration did not have to invent an entirely new narrative to push the War on Terror forward. Through the prism of Orientalism, the world already perceived and understood Islam to be oppressive, unyieldingly rigid, and zealously wed to war. We are all now accustomed, and sadly desensitized, to reading headlines like the "War Is Normal in the

Middle East" and "The Mideast Is Always at War."[77] We hardly flinch when the villain in our favorite drama or the new Hollywood block-buster film is a Muslim.[78] The Muslim terrorist has become a fixture in modern television and film, and this caricature is reproduced in line with how Washington imagines the racial and religious contours of the terrorist, and how the law is enforced against those who resemble him.

These images, and the ideas they conjure, reify the notion that Muslims are the enemy of civilization. They deepen the cruel reality that during the War on Terror, it is entirely rational and normal to perceive Muslims through the linear lens of terrorism. That vision, that idea, is repeated over and again by lawmakers, politicians, pundits, news anchors, musicians, and characters on television, in film, and in virtually every other medium. Islamic terrorism has become as natural to our senses as turning away from a bright and burning sun on a scorching summer day.

The groundwork for the War on Terror, for the Bush administration and the world's governments that capitalized on it, was deeply and firmly established before 9/11. It was part of the American fabric to fear and loathe Muslims, and in short order, that fear and loathing was pumped into every facet of the War on Terror machine. Islamophobia was the progeny of this process.

And, in the spirit of American ambition and ingenuity, whatever we consume must be packaged and shipped off to the rest of the world, to satisfy our endless imperial appetite and then feed those foreign governments that share our hunger for demonizing Islam.

The War on Terror was never intended to be an exclusively American crusade. It was framed, at its very inception, as a "civilizational fight" by President Bush, and then peddled and promoted as such by the cabinet of hawks that steered his administration.[79] Like most everything produced in America, the War on Terror was peddled globally—and pushed with the capitalistic zeal that distinguishes the United States.

It was then, and remains, a crusade in which the United States served as the front runner and enlisted nations to fight alongside it. Washington then managed a motley crew of nations keen on exploiting the War on Terror for their own political gain and for fundamentally domestic pursuits; local Muslims were both the practical means and the political menace to achieve those ends.

The days of "shock and awe" were behind us, and the War on Terror ushered in a new era of smash and grab.[80] This new model offered other nations a template of propaganda and punishment they could emulate that was endorsed by the world's principal superpower. A superpower that exported "democracy" with bullets, bombs, and bullying of weaker nations, and in line with its new "with us or against us" directive, threatened the world to align itself against Islam or feel the might of that terror itself.[81]

President Bush made that ultimatum plain on September 21, 2001. His immediate spectators were members of the US Congress, but his real audience was the world and everybody in it. Bush spoke ten days after 9/11, announcing a global war that would usher in a terror that would dwarf what took place in New York City: "This is not . . . just America's fight. And what is at stake is not just America's freedom. This is the world's fight. This is civilization's fight. This is the fight of all who believe in progress and pluralism, tolerance and freedom. . . . The civilized world is rallying to America's side."[82] This was no impassioned plea or persuasive appeal to an audience that had any choice; this was an ultimatum. An ultimatum delivered by a global superpower turned bully, an ultimatum that drew a clear line between civilization and Islam, democracy and terrorism, at a moment when labels meant nothing and might meant everything.

This global crusade had only one boundary, one consequential dividing line. And the world's nations pivoted and plotted, raced and rushed across that line to evade the aim of America's ultimatum and the pain that could follow if they did not capitulate to it. Many nations picked up arms alongside the United States and directed them against their own Muslim populations. Every Muslim was now subject to a war that marked them as a prospective enemy on account of faith, and faith alone.

In 1984, George Orwell wrote, "The object of waging a war is always to be in a better position in which to wage another war."[83] Perhaps no war has been more prolific than the War on Terror in birthing equally or more destructive progeny.

The United States rushed into war with Afghanistan and Iraq, then turned its guns against its own people, specifically against Arab and Muslim Americans, who were profiled as terror threats on the basis of race, religion, and a perceived "disloyalty" tied to these characteristics.[84] Muslims in Myanmar and India were no longer second- or third-class citizens, but "terror threats" that warranted punishment instead of protection.[85] Third- and fourth-generation Muslims in France and Germany, who strove to harmonize their nationalities with their faith, were no longer countrywomen and countrymen, but in terms more forceful than ever, dubbed "foreigners" in the only country they had ever known and called home. As Volpp states, their citizenship was politically "undone" on account of their ethnic, and more forcefully, their religious identities.[86]

The War on Terror birthed new wars and resurrected old ones, emboldening governments to scapegoat their Muslim populations for any political or economic woe, real or fabricated, that troubled their regimes. The Islamophobia reared by the War on Terror blazed a new path for populist movements and the demagogues who led them. They led anti-Muslim campaigns and planted the flag of a "clash of civilizations" atop their nation's political terrain to stir hysteria, turned their ire and guns on Muslims, and then seized power.

These new wars spread like a plague across the globe. They were political and propaganda wars, military crusades and genocidal campaigns. All were granted license and fueled by the United States, the old and new "arsenal of democracy" that armed the world with the ammunition for these new crusades against Muslims.

Islamophobia equipped nations around the world with the capacity to level their Muslim populations without firing a single bullet. Governments in China and India, for instance, that had long relegated their Muslim communities to inferior status now had an American blueprint for persecuting them with impunity, and even more importantly, a thumbs-up from Uncle Sam to crack down like never before.

However, as this book reveals in the coming chapters, these new crusades against Muslims were anything but protective and defensive; instead, they were offensive and violent at their very core. The objective of "countering terrorism" or "shoring up national security" functioned as a modern disguise for a pernicious and hidden campaign: policing, punishing, and persecuting Muslims.

Words meant little and war spoke volumes. This theme continued after the architects of the War on Terror made way for a president who marched into history and marched the crusade forward. President Obama brandished his words with brilliant precision, replacing the Bush administration's civilizational sword with oratory traps of seduction.[87]

The first trap was perhaps his most seductive. He laid it in the heart of the so-called Muslim world eight months after becoming the United States' first Black president. From Cairo, a crossroads of civilization and a citadel of Islamic teaching, the president with the middle name

Hussein declared, "I've come to Cairo to seek a new beginning between the United States and Muslims around the world, one based on mutual interest and mutual respect, and one based upon the truth that America and Islam are not exclusive and need not be in competition."[88]

These were lofty words. Moving words, in fact, that promised to heal eight years of wounds inflicted by the War on Terror. I was convinced when I first heard them. In fact, everybody was smitten by those remarks, and Muslims near and far lauded President Obama and the hope he sold. Obama symbolized racial progress and a new day of "inclusion," buttressed by the ability to disarm almost anyone with his oratory brilliance.[89]

That was, after all, Obama's genius. Words were weapons designed to lull and disarm and then, when all defenses were down, the drones were deployed abroad and informants were carefully placed in American mosques.[90] President Obama was fully wed to the War on Terror, but an iteration of it that aligned with neoliberal strategy and sensibilities. As the number of days between Cairo and reality increased, his "historic" speech revealed a hidden agenda.

The force of Obama's words crumbled along with new fronts of Orwellian aggression. While unfurling spellbinding oratory smoke screens, Obama deepened the wounds of the War on Terror and opened new ones. Behind the veil of progressivism, he deployed a nonstop fleet of drones that killed scores in Yemen, Somalia, Pakistan, and Afghanistan—all Muslim-majority countries.[91] These attacks flouted common principles of international law and wiped scores of innocent Muslims from the face of the earth.[92] In addition to the drones, Obama carried forward the war in Iraq, established and expanded counter-radicalization policing, and failed to close the detention camps in Guantanamo.[93]

From the symbolic perch of mutual understanding and tolerance, he ushered in a modern network of surveillance that flipped imams into informants and entrapped Muslim youth on the internet and in the heart of Muslim communities in the United States and abroad.[94]

Eight years of Obama's War on Terror dissonance laid the groundwork for an unfiltered era of American Islamophobia. The door was opened for the same unhinged anti-Muslim populism that took hold in Europe to make its way across the Atlantic and to an orange-skinned huckster keen on marketing anything, even Islamophobia, to claim the White House.

Donald Trump rose from the political fringes to the most powerful post in the world. He did so on the back of explicit proposals to "ban Muslims" and by ratcheting up the clash-of-civilizations speak that fueled formative War on Terror rhetoric.[95] "I think Islam hates us," Trump said, and did not stutter as he stared at CNN's Anderson Cooper and the world that was watching. Unequivocally disavowing the beautifully packaged blows delivered by President Obama in exchange for fists clad with thorns, Trump ushered in a new era of explicit Islamophobia.

Trump, and the brazen administration he oversaw, must be understood as progeny of the War on Terror.[96] The culture of Islamophobia mainstreamed by the war conditioned the people to want a leader made in its image, one who made explicit the Islamophobia buried under the technical language of the law and the oratory giftwrapping of President Obama. And Trump, a salesman of the highest order, gave the people what they wanted.

Trump was never an ideologue. He was always an opportunist, willing to meld his views and manufacture a platform that would deliver him profit, whether political or financial. Fifteen years of the War on Terror primed a growing segment of the American people to hate Muslims, and Trump fed that hatred with oratory raw meat at every campaign stop and stump speech.[97] When he claimed office, he fully wed his administration to the War on Terror's core objectives and language, pushing the message that won him the presidency and further fueled the new crusades that were unfolding before he claimed that seat: that Islam is an enemy that must be vanquished at any cost.

From Bush to Obama to Trump and now Biden, each executive presiding over the War on Terror steered it forward globally. This war was created in the name of protecting civilization, supplanted by a campaign where drones and spies donned the thin mask of harmony, and back to a *trumped-up* clash of civilizations orchestrated by an apocalyptic demagogue.[98] A fluidly remade War on Terror that offered the world, and the constellation of nations that fed on the war, an American template for unleashing their own domestic crusades against an entire faith and its followers.

"Every empire tells itself and the world that it is unlike all other empires," Edward Said proclaimed from the center of a stage that would be his last, an appearance he would later memorialize in a *Los Angeles Times* article, one of the final pieces he would publish.[99] While his world was nearing its end, the might of his work and the force of his words would never be more alive or more urgent.

I rose from my seat in UCLA's Royce Hall alongside Professor Crenshaw and my classmates. Ready for the world—and the new wars being waged—with a clarity and purpose I could not have imagined before. Only months before he transitioned, Said paved the way for a new crop of scholars, activists, and scholar-activists committed to the very project he pioneered. A community, I decided that day, that I would be part of.

That "everything of consequence either had happened or would happen in the West" was a great lie of the past, Said revealed. That pushed me to search for that truth, then fight for it, wherever that hate that still did not claim its name, Islamophobia, sprouted from the earth.

NEW WORD ORDER

> Political language is designed to make lies sound truthful and murder respectable, and to give an appearance of solidity to pure wind.
> GEORGE ORWELL, "Politics and the English Language"

It was a warm spring day in Chicago. But a day when the city, known for its strong winds, would see new voices of scorn and alarm blow in. I was in the city visiting my younger brother, Mohammed, who was prepared to launch a fleet of halal food trucks in a world where anything *tied* to Islam, even falafel and kabobs, could trigger suspicion and invite violence.

Islamophobia was becoming standard American fare. Fare with a fluidly shifting menu, and by September 2015, as the propaganda machine turned to podcasts and new age pundits claimed new age platforms, the War on Terror looked and sounded dramatically different than it had in September 2001.

While on a walk through the Loop, I tuned in to a discussion between Sam Harris, part of the intellectual vanguard of the new atheist movement, and Ayaan Hirsi Ali, the Somali Dutch pundit who called Islam a "mental cage" in her widely read book *Infidel*. This book made Hirsi Ali a staple of the anti-Muslim movement in Europe, and later, the United States.[100] Harris and Ali were eloquent, and their analysis was clear and accessible. This, along with their liberal sensibilities, wooed massive audiences from the political left and center. I could understand, listening to their discussion, why they were so effective in reeling in legions of listeners from across the political spectrum.

The days of the last decade, when aging Orientalists like Bernard Lewis and Samuel P. Huntington steered the discourse against Islam from inside their ivory towers, were waning, replaced by new, sharper voices. Calls to "wage war on Islam" were not only coming from fringe evangelical voices in the Deep South, but were being sounded by liberals on bright stages with big stars like Bill Maher, or on massive podcasts like the Joe Rogan Experience.[101]

The new voices spewing new fictions were younger, smartly dressed, and smarter in word. They often championed liberal values, like same-sex marriage and gender equality, and touted the virtues of multiculturalism and inclusion. Their followings and influence swelled by the day, along with a singular blind spot that at first appeared to be a philosophical caveat to their modern worldviews. A caveat that, upon closer scrutiny, was in fact a catapult: a vehement aversion to Islam.

Islamophobia lifted Harris, Hirsi Ali, Ben Shapiro, and their ideological allies to new levels of acclaim. They dismissed Islamophobia as a "myth," a Trojan horse used by Muslim civic organizations to push extremist agendas while "masquerading as a human rights organization."[102] Although self-styled "progressives," Harris, Hirsi Ali, and those who shared their views discounted the suffering inflicted upon Muslims by the American War on Terror, or dismissed the gravity of the new crusades it fed. Islamophobia served as an ideological meeting point for pundits with disparate ideologies. For instance, right-wing pundits like Jordan Peterson found rare agreement with the likes of Bill Maher, who similarly delivered "messages to Muslims" that claimed that the struggles of its adherents came exclusively from within the faith, its scripture, and its sectarian fault lines.[103]

This new word, "Islamophobia," and the truth it spoke to power rattled proponents of the War on Terror, old and new. Christopher Hitchens, a prominent contrarian turned War on Iraq apologist revered by this new anti-Muslim vanguard, spurred on Islamophobia denialism with his 2007 book *God Is Not Great*.[104] The book and its title, a direct swipe at Islam's signature proclamation of *Allahu Akbar*, weaponized atheism as a new liberal sword against the prolific anti-Muslim hate that percolated post-9/11. Hitchens, once an intellectual giant among progressive and liberal thinkers, embraced the hawkish posture of the Bush administration and its war on Iraq, and pivoted markedly to the right on account of his swelling Islamophobia.[105]

Hitchens did not make that pivot alone. While remaking himself, Hitchens led the making of a new cottage industry of liberal Islamophobes. These voices anchored their Islamophobia in atheism and disseminated it through mainstream outlets like HBO. Muslim intellectual Hamid Dabashi observed, "I would say, without a moment of hesitation, [Bill] Maher and [Sam] Harris, and before he passed away that careerist Christopher Hitchens, are far more dangerous Stormtrooper lieutenants of Islamophobia. These liberal Islamophobes are finagling their hatred of Muslims with smiling faces, silly jokes, phony arguments, forced laughter and manufactured consent—with the full cooperation of otherwise perfectly respectable outlets."[106]

Hitchens and his acolytes made no bones about the stridence of the "clash of civilizations" or the scale of the War on Terror that claimed millions of innocent lives and left entire nations forever fractured. Proportion did not matter, and the gravity of human suffering wrought by words took a back seat to ideology and the egos sitting in front. For Hitchens, Maher, Harris, and this liberal crop of new atheists who believed "religion poisons everything," Islam always stood apart as exceptionally and especially dangerous and utterly irredeemable.[107] In *The Guardian*, I wrote, "For these new atheists, Islam is illegitimate because it is a religion, but unlike other religions, is distinctly threatening because it is inherently at odds with liberal values."[108] For Hitchens, Harris, Maher, and the next crop of liberal Islamophobes seduced by their polemics, religion was not necessarily the threat—Islam was.

Political language—as Orwell spelled out and Edward Said incisively oriented in relation to war, terror, and Islam—is a tool exacted by power. Selectively and strategically. The old auteurs of Orientalism crafted new concepts and phrases that scorched the earth for the crusades to follow, while their ideological offspring disavowed the word

"Islamophobia" while disseminating its most damaging stereotypes to new audiences across the political spectrum.

The word frightened them. And rightfully so. Instead of debating on their terms, the word "Islamophobia," and its accompanying theory and lexicon, turned the tables. The finger was now pointed at them, as it had been with the two agents in Kenya. They were now required to explain instead of merely indict; to justify instead of judge. Islamophobia, as concept and analytical tool, enabled the unmasking of anti-Muslim bigotry. And perhaps, one day, the unmaking of that bigotry and the War on Terror that intensified it to endemic proportions.

In his landmark book *Black Skin, White Masks*, the postcolonial giant Frantz Fanon wrote, "To speak a language is to take on a world, a culture."[109]

These words sprang from the creased pages of my book as I sifted through it before taking the stage in Seattle. I always read from a book that has inspired me before giving a public lecture. Fanon was my muse that evening in the Emerald City.

I was in the thick of a tour for my first book, *American Islamophobia: Understanding the Roots and Rise of Fear*. Seattle, with its venerable backdrop of gray skies and its grunge mystique, battled against the corporate *amazon* that was rapidly eroding its identity. Wars were always unfolding somewhere, some in plain sight and others concealed by the slow and streaming pace of life that blinds us to what is taking place right in front of us.

Seattle is home to Pearl Jam, Nirvana, and Soundgarden. It is the city where two of its most iconic figures, Eddie Vedder and Chris Cornell famously sang about the perils of poverty and how the powerful exploit society's most vulnerable segments.[110] The grunge sound was quintessentially Seattle and scored the spirit of a city that championed the plight of those living at its fringes. A city that rebelled against corporate greed and sang odes for the subaltern, then matched its words of protest by putting its body on the line against unchecked and unhinged power.

This spirit of Seattle summoned me to rise to *its* grassroots ethic on that stage. I read Fanon while listening to the *Temple of the Dog* classic "Hunger Strike," excited to meet and engage with the audience. In the meantime, ideological crusades and corporate wars that streamed from the very source of greed Vedder and Cornell sang about, and that fed off the powerless, raged forward, around the whole city and the Fourth Church of Christ, where my event was being staged.

Seattle, like Fallujah or Kabul or New Delhi or Paris, was another front of the *new war order* where words were the most potent weapons. It had been nearly fifteen years since I had watched Edward Said on the stage of Royce Hall at UCLA. Now here I was, in June 2018, on another stage fighting the *very* same fight. Instead of sitting in the crowd trying to make sense of a world that had been spun out of control by the War on Terror, I found myself on a church stage preaching the word against the new American empire.

The landscape of the War on Terror had changed dramatically since 2003, as had the faces of the adversaries and the theaters of engagement. But the core of the War on Terror, decaying from within as it plagued the world from without, remained its rotten self. And with a new wave of demagogues and populists that wielded Islamophobia as a bludgeon, it had never been more violent.

I took one more sip of my coffee, then walked to the back entrance of the stage.

The coffee was sour, but the words of another muse, describing a Syrian city brought to its knees by another war, left an even more bitter taste.

"My home was wiped off the face of the earth."[111] I had no words as I looked down, staring into the black of my coffee in a sour attempt to compensate for my silence. "Everything turned into rubble," Jihan recounted of her final days in Aleppo. She was now living on the other side of a war that had buried so many loved ones beneath it.

I was in the other Washington, DC, the city where the War on Terror was conceived, the seat of the "civilized" world, with a young woman who had just turned twenty-four and had left behind a country that bore no resemblance to the place of our youth. Eastern Aleppo was no more.[112] And Syria seemed poised to follow Iraq's fate of being dismembered into a wholly unrecognizable form. We often think of the colonial laws that fractured Muslim-majority nations, like the Sykes-Picot Agreement, as relics of a bygone era. Yet modern crusades are quick to smack us in the head and open our eyes to the plodding disfiguration and division of nations unfolding today.

I stared across at another victim of the War on Terror, a victim who appreciated that the aims of this crusade were taking shape, and reshaping lands, for the benefit of American empire. She may not have fully understood it, but she could feel its impact. The full-scale, multi-dimensional impact of Islamophobia that had a hand in the proxy wars that decimated her country and closely shadowed her almost immediately after her plane touched down in New York City.

Jihan and I met roughly a year after the US Supreme Court upheld President Trump's Muslim ban. By a split five to four decision, the highest court in the land ruled that the executive orders signed by the president that claimed that "a lot" of Syrian refugees like Jihan "are aligned with ISIS" was constitutional.[113] The Supreme Court ruling stopped me, but being a professor of constitutional history and law, I was hardly surprised.

Jihan's country of origin, Syria, found itself on all three versions of the Trump ban, which prohibited her family members scattered in Syria and around the world from reuniting with her.[114] They also marked her as "illegal" because of her nationality, and ominous on account of her faith. Burdens she carried, nobly, while navigating a life that she did not want in a strange land where its president demonized her through the enmeshed power of executive orders and rhetoric.

This was "structural," or state-sponsored, Islamophobia: the enforcement, through law, policy, or formal state activity, of the presumption that Muslims were tied to terrorism. And in Jihan's experience as a Syrian immigrant newly arrived in Maryland, being targeted by a presidential executive order upheld by the highest court in the land.

"How are you adjusting to life in Maryland?" I asked Jihan in our common Levantine Arabic. "The people are welcoming, especially the family I am staying with," she shared. "But I don't like how people stare at me when I cross the street, or shop," she continued. "My hijab invites too much attention . . . attention I'm not accustomed to," she confided in me as she gripped the bottom of her headscarf. *Hijab* means "to cover" in Arabic, but Jihan's hijab could not conceal her fear and anxiety.

"I have heard of the girls that were killed in that college [University of North Carolina at Chapel Hill]. Their families came from Syria too." This was true. Although she had been in the US for less than a year's time, Jihan knew about the three Muslim students massacred in Chapel Hill in December 2015.[115] Two of them—Razan and Yusor Abu Salha—had been gunned down on account of the same scarf Jihan wrapped around her head every morning.[116]

This massacre was a tragic manifestation of "private Islamophobia."[117] This dimension encompasses the slurs and bigotry, mob and vigilante violence inflicted on Muslims, or people mistaken to be Muslims, by private individuals and institutions. It is the front of Islamophobia carried forward by the people, who are ordered to "see something, say something," and relentlessly, through propaganda and law, to *do something.*

"I can't bear to watch the news, especially Fox." Jihan was fully inducted into American culture and was familiar with the leading network that foments popular zeal against Muslims in the United States and beyond its borders. The most potent of the mainstream media platforms where presidents, congresswomen and -men, and other state actors push rhetoric that endorses the notion that Islam is wed to terror, and where hatemongers are emboldened to take up arms in the crusade against its adherents.

This forms the final dimension of Islamophobia—"dialectical" Islamophobia. The fluid and dynamic discourse where state action, based on the notion that Muslim identity is predictive of terror, authorizes and emboldens the populace to join the national project of punishing and persecuting Muslims. Through the ongoing process of dialectical Islamophobia, the law itself instructs people to hate or hurt Muslims.

These three distinct but connected dimensions of Islamophobia—structural, private, and dialectical—comprise the new word order I constructed to combat the new world order. These conceptual frames are vital for fully understanding global Islamophobia—and its diverse and divergent tentacles—for what it is. However, breaking them down as ideas and theories alone renders an incomplete portrait of how Islamophobia is experienced in places across the world where it is most ominous and destructive.

Islamophobia, at its very core, is about people. People like Jihan, who sat across from me in that café on 14th Street in Washington, longing for a home buried in her memory and loved ones banned from entry into the country where she would make her new home.

We sat across from one another, two Muslims on the *right* side of civilization adhering to the *wrong* religion. Both struggling to make sense of a senseless world through words; words that came from the mouths of two distinctly situated victims of the War on Terror. Both of us, however, seeking to craft new words to mount an attack against the language and laws deployed, from the very top, against us and billions more Muslims implicated by the War on Terror and the new crusades it incited.

While its principal propagators insist that it is a myth, Islamophobia persists as one of the final forms of acceptable bigotry. It is, as I have stated time and again, that *last bastion of tolerable hate* that is not only palatable in the popular sphere, but a hate that pundits build careers off of, politicians claim power through, and hatemongers—seated before church stages and carrying tiki torches across college campuses—openly spew.[118] In 2022, it is mostly acceptable to be Islamophobic. Engaging in it, by way of political statement or slur, will likely not invite the sort of reprimand tied to anti-Black, anti-Semitic, or homophobic expressions.

Perhaps denying the existence of something is what enables it to swell, spread, and garner sanction. This was true for French and American politicians' claim that "racism does not exist" because their societies were, magically, colorblind.[119] Or more ominously, when the Chinese government expels all foreign journalists and brazenly claims, despite mounting evidence, that there is "no such thing as [Muslim] detention camps" in the country.[120] If Donald Trump can shout down facts by screaming "fake news," just imagine what authoritarian regimes can do to suppress the truth in societies where discipline, control, and punishment are blurred by blunt rule.

A new language exposes these lies that distort and lies that conceal. It also arms the powerless with the possibility of taking on a world that flattens them into terrorists, and at the same time, counters pundits who claim that Islamophobia is a myth and their pain is not real. This new language of fighting Islamophobia, and naming it for what it is, furnishes the powerless with the intellectual ammunition to fight back and fight forward.

Jihan, seated in a Washington café with her mind still in Syria, was new to this fight. But she had been thrust into it as soon as she stepped into the United States. Jihan had no choice. She knew that her identity placed her in the middle of a clash of civilizations, a War on Terror that pushed her far from home and pulled her into a new battle.

The Tunisian Jewish postcolonial thinker Albert Memmi wrote, "Just as I sat on the fence between two civilizations, so would I now find myself between two classes; and I realized that, in trying to sit on several chairs, one generally lands on the floor."[121]

Jihan sat across the chair from me, and her pain was clear to me. Regardless of what Jordan Peterson, Hitchens, or Harris or Hirsi Ali said or did, to deny what the world did to her and took from her, her pain and suffering were real. She was real.

Islamophobia was real. And it sat across from me in a chair that would not throw her onto the floor. But, as I heard the strength in Jihan's voice, a chair that would inspire fight.

I had no chair on that stage in Seattle, just a stool that stood alone behind the podium. I closed my remarks, walked forward and stood between the podium and the audience, ready to field questions from people I did not know, but who knew me.

After a young Black woman inquired about the history of enslaved African Muslims in the antebellum South, a man seated several rows behind her raised his hand. The young man assigned the task of holding the microphone dashed up the aisle and made his way toward the audience member. The man read out loud, pausing strategically for emphasis:

> But when the forbidden months are past, then fight and slay the Pagans
> wherever ye find them, and seize them, beleaguer them, and lie in wait for
> them in every stratagem (of war).

I realized, before he finished reciting the passage, that he had no intention of asking me a question. Neither was he interested in engaging with the substance of my book or the presentation I had made. This was performance. Political performance.

"That is verse 9:5, from the Islamic Qur'an—the part of the speaker's book that he forgot to bring up today," he announced, beaming with pride. The young man holding the microphone looked nervously around the room but stood in place as the man continued to *misquote Muhammad* and the message revealed to him.[122]

"That was the first of the Qur'an's 'sword verses.' The second— verse 9:25—says," he announced with strange glee, then read,

> Fight those who do not believe in Allah in the Last Day and who do not consider unlawful what Allah and His Messenger have made unlawful and who do not adopt the religion of truth from those who were given the Scripture.

He rambled through the text, mispronouncing words, which signaled that he was no scholar of religion nor a neutral arbiter of the faith. He came to the text, like Harris and Hirsi Ali, with preconceived notions of Islam that colored his conclusions. Islam was the enemy, and from his vantage point in the crowd, so was I.

This was his moment. Or so he thought. He had sat in that seat during the ninety-minute lecture, prepared to parrot what he learned from a podcast or social media, a liberal pundit or populist in the White House. In 2020, these divergent sources of information, which disagreed on almost everything else, found common ground with regard to Islam—namely, in their disdain for it and its adherents. Islamophobia was a bipartisan commitment that spilled across the political spectrum.

The man made no mention of Christian or Jewish fundamentalism, or the Hindu supremacy marching through India, or the weaponized secularism driving modern French nativism, treating the terms "fundamentalism," "extremism," and their modern cousin, "terrorism," as inherent and exclusive to Islam. In fact, these descriptors were not only exclusive to Islam, but synonymous with it. But how could I blame him for what the War on Terror, and the three presidential administrations steering it, had taught him?

To paraphrase Albert Camus's *The Stranger*, one always has exaggerated ideas about what one doesn't know, a revelation true of that book's forlorn protagonist and the foolish character standing before me in that Seattle church.[123]

It was as clear as that rare sunny day in Seattle: the man had no interest in a constructive exchange, or any exchange at all. His goal was pointedly political, and he had cherry-picked text from Islam's holy book in the same sloppy fashion that radio pundits and podcast crusaders did.

He stopped reading and raised his head from his notebook, then pointed the same scorn he had for the Qur'an toward me, its walking embodiment planted on that Seattle stage.

"What do you have to say about these verses, professor? What does *your book* say about this?" the white man in the white shirt asked, launching an anemic attack in the form of a question. I was not sure, at the time, what he meant by "your book." Did he mean the book *American Islamophobia?* Or the Qur'an? It didn't matter then and matters less now, as I write this book.

It meant even less that, to this man, my book and prepared remarks were not some sort of spiritual convocation or skewed defense of Islamic scripture. I was not in Seattle to proselytize or present Islam as some pristine faith. My writing, both popular and academic, has emphasized, ad nauseam, that Islam is hardly monolithic, and that the global ecosystem of Islamic thought encompasses worrisome factions, many of which are deserving of both concern and scorn. I have, in my broader body of writing and the very book I presented in Seattle, condemned Wahhabi and militant Shiite movements—for instance—and fanaticism of the Muslim and non-Muslim variety. Muslim terrorists certainly exist, and they commit vile acts—particularly against Muslims. But conflating Muslims at large with the entirety of terrorism was a myth, and a myth that I was wholly committed to destroying.

Further, as a constitutional law scholar, there are very few principles I hold as dear as the Free Exercise Clause of the First Amendment. My work and intellectual commitments are driven as much by that single liberal principle that is denied to Muslims, in America and the world over, as by Islamic scripture. If Islamophobia is anything, it is the systemic denial of the free exercise of religious liberty to Muslims in the country that I call home, and even more sharply in places abroad—including Muslim-majority countries.

But that, and everything else I had written in my books and academic articles and media insights, meant nothing to that man. He condemned me for what I was in his mind, not for who I was in reality. In the words of James Baldwin, "I was being spat on and defined and described and limited" by a man wed to the new crusade against Islam, who saw me through eyes conditioned to revile the very sight of me.[124] I was caricatured in his mind well before I stepped onto that Seattle stage.

He did not see an author who wrote on matters of secular and civil rights. He saw a Muslim: a subject of war and an object of terror. He did not see a constitutional law professor who combed through the Federalist and anti-Federalist papers, the original sources that spawned the freedom he enjoys today. He saw an enemy wielding the "swords of Islam" on that church stage in Seattle. He did not see a fellow American dressed in a suit and tie that would command his respect if I were a white and Christian professor. He saw a man peddling "Sharia Law" while never uttering a single word from the Qur'an and its supplementary sources of canon.[125]

He saw me in the precise frame that Islamophobia intended him to unsee me. That indictment, spurred by bigoted imagination, is the very essence of Islamophobia. An essence exported globally and ascribed to anyone and everyone that adhered to the faith.

This was the theater of Islamophobia, performed by a willing character rows away from the stage. I stood there, alone behind the podium, fielding a barrage of questions and assaults guised as questions. "I knew the tension in me between love and power, between pain and rage, and the curious, the grinding way I remained extended between these two poles—perpetually attempting to choose the better rather than the worse."[126] Like Baldwin, I wanted to lash out and scold the man for all to witness. It would vindicate me, a voice inside me spoke, seducing me to shout thunder and spit lightning in the hall of that Seattle church.

But that is precisely what he wanted. His performance would only be successful if it prompted the aggression and anger he conspired to incite from me. The very aggression and anger he conflated with Islam, which, in his mind, would conjure up the threat of violence on that stage, for everybody in the audience to behold.

I ignored that familiar voice of pain that rolled off Jihan's lips, and the rage it summoned from deep within me. I would not let him, this stranger in the audience, set the terms for making me and unmaking me as I stood, alone, on that stage.

It was, after all, my stage. And the land where we both stood was *our* country, just as much mine as it was his. And I was intent, that day in Seattle, on taking my place in it.

By not giving in to rage, I foiled his plan, and set the terms of our exchange. "Come speak to me after the question-and-answer period," I finally responded. That ended his performance, and ended the war he wanted to wage with me. I did it without firing one hostile word. Not a single bullet of rage.

He was disarmed. And there was no war, that day, at the Fourth Church of Christ in Seattle.

However, the War on Terror raged onward. But new fronts of understanding were developing—and new languages, robust languages of resistance and reclamation, possibility born from pain and trenchant ideas born in the trenches of war, were being crafted to arm the targets of this War on Terror. Weapons that foreshadowed that it too could, and would be, toppled one day.

The pen is mightier than the sword.[127]

CHAPTER THREE

BLOOD AND SOIL

GOODBYE, INDIA

> The world, somebody wrote, is the place we prove real by
> dying in it.
> SALMAN RUSHDIE, *The Satanic Verses*

"I would love to travel the world, try exotic foods, and treat ill people," shared Mrinal. The voice of the young college student studying biology at Jawarhalal Nehru University roamed with wonder, not yet bound down by life's trying verses.[1]

During our hour-long conversation, Mrinal, a self-described "Hindu activist for justice," talked about building bridges and shattering barriers. She saw the world through that prism, guided by a faith that instructed her to unify people in her country. When she spoke about Muslims or Jains or Christians in India, Mrinal referred to them as "my people." Religious diversity was something Mrinal loved about India, and she traveled past artificial barriers to build ties with Indian friends of all faiths. The young student, living in the "largest democracy in the world," embodied what India had aspired to be since its inception as a modern nation-state.

Her words reminded me of another traveler and bridge builder: Anthony Bourdain, the globetrotting chef who dined on life and broke bread with people of all walks and cultures. Anybody who watched Bourdain's adventures loved the renaissance man and came to see the world through his curiosity and his voracious appetite for life. The man the *New York Times* dubbed the "renegade chef" lived life without restraints or constraints, drinking from its overflowing cup and dining on its delicious tapestry of foods everywhere he went.[2] Everybody, including Mrinal and I, watched with envy and adoration and believed that Bourdain had reached the very pinnacle of life.

From the confines of her screen, Mrinal watched Bourdain immerse himself naturally in the world's cultural capitals and its most remote villages, moving freely and appearing to fit in easily wherever he went, truly living life with "no reservations." Bourdain learned about the countries he visited through his love for food, and the local cast of characters he dined with brought native flavor to the places he reported from, the very places Mrinal and I hoped to visit one day. Millions of people like Mrinal learned about places unknown through the eyes of Bourdain and the camera that followed his enviable life.

Like me, the young Indian college student loved Bourdain, and like most of his greatest admirers, we were inspired to one day travel the world like he did—to visit countries far from our own and immerse ourselves in cultures far different from the ones that had shaped us. But in the interim, like millions of others who tuned in to his television programs, Mrinal and I could only see the world through his eyes. Or, far more intimately, learn about the world and its sublime diversity through places of worship and restaurants, neighborhoods, and eateries at home.

Bourdain's passport was a love for food, which opened pathways to learning about different cultures and faiths, history and politics, and the world of wonder and possibility in between. He saw the good in everybody, or at least tried to, and roamed the globe finding what ties people together, instead of what drives them apart.

Disunity, for a man whose name circulated furiously through India, was at the top of the menu. Unlike Mrinal or Bourdain, Narendra Modi saw a nation comprised of past castes and existing divisions to be inflamed for his political benefit. Modi, the Hindu nationalist who rose to power in India in 2014, sparked the rise of Islamophobia on the subcontinent.[3] I began tracking, with concern that gradually devolved into horror, the hate crimes and mob attacks targeting Muslims in India. Eventually, I built relationships with people on the ground, like Mrinal, who shared my affinity for social justice and travel.

Yet it was Anthony Bourdain and his travels through Rajasthan, a state in northwest India, that spurred my desire to visit the country.[4] The warmth and pride of the people, the majestic Hindu temples and Sikh gurdwaras, and the color and flavor of the food that poured through the screen whetted my appetite. I wanted to visit Rajasthan and experience the richness of Indian culture. I wanted to follow in Bourdain's footsteps and see the nation that blended the distinct traditions and rich histories of its peoples into a beautiful tapestry.

However, more than cuisine or culture, it was Rajasthan's religious diversity and apparent harmony that convinced me to book a ticket. Hindus were not only living alongside Muslims and Sikhs, Jains and Parsees, Christians and a broader mosaic of faith groups, but from my vantage point watching Bourdain, coexisting in harmony.

On screen, Bourdain broke bread with Hindus, who shook their heads with delight as he fawned over their food. He walked the streets with Sikh friends who beamed with pride at his praise for the city. He dined in the homes of Muslim Indians, sitting alongside them as if he were a family member. He felt at home with anybody, including Muslims, while the Modi regime began to push propaganda that India was *no home* for Muslims.[5] Propaganda, later enshrined into law, that held that India was the exclusive land of Hindus.

These intimate gatherings, with Muslims in India and a host of other nations, moved Bourdain to claim, "I've spent much of my life in the Muslim world where I've been treated with overwhelming kindness and generosity."[6] For Bourdain, sitting with members of other cultures and other faiths was not only commonplace, but *soul food*—the spiritual nourishment that makes life worth living.

Bourdain, an atheist, seemed to understand that faith and religious harmony more deeply than most devout theists. Most notably, more than Modi, dubbed by *Time* as India's "Divider in Chief," who was primed to split and segregate the nation along religious lines.[7] All seats at the Indian table, he proclaimed when elected, were reserved for Hindus and Hindus alone. That left no room for Muslims, who were pushed to the margins by Modi's rhetorical fury and the fiat he peddled in the following years with the ultimate aim of removing them entirely from the table.

Bourdain told the story of Rajasthan through the promise of India, the modern nation established in 1947 on the principle of secularism. A secularism that aspired to glue the nation's vast religions into one integrated community, instead of the fractured castes with fault lines drawn in blood. Although young, Mrinal knew this history quite well, as did the some 200 million other Muslims who called India home.[8]

Bourdain's episodes filmed in Rajasthan offered an aspirational portrait of the India that *could be*, and what its forefathers envisioned it might be, one day, if their successors steered it away from its bloody past of enshrined caste and internalized colonialism. That history that is very much a lurid and living part of India's present.[9] Modi, India's new strongman, had an appetite for a different kind of nation, and for revitalizing caste in the modern image of religious populism. His Bharatiya Janata Party's vision of the future was rooted in the past, and caste, partition, and cross-religious violence would determine the flavor of his regime.[10]

The "Butcher of Gujarat," a title Modi earned for unspeakable violence against Muslims while chief minister of that state, was setting a new table for India.[11] A table where Hindu nationalism was the main and only course, and where India's commitment to secularism would be diced up and disposed of.

Muslims no longer had a seat at India's table, but found themselves on the menu that Modi remade, ready to be served up and swallowed whole by a rabid and revitalized Hindu supremacist movement primed to unleash the rage of the past with the hate of the present.

For decades, modern India has struggled to shed a dark history tainted by caste. This history haunts the present, and its vestiges intersect with the religious tension, classism, and colorism pervasive throughout the massive nation. In Modi and his ascending BJP Party, these vestiges found an ideal political vessel in which to harden caste and religious divisions.[12]

"If a Muslim living in India chooses their god before India, then why should he be allowed to live in our country? This country belongs to Hindus first."[13] These were the words of Ramapada Pal, a formative Hindu supremacist thinker whose ideas saturate the BJP's modern vision. For Hindu nationalists like Modi, dubbed Hindutva in India, nationalism was a matter of faith, and Hinduism was not just the official faith of the land, but one synonymous with Indian identity. Audrey Truschke, a historian of India, has defined Hindutva as "a political ideology, not a religion" which seeks "to restrict the many permeations of Hindu practice to a single political doctrine of supremacy."[14] Modi strategically "racialized" Hindu identity, flattening it into a status synonymous with "Indian." According to him, and his swelling legions of followers, anybody who was not Hindu was not legitimately Indian. This perspective matched what ardent white supremacist Americans believed, that whiteness and Americanness were one and the same, and those who lacked the former could not become the latter.

The War on Terror created a gaping entryway for Modi's Hindutva vision. By 2014, demonizing Muslims had become a global phenomenon, and as lucidly illustrated in American media and European newsprint, one of the last remaining acceptable forms of bigotry. Modi drew up a strategy to seize power by turning back the clock and restoring the vision of Bharat—the belief that India is the holy land for Hindus— as the center of his campaign to take power.[15]

Modi's quest to realize Bharat is rooted in a cultural movement that many Indians, including Hindus like Mrinal, have analogized to Nazism. The Rashtriya Swayamsevak Sangh (RSS) is the ideological engine for Modi and the BJP party. Its founder, Vinayak Damodar Savarkar, published the cornerstone text for the RSS movement, titled *Hindutva: Who Is a Hindu?*. In that seminal text of Hindu supremacy, Savarkar wrote, "To be a Hindu means a person who sees this land, from the Indus River to the sea, as his country but also his Holy Land."[16]

Thus, Hinduism was not merely a faith and more than a racialized identity. It was in fact a political identity and movement, and for the RSS, the BJP, and the man who would become prime minister of India in 2014, an identity that obliges its adherents to actively work toward the realization of Bharat. A vision of India as the Hindu holy land that mandates the removal of Muslims—a population that BJP leaders have dubbed "termites" (Amit Shah, minister of the interior) and "foreigners" (Yogi Adityanath, chief minister of Uttar Pradesh), and that swelling numbers of Hindutva loyalists have labeled "Pakistanis."[17]

The more power the BJP has garnered, the more unhinged and unfiltered its hatred has grown. During a campaign rally in 2020, Adityanath declared, "It is the need of the hour to remove Muslim women from their graves and rape their dead bodies," recalled Mrinal; words that highlight that the threat of saffron terrorism does not even spare the Muslim dead.[18]

Adityanath, who makes explicit what Modi guises in dog whistles, also stated, "If they [Muslims] kill one Hindu man, then we will kill 100

Muslim men."[19] It was precisely because of this rhetoric that Modi handpicked Adityanath to govern Uttar Pradesh, India's largest state. Rhetoric that regularly incited mob violence against the state's Muslims and vigilante attacks on its mosques, Muslim businesses, and communities.

He spoke, in terms unfiltered and in a tenor of terror, what the RSS outline of Hindu supremacy espoused. Modi presented a palatable version of the BJP to the world, while he surrounded himself with firebrands who articulated—with violent clarity—his Hindutva vision for India. Good cop and bad cop, presenting a two-headed monster that unleashed renewed fury against a Muslim population that has always known India as its home. That only knows India as home.

At the very core of Hindu supremacy was an Islamophobia native to India's historical and political imagination. Muslims were believed to be Moghuls, a foreign people, and Hindus the indigenous people of India. This grand narrative drove Modi's political agenda and made conceptions around citizenship a matter of blood and soil instead of birthright or naturalization.[20]

To be Hindu was to be Indian, the Modi regime proclaimed by way of rhetoric and then policy. And to be Indian, Hindutva lore held, was to cast out Muslims regardless of their legal status or ties to the land. Indian Islamophobia, as devised by the Modi regime, was a full-fledged remaking of Indian identity, one driven by a demographic reengineering of society that used federal and state law to push forward a slow-moving ethnic cleansing project.

"The biggest threat with Islamophobia in my country . . . is [it has] now started to damage the secular status of India, most of the people are becoming more conservative and started hating Muslims around them. People are now calling Muslims 'anti-national' and 'traitors,'" shared Syed Mohd Gulam Baquer, a twenty-four-year-old Indian Muslim professional living in New Delhi.[21]

The Islamophobia deeply rooted in Hindutva supremacist lore was rising politically and spreading in Indian society. It became common for everyday Hindus to peddle the claim that "Muslims have fifty other countries, we Hindus only one," shared Jaiwanth Reddy, an eighteen-year-old Hindu student from Hyderabad.[22] BJP leaders echoed this claim, or some variation of it, at the federal and local levels in India, which were puppeted by their followers on the ground and on social media. Indian Islamophobes holding the highest offices, and their growing legions of loyalists, were "tearing India apart."[23]

Hindutva supremacy and the Islamophobia it summoned was no longer fringe in India, nor was it confined to members of the political class and sphere they commanded. Modi and the BJP thrust it back into the marrow of Indian society and deep into the most intimate and unexpected spheres of Indian life.

"I have seen people whom I respected my entire life, professors of great and national institutes, certain family members blatantly blaming Muslims for anything and everything without even giving a thought," said Dr. Sharath R., a Hindu physician from Bengaluru, India. "Of course [Islamophobia is] propagated by the politics and the media."[24] If the nation's intelligentsia were infected by Modi's hate, then it is safe to assume that its imprint on the lay and working classes would be just as potent, if not more so.

This is, perhaps, Indian Islamophobia's most sinister dimension, and the Modi regime's most damaging effect: the fact that, in only a handful of years, the appeal of Hindutva supremacy and Islamophobia could resurface so prominently within universities and professional settings, in lay contexts and cultural centers, testifies to its mainstream appeal.

The prominence and pervasiveness of Islamophobia also testifies to the widespread popularity of Modi and the BJP, who converged on a global moment to launch a crusade against India's Muslims and the country's secular foundation. The War on Terror kicked open the door for Modi and the BJP, who marched through it with the ideological mandate of Hindu supremacy and the war's aligned tenet that branded Islam as a pariah to be condemned, then cast out.[25] American Islamophobia, packaged and promoted via the global War on Terror, opened the door for demagogues like Modi to seize their moment and capitalize on the vocabulary and violence that drove the new American crusade.

As the War on Terror breathed new life into the BJP and its archetype at the top of Indian government, the coffin for Indian secularism was being prepared. The portrayal of Muslims "as Pakistanis, or Jihadis or evil conspiracists is very much in vogue," a student shared, testifying to how the War on Terror conflation of terrorism and Islam took form in India.[26] But the worst was yet to come for India and its massive Muslim population. Greater perils, in the form of violent mobs and bloody massacres intent on filling those coffins, hijab bans and the vision of India as the holy land for Hindus, would descend on a nation that tried to cling to its formative commitment to secularism and democracy.

For some, death is preferable to living a nightmare, a nightmare where sleep is the only escape, and during the most terrifying of days, no escape at all. Jean-Paul Sartre's existential play *No Exit* constructs an image of hell where individuals are confined in a small space with other individuals and forced to interact and engage with one another without pause and without escape.[27] There is no exit from this hell, which for Sartre's characters is fiction but for India's Muslims a reality. As Sartre famously wrote and Modi infamously embodies, "Hell is other people."[28]

This is the state of being for Muslims in India, a nation home to the second-largest Muslim population in the world, and which by 2050 is predicted to overtake Indonesia for the top spot.[29] A place where former neighbors and colleagues, classmates and friends have been remobilized as enemies by Modi. A place where a state that once integrated Muslims and members of other minority faiths as full-fledged citizens currently brands its non-Hindus as second- or third-class Indians. Or, in the case of Muslims, as not Indian at all.

India's vast and distant borders are rapidly closing in on Muslims. They draw closer and closer by the day, like a noose around the throats of Muslims in both the hinterland and India's major cities. The hangmen are Modi and his BJP brass, zealously tightening the Hindutva supremacy of the RSS forefathers, remade in the modern image of Indian Islamophobia.

While young Mrinal views Hinduism, a faith that fuels her commitment to social justice, as a unifying force, Modi has weaponized it as a knife, a sharp instrument used to cut and divide Indian society. And then, when the butcher finishes his job, is quick to dispose of every part of the county's religious body except its Hindu majority. For Modi and the Party he bleeds for, Hinduism is not only supreme in India, it is *synonymous* with India.[30]

This hit close to home for the young college student. Mrinal's family was gradually growing suspicious of Islam because of what they heard from friends and read in the newspapers. Her mother once told her, "Be careful of your Muslim friends at school, they stick together above everybody else." Her father, an educated man, stated at the dinner table, "If you give them [Muslims] a finger, they may take away your whole hand." Mrinal sat at the table in horror, realizing that the Islamophobia that ripped across her campus had come into her home. She thought, as her mother and father—the most beloved people in her life—spewed vile notions of Muslims, in fact, of friends of hers they had met, that "everything had changed."[31] Her world, and her place in it, was changing by the day in a country where the War on Terror and Indian Islamophobia converged, then descended to the top of her family dinner table.

She excused herself from that table, collected her things, and left for campus, ready to give her Muslim friends that hand her father warned her about for a protest against a new law. That new law, dubbed the Citizenship Amendment Act (CAA), aimed to deny naturalized citizenship to Muslim immigrants. This was another step toward the Hindutva vision of binding Indian citizenship with Hindu identity.[32]

Mrinal raced out, the door slamming behind her, and traveled back to campus as fast as she could. There, Hindutva mobs marched alongside police in a united "blood and soil" front against Muslim students and allies from other faiths defending what remained of Indian secularism, and when the mobs and the blows came, their very limbs and lives.[33]

The mobs advanced and trounced the students and the secularism they stood for. The aspirations of multiculturalism and harmony and the "imperfect experiment of India" were dead, and the dreams Mrinal once held—of traveling through her vast country and the world beyond it—were killed along with those aspirations and the limp bodies of students that were spread on the ground.[34]

A wandering spirit of innocence was replaced by the sobering reality of violence, bloodshed, and death. Mrinal stood still, the dreams she had for India and herself stifled, permanently it seemed, by Modi and this Indian strand of Islamophobia that hung Indian democracy in the balance.

On June 8, 2018, the man who moved Mrinal to dream and inspired my visit to India hung from the ceiling in a French hotel room, dead and alone. A life that had seemed so unreal, so enviable, and that had inspired Mrinal and me and millions more to dream that we could have it, was real. So real that Bourdain was moved to take it with his own hand.[35] He was only sixty-one, roughly ten years younger than the modern state of India, which too found itself swinging toward death.

On the other side of the planet, and in the streets of Rajasthan and in the cities and streets Bourdain toured on- and off-screen, the dream of India was dying. Dalits and Sikhs and Muslims, especially Muslims, were meeting their maker in large numbers. Bourdain, the man everybody loved and felt they knew so well, was dead, and the promise of India as good as dead.

"Beauty is unbearable, drives us to despair, offering us for a minute the glimpse of an eternity that we should like to stretch out over the whole of time." The despair that Albert Camus romanticized gradually ate away at the beauty of Bourdain's life and at that sublime "idea of India" as a secular nation, an idea now ravaged by the Modi regime.[36]

"India is no longer India," Aatish Taseer eulogized in *The Atlantic* in May 2020, bidding farewell to a nation that pounds its chest as "the biggest democracy in the world" while burying its own.[37] The sun has set on that India and the beautiful dream of secularism that traveled, wildly and wondrously, through the minds of its citizens young and old.

Life is tragic simply because the earth turns and the sun inexorably rises and sets, and one day, for each of us, the sun will go down for the last, last time.[38]

Goodbye, India.

BETWEEN VIRUS AND VIOLENCE

What is left for a virus to kill in a morally corrupt nation?
RANA AYYUB

"My cousin was murdered during the Gujarat massacres."[39] Abdul, an Indian American engineer from Houston, recalled the bloody pogrom of 2002, pointing to the picture of Narendra Modi on his computer screen. "This man is responsible for his death, and all the deaths that took place there years ago. Now, he's prime minister of India."

Memory was now reality, and for Abdul, the past and the present blurred together into an indistinguishable whole.

I sat down with Abdul a week after Modi held a massive rally in Houston. The September 2019 rally, attended by 50,000 people and President Donald Trump, forced Abdul to relive the darkest period of his life. It was a three-day stretch in Gujarat in 2002, when Muslims were accosted by violent mobs. Gujarat had witnessed explosive riots in the recent past, and those had bled into the identity of the state and shaped a "template of violence" for future agitators to emulate.[40] A year after the War on Terror commenced, violent mobs in Gujarat were incited by no other than Narendra Modi, who was chief minister of the state during the massacre.[41] "I get sick every time I look at his photo," Abdul shared, "this deep sickness in my stomach every time I see his face . . . or hear him speak."

At least 800 Muslims were killed during the 2002 Gujarat massacre. Some researchers believe that the number was far higher, and that the death toll was intentionally diminished by Modi.[42] That very man, Modi, who Abdul thought he had left behind in 2002, haunted him again in Houston on September 22, 2019.

The past was the present, again, and Modi was lobbying in Texas—the heart of American Republican country—to make Hindu supremacy a permanent fixture of India's future.

"Whether it is the 9/11 attack in America or the 26/11 attack in Mumbai, where are its conspirators found?" Modi roared toward an American audience where red "Make America Great Again" hats and saffron flags ominously blended together.[43] He continued, with Trump standing behind him, "The time has come for a decisive fight against terrorism and those who support terrorism. I want to stress here that President Trump is standing firmly against this."[44]

Modi knew that fight quite well. He had unleashed its fury upon Muslims in Gujarat nearly two decades earlier. And with Trump at his side, he was lobbying that in order for India to become the holy land for Hindus, the War on Terror would have to come crashing down on the some 200 million Muslims who call India home.

In *Gujarat Files: Anatomy of a Cover Up,* journalist Rana Ayyub observed how the bureaucrats, the police officers, and the people were given "a free hand to kill Muslims during the riots of 2002" by Modi himself.[45] Eighteen years later, the Gujarat of 2002 would become the India of 2020. This time, the violence would happen on a national scale and had found an ally in the world's most visible orchestrator of Islamophobia: Donald Trump.

Abdul, sunk in memories of the past, signaled that the bloodiest struggles against Hindu supremacists were yet to come. "I left that country knowing what it could one day become," he said, standing on the other side of the world, suffocating between Trump's Muslim Ban and Modi's Hindu supremacy.

On December 11, 2019—less than three months after Modi stumped with Trump in Texas—India enacted its very own "Muslim Ban." The Citizenship Amendment Act (CAA), which many—including myself—compared to the executive order that President Trump signed and the Supreme Court later upheld, was more draconian and more destructive than its American counterpart.[46] Its enactment hammered another nail in the coffin of the "promise" of Indian secularism.

Unlike Trump's ban, the CAA did not seek to restrict Muslim immigrants from entering India. It sought to wholly redefine the bounds of Indian citizenship and mark a legal stride toward realizing Modi's vision of remaking India into Hindustan.[47]

The law prohibited Muslim immigrants from three bordering states—Afghanistan, Bangladesh, and Pakistan—from becoming naturalized citizens of India.[48] Its immediate effect was to draw explicit lines around Indian citizenship that endorsed and entrenched religious caste, whereby Hindus stood on top and Muslims on the bottom. Or, if Modi has his way, whereby Muslims are entirely removed from caste and country.

The CAA, however, transcends the bounds of Muslim immigration and should not be narrowly understood as an "anti-Muslim immigration or citizenship measure." While on the surface it targets these fronts, the CAA is another strike against Muslims by a regime poised to emaciate it from within and without. While technically geared to prohibit "illegal Muslim immigrants" from three nations, the CAA is just as concerned with policing and punishing the indigenous Muslims, now some 200 million, who have called the nation home for generations.

The CAA functions in conjunction with India's National Register of Citizens (NRC), which tracks the presence of Muslims in the country. The NRC has been compared to Donald Trump's proposed "Muslim Registry," and more ominously, to Nazi Germany's Nuremberg Race Laws, which excluded Jews from German citizenship.[49] "Under [the] NRC, first we [Muslims] will be asked to prove our citizenship; if we Muslims fail to prove [it] then they will put us in detention centers and strip us of citizenship," stated Mohammed Asif Khan of Mumbai.[50]

This bleak horizon of lost citizenship is symbolic of the mass stripping of dignity from Indian Muslims like Mohammed, which law scholar Bernadette Atuahene calls a "dignity taking."[51] Citizenship ranks among the most prized of possessions, but robbing a people's freedom to practice their faith through an intricate system of laws, including an anti-beef law and religious registries, sows the soil for ethnic cleansing, or far worse.

Shoaib Hussein, a thirty-seven-year-old resident of New Delhi who witnessed firsthand the mob attacks that took place in that city in 2020, drew a direct line from the Modi regime to its Nazi predecessors. "The Hindu right reveres Hitler and *Mein Kampf* is the best-selling book in India for decades. You can find it at all major bookstores and street-corner book stalls. We [Muslims] are sitting ducks."[52] Closer scrutiny of BJP ideology reveals intimate connections between its Hindutva aims and Nazism, rooted in the RSS's reverence for the white supremacist ideology that spread through Europe in the early twentieth century and incited World War II.

Mohammed and Shoaib's fears are not unfounded. The Modi regime has begun constructing massive internment camps in Assam, modeled after the Uyghur concentration camps in China and the Nazi camps of World War II.[53] This is where the Modi regime plans to imprison undocumented Muslim immigrants as well as citizens like Mohammed. To make way for Hindu settlers, this is where it will relocate Muslims who are too poor to produce documents proving their citizenship or too marginalized a population to have even been extended paperwork.

Together, the NRC and the CAA are great leaps toward making Indian citizenship synonymous with Hindu identity. These policies were enacted less than two months after Modi said "howdy" in Texas and spoke alongside the only other world leader whose Islamophobia rivaled his own.

September 22, 2019, in Texas was a raucous reminder, for Abdul and the world at large, that the fate of Muslims in Gujarat in 2002 would be sowed against Muslims throughout the body of the nation. Another reminder would take place not in Houston, but in India's capital, New Delhi, where Modi and Trump would share an even bigger stage at one of the world's largest outdoor arenas, then called Motera Cricket Stadium and now renamed Narendra Modi Stadium, a standing shrine for the horror that unfolded in the days to come.

While Trump declared that both India and the United States have to "defend ourselves from the threat of radical Islamic terrorism"[54] and the two heads of state embraced inside the walled-off stadium, the city surrounding it was beginning to burn with rage. A rage it sourced from within that stadium and swiftly unleashed onto the 2 million Muslims in New Delhi. A rage that felt like the Gujarat riots of 2002 all over again, helmed by the very man who gave everybody a "free hand to kill Muslims."[55]

This fury was not an unfamiliar one to Modi or his guest of honor, Donald Trump. Nor were the hate crimes that left Muslims' homes and mosques vandalized and tens of people killed by impassioned mobs only miles from the stadium, the source of the fire, where the American and Indian dividers-in-chief addressed a nation that was reeling back into its dark past.[56]

CJ Werleman, a journalist who closely examined the New Delhi massacre, wrote, "Attackers also marked Hindu-owned properties with saffron-colored flags to help their terrorists-in-arms identify Muslim targets . . . thus mimicking a sinister measure used on the eve of the 2002 Gujarat riots, which left more than 2,000 Muslims killed and thousands more battered, raped, and abused."[57]

History was repeating itself. And the Islamophobic rage ripping through New Delhi was directly authorized by the Butcher of Gujarat, now the prime minister of all of India. The rage was sparked not just by their rhetoric, but by Trump's and Modi's policies, and perhaps most powerfully, by the ferocity of their shared worldview that Islam posed a threat to society, security, and civilization.[58]

This was the central tenet of the War on Terror, which the United States had been disseminating across the globe for over two decades through fluid policy and fervent propaganda.[59] Those decades witnessed Modi's rise from a butcher with blood on his hands from masses of dead bodies in Gujarat to India's reigning Islamophobe-in-chief.

Shortly after Trump left India, the mobs burned the homes of Muslims to the ground. They desecrated and destroyed longstanding mosques. They violently accosted elders and Muslim women wearing the hijab while walking with children in their very own neighborhoods. They raged and rioted, ransacked and ripped through anything and everything that appeared to be Muslim. When all was said and done, Hindu extremists had killed more than fifty-three people and maimed thousands more.[60]

Modi stood idly by as the city burned and Muslim citizens were assailed. His "failure" to reign in the mobs and stop the massacre was perceived by many beyond India, and even more within, as approval. Mira Kamdar, an expert on modern Indian politics, concluded in a compelling article written in the early stages of the violence that "what happened in Delhi was a pogrom."[61]

Modi had seen this before, in 2002 in Gujarat. And with renewed vision and rising power, he sowed that very violence again in the heart of the nation's capitol in 2020. With the same hands of hate with which he ruled Gujarat, the butcher's hands grew sturdier with time.

Violence fell upon India and its Muslim population. Then came the coronavirus, which descended squarely on their collective back. A back that could not take any more yet would face a novel strand of Islamophobia in the very city, Delhi, where the Muslim massacre unfolded.

"India is a gorgeous place," shared Sabina Basha through a March 3, 2020, message, "except that it has caught this disease of Islamophobia. We have existed together for a 1000 years and then, wham." The Indian college student's note, dubbing Islamophobia a "disease," came at a time when a novel virus of pandemic proportions gripped India and the world at large.

The coronavirus preyed on the immune systems of individuals regardless of location, race, or religion, and in India it converged with

Modi's rapidly spreading Islamophobia.[62] Three months after the CAA was enacted into law, Muslim citizens were forced to face the compounded effect of hateful policy and popular scapegoating, during a global pandemic that was infected by a hysteria that knew no ceiling and had no exit. Islamophobia in India took its most vile turn yet as Hindu extremists, seeking to scapegoat Islam through any measure and purge Muslims from India by any means, blamed the outbreak of COVID-19 in India on no other than the country's Muslim community.[63] As a pandemic was shutting the world down in March 2020, Muslims in India found themselves locked between intensifying Hindutva violence and what became one of its deadliest weapons: the coronavirus.

On March 1, 2020, Tablighi Jamaat—a Muslim missionary organization—commenced its annual conference in New Delhi.[64] The conference took place a week after Trump's rally in the Motera Cricket Stadium, and the riots were still ongoing when the meeting convened.

The Muslim conference, planned months in advance, converged with growing concern within India about the domestic spread of COVID-19. The state had not yet issued a lockdown, and Tablighi Jamaat conference, and religious gatherings of other faith groups, particularly India's majority Hindu congregations, continued without interruption.[65] Modi himself even staged events attended by tens of thousands of people. The crowds at Modi's rallies were far greater than those at the Muslim groups' meetings, and his massive events were far more frequent.

However, the ire of the popular media—and of the extremist mobs that ripped through the city that hosted the Muslim conference—found a convenient scapegoat for the domestic spread of COVID-19: Muslims. Not only the organizers of the Tablighi Jamaat conference, and the 2,000 attendees, who were dubbed "super spreaders," *but the whole of the* Muslim population in India.[66]

All 200 million Muslims throughout the nation were singled out and scapegoated as disseminators of the coronavirus in India. A people already accosted by mob and vigilante violence and state policies that equated Muslim identity with foreignness and terrorism, and who were oriented as the very enemy of the Modi regime, were cast—at the height of a global pandemic that carried the "threat of universal extinction" over everybody's head—as the disseminators of its domestic outbreak.[67] This intensified the ire of Hindu extremists and exacerbated the already frightening violence directed at Muslims in India.

News headlines and stories throughout India ran with the story that the Tablighi Jamaat conference was the source of the national COVID-19 outbreak.[68] This was not journalistic work, but media wed to the state mandate of blaming Muslims for a viral terror spawned by Mother Nature. Islamophobia was already a violent dialectic, but it became far more furious when the manufactured scapegoats of the state were endorsed and disseminated by mainstream media outlets.

In swift order, Hindutva nationalists took to social media, dubbing the virus "Corona Jihad" and Muslims "human bombs."[69] These labels were accompanied by vile caricatures of Muslims spitting on bystanders and physicians, bigoted political cartoons spread in newspapers and disseminated on social media. Then doctored videos of Muslims disobeying stay-at-home orders went viral online, shared millions of times over within the country and beyond.

In Modi's India, the facts meant little and the fearmongering meant everything. The outbreak and accompanying media coverage created another opportunity to push the narrative that Muslims were damaging to the Indian body, and in line with the CAA and other policy, to push Muslims out of it.

A novel strain of the Hindutva menace was now spreading, capitalizing on national anxiety around a global pandemic that bore the face of a relentlessly persecuted and pummeled people: India's Muslims. Islam in India was deeply rooted, and the world's third-largest Muslim population was the target of unhinged pandemic paranoia spread by Modi.

After the lies came the batons, cricket bats, and boycotts. Hindu extremists mobbed and then pounced on Muslims in New Delhi. Muslims were being beaten physically, then financially. "In Punjab State, loudspeakers at Sikh temples broadcast messages telling people not to buy milk from Muslim dairy farmers because it was infected by coronavirus,"[70] and shops owned by Muslims in both big cities and small towns were boycotted as sources of COVID-19 outbreak. "We wanted to pick up our things and leave, go somewhere far away," shared Abdullah, who owned a store targeted by mobs in New Delhi.[71] Those with money could flee. For poor and working-class Muslims in Delhi, which comprised a sizable segment of its population, there was no exit.

Again, for Modi and his swelling following of Hindu nationalists, Indian identity is fundamentally a matter of "blood and soil." A familiar phrase to the lips of white supremacists in Europe and the United States, and in India, Hindu supremacists who view India—despite its unrivaled religious diversity—as the exclusive homeland of Hindus.

But instead of carrying tiki torches through college campuses like white supremacists in the United States, Hindu supremacists hold federal power in India.[72] And, with that power firmly in their grasp, they are exacting their vision through the might of state policy and mobs of private extremists, forming a violent dialectic that punishes Muslims at every turn and actively seeks to push them out of the country by way of political and legal dictates and mobs given license by both to accost Muslims.

"I am more afraid of extremists than I am of the virus," shared Yusuf, a father of two living in Uttar Pradesh. "I know more people hospitalized by Hindutva than the sickness."[73] So Yusuf, and millions of Muslims in Uttar Pradesh and the rest of India, stay locked inside—for as long as humanly possible—to safeguard themselves and loved ones from two parallel pandemics that are on a violent collision course.

Staying at home and social distancing, for Muslims in India, may be a matter of life and death. Not as much out of fear of the global virus that has had much of the world confined and quarantined, but out of fear of a far more ominous and deadly pandemic—Indian Islamophobia.

New Delhi was on fire. Donald Trump's visit to the seat of Indian government on February 24, 2020, set its streets ablaze minutes after he spoke. With his patented grin, Trump took center stage in the massive cricket stadium with his populist partner, Narendra Modi, standing alongside him. Modi blazed the ideological pathway for the enactment of India's own "Muslim Ban"—which immediately restricted Muslim immigrants from bordering Afghanistan, Bangladesh, and Pakistan from becoming Indian citizens, but had far broader implications. Like Trump's travel ban, the CAA marked the apex of an Islamophobic vision that was rapidly becoming reality in India.[74] But as forthcoming events within India and Kashmir would illustrate, that apex was only temporary.

To the roars of a massive crowd, Trump and Modi stood side by side and affirmed their nations' commitments to each other. Their words reverberated through the cricket stadium, but the symbol of the world's two most prominent Islamophobes—locking hands—was far more powerful than anything they could utter.[75]

The coming together of Modi and Trump, the world's two chief Islamophobes, incited an immediate storm that ripped through the streets of New Delhi, gripped it for nearly three weeks, and left Muslim families and communities in shambles.[76]

The eye of the storm descended on the Badi Mosque in Ashok Nagar. This district of New Delhi is home to a large Muslim and immigrant population. Hindu extremists marched into Ashok Nagar to unleash the anti-Muslim furor of the American and Indian heads of state who had spoken in the cricket stadium only miles away.

Around the periphery of the mosque, Hindu extremists armed with weapons, and others brandishing only bare fists, shouted the Hindu nationalist slogan "Jai Shri Ram" as their feet pounded the pavement. This chant signaled, for Muslims who heard it, that violence was coming their way. And that violence came in droves.[77] In the India remade by Modi, those words were not only a spiritual chant for a Hindu deity, but also the "three most polarizing words in India," which could signal anti-Muslim violence.[78]

The mob converged on Muslims and their homes chanting those three words, which grew louder and more menacing as those in the mob came closer. They punched, kicked, and struck anybody who looked Muslim as they marched down the street, increasing in number and expanding in rage as they arrived at their destination. Surveying the mosque and the towering minaret that overlooked the neighborhood, they were poised to memorialize their carnage with their own lasting symbol, a symbol that would serve as an emblem for the Hindu nation their prime minister was bent on bringing into existence.

For Muslims living in Ashok Nagar, the minaret and the *adhan*, the daily call to prayer that rang from it, symbolized *home*.[79] Yet, the Hindutva mob was summoned to the Islamic house of worship by another dictate, namely, proclamations from their beloved prime minister that Muslims were not genuinely Indian, but foreigners. This view was corroborated by an Indian version of the US Muslim Ban, a version that prevented a large number of Muslim immigrants from becoming citizens, and more ominously, laid the groundwork for stripping bona fide Muslim citizens of their status. As law scholar Leti Volpp writes in relation to American Islamophobia, Muslim identity "undoes" political citizenship in the United States, a phenomenon that took violent form on the streets of Delhi.[80]

The mob finally stopped at the entrance of the mosque. Then one of its members torched the building, setting it ablaze as scores of extremists stormed inside to desecrate the walls, destroy the prayer room, and exact the populists' message that Islam is a foreign faith and India a Hindu state.

Hindu extremists mercilessly beat Muslim children and women outside of the mosque as it was set ablaze. As the mosque burned, a member of the mob climbed its minaret while his friends cheered him on with "Jai Shri Ram" and "Hinduon ka Hindustan," Hindu nationalist chants. Their cheers drove him higher and higher, until he reached the pinnacle of the minaret and placed the Hanuman flag, symbolizing a Hindu India, atop it.[81] The man's face beamed with pride—the same hateful pride displayed by Trump and Modi at the cricket stadium in Delhi and the rally in Houston—as the mosque underneath him burned. It was a mortifying scene, and a stunning metaphor for a nation that burned around it. The Islamic call to prayer that rang from that mosque was silenced, supplanted by an Islamophobic call to prey on the 2 million Muslims who called Delhi home.

This was Modi's India. A nation he believed to be the exclusive homeland for Hindus, ravaged by vigilante mobs ready to do his bidding on the burning streets of Delhi and beyond. These fires burned violently, but the fires next time would be even more vile.

I thought about Abdul when I saw images of that mosque, and the many others torn and torched to the ground in India, in newspapers and online. These were new images for me, but for Abdul, they matched old ones, scenes of massacre and memories of murder.

"The struggle of man against power is the struggle of memory against forgetting," states Rana Ayyub in *Gujarat Files*, a lucid testimony of that stretch when Muslims were brutally slain under Modi's watch in 2002.[82]

Forgetting is only permanent in death. And when Modi flew into Houston, the place where Abdul thought he had found escape, forgetting was permanently suspended for Abdul.

The horror of the past was linked to an even more horrific present. A present that spread like a virus through India and beyond, unleashing violence of such scope that there was no hope of slowing it down. A virus that in the years to come would spread into Karnataka, where hijab bans at public schools and colleges would prohibit Muslim women from pursuing their educations.[83] A virus that devolved into new forms, including the bulldozing of Muslim homes and businesses, a form of state-sponsored Islamophobia that destroyed the brick and mortar symbols of Muslim life in cities across India, foreshadowing more violent stages of ethnic cleansing still to come. A virus that spurred the assembly of a developing network of prison camps in Assam, on the eastern edge of India, where undocumented Muslim citizens would be cast as "immigrants" under the CAA, uprooted from their homes and incarcerated indefinitely. A virus that would police the dress of Muslim women and punish the bodies of Muslim men, with limitless impunity and without stop, comprising a front of Islamophobia that stands as one of the world's deadliest.

Under Modi and the BJP, Islamophobia is far more than an epicenter of global Islamophobia; it is a laboratory for one of its most virulent strands.

TELL IT TO THE MOUNTAIN

> Do not walk proudly on Earth. Your feet cannot tear the Earth apart nor
> are you as tall as the Mountains.
> QUR'AN, 17:37

There are the Seven Wonders of the World, and then there is Kashmir. It stands so far above those other so-called wonders that it needs its own distinction, its own title.

It is a place so sublime, so celestial, that it outgrew its original earthly plot between the Great Himalayas and the Pir Panjal mountains. Today, it encompasses a stretch that touches India to the south, China to the east, and Pakistan in the direction where Muslims bow their head five times every day. And in every direction are mountains so majestic and so heavenly that they lift you from the very ground on which you stand.

The mountains, and the beauty between them, have inspired photographers among generations of smitten Kashmiris. Many, like Ahmer Khan, know no home except that land that sits between those mountains and the heavens. From there, they have snapped award-winning photos for the *New York Times* and earned Pulitzer prizes for capturing the beautiful struggle many beyond Kashmir do not see.[84]

"As a photographer, Kashmir has been a Muse, not necessarily a happy one. It [is] more of a forlorn atmosphere amidst a natural beauty which I try to depict in my pictures," Khan wrote me on June 25, 2020. That period marked a crossroads moment for the slice of heaven sitting between two mountain ranges and two regional powers with deep-rooted tension.

Kashmir is, if anything, a land of living and lurid juxtapositions. A place so breathtaking, so overwhelming to the senses, that it seems destined to attract foreign devils, and in some instances, devils who have eyed it for decades. They have created a hell that seems to sink lower and lower, and when India functionally annexed Kashmir in October 2019, it reached a new bottom.[85]

Kashmir is as much a metaphor as it is a place, sitting, as it does, in front of mountains so grand and ranges so endless. Only man's hand can turn a place so heavenly into a crucible of perdition. The mountains are at once a reminder of the divine and the bars of purgatory, with photographers capturing the precarious tap dance of life in between.

For Kashmiris, living in flux and under an Indian military siege, photographers like Ahmer are their poets, their reporters, and their intellectuals. All at once, their photos *speak* because activists and politicians and freedom fighters cannot. There is no freedom of speech or tolerance of dissent in a Kashmir suffocated by India, where the slightest acts of individuality are branded subversive, and in a world where the War on Terror seeps into every crevice.

The images of Kashmir's photographers, perhaps the final embodiments of Kashmiri independence, are acts of protest on behalf of a people who have no right to speak freely, assemble, or march. Their cameras are *weapons* that tell stories of survival between the two nations warring on either side of them and the mountains that watch from high above. Kashmir, that beautiful but cruel muse, is being torn apart by small men with outsized imperial ambitions.

The three-year-old child sat there, still and frozen, his legs pointed to the east and his face fixed in that same direction. His little green sandals matched the green hue of his button-up shirt, and his khaki pants were camouflaged by the dirt around him. He sat there, static, looking toward the horizon.[86] Perhaps taking a mental photo of a scene that he could not yet fully absorb.

His cheeks and eyes were red. He sat alone, or at least appeared to be alone in the photos. Indian media disseminated pictures of this Kashmiri boy sitting, and then walking toward an Indian military police officer.[87] The most ubiquitous photo shared by Indian media outlets showcased the young boy being held in the arms of a lionized Indian military man who patted him on the cheek and appeared to speak softly to the shaken boy, accompanied by headlines declaring that the occupying soldier "saved the boy from Kashmiri terrorists."[88]

It looked like a carefully plotted photo opportunity for the state of India. It could not have been staged better on a set in Hollywood or Bollywood. The young Kashmiri boy, a victim, caught in the crossfire of a war-ravaged land that needed a hero, the state of India, embodied by that soldier who held the boy to his bosom and safeguarded him from "terrorists."[89] So-called terrorists that included members of the boy's family, including his dead grandfather, who were given that label because they demanded independence and dignity.

The images were so potent, so powerful, that they were far more than mere pictures. They embodied an irresistible metaphor for those who saw them, one in which a gallant nation, Modi's India, stood as the only hope for the land between those mountains. It could not have been staged any better, except that it was—by photographers and their media handlers in India, and the mobs that took to the internet and the airwaves to tell a story that never happened.

These Indian handlers were dramatically unlike Kashmir's native photographers, who organically captured the divine images in front of them, those sublime places and familiar faces they knew so well, without the need to distort or fabricate. The Indian cameras were ignorant of the terrain, and thus had to doctor images in order to push forward old lies and new fictions so they could claim a land that they knew, deep inside, was not theirs.

That little Kashmiri boy was not sitting on the ground. Despite what India showed us with its fictive frames, he was not alone. He sat on the stomach of his grandfather's limp body. The grandfather, Bashir Ahmed, was dead. He had been murdered.[90]

Bashir Ahmed was killed by crossfire that would not have taken place had Indian military not been in Kashmir. Blood stained his white shirt. His arms were stretched above his head, as if he had been signaling to the Indian soldiers to halt their gunfire before they took his life, and as if he were reaching for the mountains and making his way back home.

Pictures are powerful. But in Kashmir, where land is sacred, pictures are terrain for propaganda wars. Disputed terrain where the images we see before us, more often than not, are not what they appear to be. These images and everything else, except those mountains, are vulnerable to being manipulated by that powerful foreign hand. A hand intent on capturing those mountains, and all that lives and dies between and beneath them.

Modi's portrait of a Hindu India did not stop at its current borders. "To be a Hindu means a person who sees this land, from the Indus River to the sea," goes the RSS lore that drives the modern Hindu supremacy spearheaded by Modi.[91] The Indus flows through the heart of Kashmir, thus making the territory—which has long held semi-autonomous status, a designation established to avoid war—vulnerable to full-fledged annexation.

That ended in August 2019. On August 5, the Indian parliament enacted the Jammu and Kashmir Reorganization Act, which opened the door for greater military presence and Indian state control of the disputed territory. It was tantamount to annexation.[92]

The law was viewed as a provocation by Pakistan and China, who also make claims to the coveted lands of Jammu and Kashmir. Despite being locked between a sibling rival and a global superpower, Modi acted—and acted aggressively—to begin making the Hindu state he and his BJP counterparts had pictured in their minds for so long.

The Jammu and Kashmir Reorganization Act did away with the Indian constitutional provision (article 370) extending quasi-autonomy to Kashmir. "We were not free before, but at least we didn't have to stare down the barrel of an [Indian] gun every time my children walked to the school," shared Yusra, a mother of two living in Srinagar, the urban center of Kashmir.[93]

Indian military police and soldiers were everywhere after August, stationed at intersections, mounting checkpoints that stymied and slowed once fluid streets and avenues, and standing ominously in front of mosques. Kashmir state is approximately 67 percent Muslim, while the entire Kashmir Valley region is overwhelmingly populated by Muslims (98 percent). For Kashmiri Muslims like Yusra, being under the thumb of a Hindu supremacist regime made for an ungodly existence: "We see what he's [Modi] done to Muslims in his country, just imagine what he has in mind for us here in Kashmir. We cannot even go pray in peace, and our mothers and children are spat on when they walk the streets. Their own streets, in their own communities."

If Islam does not figure into Modi's portrait of India, then it surely does not align with what he has in mind for Kashmir. By exporting Indian Islamophobia into Kashmir, Modi's designs to claim the coveted territory became clear, and after 2019, built considerable momentum.[94] Designs comprised of doctored pictures staged by the state and taken by the amateur hands of a military force, designs in which Islam is excised—and Muslims excluded—from Kashmir and a sublime panorama they will only know as unwanted visitors.

As is the case for millennials around the world, Roya's phone was the center of her universe. But unlike young people her age in India and elsewhere around the world, she did not use that phone to snap selfies or document her daily jaunts on social media. The phone she wielded in her right palm was her weapon, and after India's siege of Kashmir, her only outlet to the world: "I remember when they [the Modi regime] shut down the internet. It felt like the world was coming to an end, in some ways, and we were being cut off entirely from it. We went completely dark, and they could do whatever they wanted to us and nobody would know."[95]

That was the Modi regime's very objective: black out Kashmiris, and in the process, strip them of the ability to document their daily struggles under Indian occupation.[96] Roya, and scores of activists and students, journalists and academics, were disarmed of their final weapon.[97] Once that last line of communication to the external world had been stripped away, the door was open for the Indian regime to beat innocents in the street, ransack homes and mosques, jail activists and journalists, and extrajudicially kill anybody who sought to resist the terror.

In the immediate wake of the blackout that followed the revocation of Kashmir's special status, India detained and arrested hundreds of local leaders and politicians. The objective was clear: gut Kashmir of its political and activist class and make way for Indian Hindutva rule. Prominent leaders like Farooq Abdallah and Mehbooba Mufti, the last chief minister of Kashmir and Jammu State, were imprisoned indefinitely.[98] During the blackout, Indian state violence peaked and pummeled Kashmir's intelligentsia and political classes behind its veil of darkness.

Journalists were expelled. Activists and students protesting India's siege and the blackout were jailed without charges being levied, and the process for their release was dragged out. Photographers, the last line of resistance for a people stripped of their voice, were also left in the dark.

"I fear taking photos, even mundane ones of friends or family on the street. Even on Ramadan, because I feared it would be viewed as political by the police. They are always there, and looking," shared Roya, painting a picture of a dystopian Orwellian state of surveillance.

The blackout was not temporary. It continued, full-scale, from early August 2019 until late January 2020.[99] During that horrific six-month stretch, India suspended landline and cell phone connections and internet services, and it flooded Kashmir with nearly a million troops.

The blackout was not completely lifted in January 2020. In order to maintain control over the predominantly Muslim population of Kashmir and keep tabs on the "terrorists," India restored only limited (2G) internet service.[100] That move by the Modi regime was another instance of image-doctoring, representing to the world that the blackout was lifted while concealing the challenges of carrying on with no access to social media, video communication, and a slow and often interrupted connection.

"It is very slow—and a good joke. India wants to deceive the world by saying we have restored internet, but we can't even access email with 2G speed," stated Sajeel Majid, a thirty-five-year-old restaurant owner in Srinagar.[101]

India's de facto annexation of Kashmir has become the new normal for Roya and the 13 million people who call that sublime strip of land home. "Life is what it is now. Anything we do, if they [Indian military] don't like it, can be said to be terrorism," Roya revealed. "We are Muslim, and this goes against what Modi wants for this place."

Ali Hussein Mir, a Kashmiri who lived in India but relocated to Dubai, echoed Roya. "Being a Kashmiri is a synonym of being a terrorist if you are living outside of Kashmir and inside India. If you wear a skullcap (kufi) while going to the mosque, people look at us as if we are wearing a bomb."[102] Muslim identity is intimately tied to terror suspicion, while being Kashmiri stands for the quest for self-determination that stands in the way of Modi's Hindutva designs for Kashmir. In June of 2022, I met with several leaders of the Kashmiri freedom movement in Istanbul, Turkey, who echoed the same. One of them, who is also a founder of the independent research organization that tracks Hindutva violence, Hindutva Watch, succinctly stated, "They have reduced Kashmiri identity to terrorism."[103]

Islamophobia is the familiar scapegoat legitimized by the War on Terror, readapted to suit the local interests of dictators and demagogues. In fact, American researchers and hawks within the Bush administration singled out Kashmir, during the earliest stages of the War on Terror, as a site of "cross-border terrorism."[104] That is what the War on Terror gifted to Indian imperial designs. Namely, that whenever Muslims stand in the way of ambitions of hegemony and Hindu supremacy, they can be remade, with full prejudice and without due process, into terrorists. Doctored ideas legitimized by Washington,

DC, enable the distorted images that India commissions and then circulates, images of "terrorists" stripped of any power and humanity, striving to stay alive on their own land.

If Muslim cities in India can be renamed from Allahabad to Prayagraj in the pursuit of "toppling terror," then Kashmir can be remade in the image of Hindutva lore.[105] The only obstacles standing in Modi's way are those mountains. And those millions of people whose faith marks them as targets of military guns, and of the even deadlier aim of Indian cameras.

This is Kashmir. A land of a million pictures that inspire a million more. A place where India has deployed one soldier for every thirteen residents, and swarms of photographers pushing propaganda in place of the authentic images snapped by the locals. A place so beautiful that it has spawned generations of photographers, like Dar Yasin, Mukhtar Khan, and Channi Anand, who won the Pulitzer Prize—and some like Roya and Ahmer Khan, who clutch their phones and cameras as their homeland's last line of resistance. Cut off from the world. With almost every lane of contact severed and every line of communication suspended, Roya and Ahmer and every Kashmiri walking those heavily occupied streets with a picture of freedom in their head and a camera in their hands.

With no freedom of speech or assembly or association to exercise in the face of Indian imperialism, Kashmiris are forced to *tell it to the mountain*. Those familiar mountains, hugging a land and a people who have seen it all and are destined to see far more. Standing there alongside them when nobody else will.

"What is meant for you, will reach you even if it is in between two mountains. And what is not meant for you, won't reach you even if it is between your two lips," an Islamic proverb holds. These words capture

Kashmir's alchemy of beauty against struggle, its boundless stretches of heaven surrounding the belly of hell. All of which can be found, right there in Kashmir, between those mountains that dwarf the men trying to remake that land in their image, who spit hateful rhetoric from their lips in hopes of claiming a destiny that they will not reach.

Those mountains are far mightier than men, even strongmen like Modi and his millions of soldiers, whose time will pass as these ranges continue to stand tall, strong, and proud. They embody the strength of those living below and between them. They tell the truth when manipulated pictures of slain grandfathers peddle false narratives of heroism and hegemony, and move innocent babes to speak it in the face of power: "A policeman killed grandpa. . . . A policeman shot him."[106]

In December 2021, my friend Professor Farhan Chak, a Kashmiri leader for self-determination, convened the first Russell Tribunal on Kashmir. It was held, appropriately, in Sarajevo, Bosnia and Herzegovina—another site of Muslim genocide. Among Kashmiri leaders, our Bosnian hosts, and committed friends, I spoke: "In Kashmir—at this very moment—law sits at the very center of a two-faced genocide just as concerned with murdering a culture, a history, an identity as it is with murdering the Kashmiri bodies whose very existence—whose very being—is an act of rebellion and expression of 'terrorism' to an imperial, occupying, and genocidal Indian regime."[107] There, amid the shadows of Bosnian genocide and among Sarajevo's Olympic mountains—Trebević, Jahorina, Igman, Bjelašnica—where mass murder unfolded from 1992 to 1995, we met from places all over the world to give face to a renewed struggle for Kashmir, different mountains that witnessed the same anti-Muslim hatred.

Tell it to the mountain. Mountains that have seen it all, every scene of injustice since 1947 that sank Kashmir into political flux, and every incident that was blacked out by internet cutoffs and scissored out of newsprint.

Tell it to the mountain. Mountains that know you so well, and every inch of heaven and every incursion of hell, and that are poised to inspire more photographers among you—its brothers and sisters struggling in between as they stand alongside you. Loyally. Offering unmoveable solidarity when the rest of the world cannot.

Tell it to the mountain like you tell it to yourself, in whispers the soldiers and the state cannot hear.

You are not in the mountains. The mountains are in you.[108]

CHAPTER FOUR

INTERNMENT AND EXILE

REMEMBERING AUSCHWITZ

> It is natural to believe in God when you're alone—quite
> alone, in the night, thinking about death.
> ALDOUS HUXLEY, *Brave New World*

"I was arrested on 22 May 2017. The statement says that I'm a terrorist." Before her arrest, the state tracked every terrestrial and virtual footstep Jelilova Gulbahar left behind. Every online purchase and social media exchange, every phone conversation and checkpoint stop supplied the state with a fluid stream of data, data fed into a policing algorithm that led to Jelilova's identification as a "terrorist."[1]

Immediately after her arrest, Jelilova was taken to a concentration camp. There, she learned that more than 1 million people were detained inside of China's swelling network of 1,200 prison camps.[2] The inner sanctums of these camps were theaters of mass discipline and ghastly punishment, which for Jelilova began with the removal of her hijab. Prison guards cackled as they replaced the Islamic headdress with a freshly shaved head.[3] After that initial "dignity taking," Jelilova was escorted to a cell, where she met other women who had been arrested on terror charges.[4] The majority of them were Uyghur; all of them were Muslim.

Days within the prison blended together until they blurred into one. "In the morning we had one minute to use the bathroom. If we used it longer, we got punished," Jelilova shared.[5] Following the bathroom drill, inmates were forced to sing

Communist Party jingles: "Long live the Communist Party" and "I love China."[6] After weeks, the Mandarin rolled from the prisoners' tongues and muted the native Uyghur they were restricted from speaking. These imposed disciplines were designed to treat the "illness" and systematically "wash [the captives'] brains clean" of it.[7] Their ailment?[8] The very ethnic and Muslim identity that defines who Jelilova and 15 million other Uyghurs in China's Xinjiang are, and what, in a surveillance society designed to subjugate them, they struggle to remain.[9]

But the middle-aged Uyghur woman and the vast majority of the prisoners were no *terrorists*. That very word was "stripped of its meaning" and deployed by the state to suppress a people long cast as oppositional and subversive.[10] The state deployed counterterrorism law to intensify its crackdown on the Uyghurs, doing so behind the curtains of the camps and the digital walls that surrounded Xinjiang, or what the Uyghurs call East Turkistan.[11] Eventually, Jelilova confessed to the charge of terrorism.[12]

The global War on Terror legitimized that charge, then intensified the Han supremacist campaign to suppress and stamp out the Uyghurs.[13] Supplemented by domestic counterextremism laws and the regime's "Strike Hard on Terror" Campaign, Xinjiang, the autonomous region in western China that is home to roughly 11 million Uyghurs, has been reengineered into a postmodern panopticon—an enveloping digital surveillance prison—that tracks every breath and mines every move of its Uyghur Muslim captives.[14] The new policing technologies that extend Beijing's eyes into every facet of Uyghur life are the building blocks of China's new state of surveillance, where the threat of incarceration looms throughout a society characterized by total "e-carceration."[15] One where predictive algorithms, tracking software, and facial recognition cameras are planted throughout the province and rooted inside the devices that accompany Uyghurs wherever they go.[16]

Far more than cogs of a novel "surveillance capitalism" machine,[17] these surveillance technologies form the prevailing architecture of policing in Xinjiang and societies beyond, where modern policing is creating new orders of digital surveillance.[18] These digital tools form new surveillance sites where punishment, discipline, and control ominously blur into one. A state of surveillance, manifested most ominously by concentration camps that Uyghur, Kazakh, and ethnic Muslims are forced into and where they are then confined, that sits at the center of a new state of digital subjugation and ethnic cleansing.[19] A new state of surveillance perfected in Xinjiang, a dystopian laboratory for the most cutting-edge, nefarious forms of mass surveillance that China is exporting globally and advancing to crush the Uyghur people.

I found a plot in the courtyard in front of the church entrance. The sun was shining, bright, and I took off my jacket and laid it and my bag on the grass, marking the spot where I intended to stop and pray.

"The entire earth has been made a place of prayer," the Prophet Muhammad said to his companions. And the Columbia Theological Seminary's green quad provided an idyllic setting for the third set of my daily prayers.

I turned to my right, and finished with my left. I prayed alone but was not alone, seeing the conference crowd file into the seminary hall for the next address. It was my turn, and I gathered my jacket and bag and followed the people sifting into the hall.

Beautiful stained glass provided the backdrop, and the high vaulted ceilings and rows of oak benches gave my lecture a grand, sanctified feel. I turned my talk to Abdulla, a Muslim living in Xinjiang, which he defiantly called East Turkistan, the disputed territory in northwest China that is the indigenous home of the Uyghur Muslims.

Like me, Abdulla prayed every day and night in line with Islam's mandate.[20] He prayed alone, oftentimes in the dark, fearing that the Chinese policemen who roved through his neighborhood would spot him. Abdulla lives with the fear that he, like friends and family members, could be shipped off to a concentration camp, one of the prisons where up to 2 million Uyghur Muslims like himself have been locked away.[21] Years later, in Istanbul, Turkey, I met many survivors of concentration camps; that city is home to a swelling Uyghur diaspora and the site of their rising movement for self-determination. A movement that I, through philanthropic work and advocacy, would become part of.

For me, the right to pray is protected by the First Amendment of the US Constitution, even during the War on Terror. For Abdulla and the 11 million other Uyghur Muslims who have always called Xinjiang (East Turkistan) home, prayer may be a one-way ticket to the dark and din of a Chinese concentration camp. Again, China has been reengineered into a total surveillance state, and the omnipresent digital gaze of the state is fixed most intensely on the Uyghurs.[22]

In that seminary in Decatur, Georgia, I told the story of Abdulla and the concentration camps where members of his community were locked away. I was in Georgia, but East Turkistan was on my mind. In that seminary, I delivered a speech that, for at least one audience member sitting in what felt like a congregation, took her from 2018 Georgia back to 1939 Germany. For that woman, Auschwitz was on her mind.

I saw her there in that first row, shifting uncomfortably in her seat. The stories of praying in rooms the size of closets, warding off the fear within and the fright without, fearing that knock in the night that could come at any time, unannounced, and those two words, "concentration" and "camps," benign when separated but bone-chilling when combined, shook her. They shook her every time I uttered them. And shook her so violently that she remained there, fixed in her seat, after I finished my lecture and walked from the podium.

I had noticed her, and locked eyes with her several times, before I uttered the final words of my speech. I intended to speak to her as soon as I finished. But she spoke first, inviting me toward her and into what she was feeling and thinking.

"I thought concentration camps were a thing of the past," shared the elderly woman from her seat. Her eyes demanded respect, and her question seemed rooted in a place so dark that only experience—personal experience—could have given it that tone.

Although the distinctions between present-day Xinjiang and Nazi Germany are dramatic, particularly with regard to mass deaths and mass punishment, the parallels cannot be ignored. Over 6 million Jews were killed during the Holocaust, moved from concentration camps into gas chambers.[23] To date, there is little evidence of mass deaths in China, but torture and ethnic cleansing and its concomitant project of "cultural genocide" have been widely documented. Those two words I had uttered throughout the talk—"concentration camps"—had struck a chord with at least one audience member.[24]

"I'm Jewish, and lost so many people that I love in Auschwitz," she shared, still from her seat, looking up at me—a Muslim American professor—searching for what connects one of the greatest human disasters of the twentieth century with the one currently unfolding in China.

I could not make sense of something so utterly unholy, and wholly evil, as we spoke in that church hall. The testimony of Uyghur Muslims tortured and brainwashed, raped and executed, conjured up memories of Jews in World War II Europe for that elderly woman.[25] Her words and memories drew that same connection more starkly for me.

The time, place, and faiths of the two persecuted groups differed in myriad ways, but the hateful motive was one and the same. Religion was the scapegoat for two morally decayed regimes that vilified an entire faith and its adherents through meticulous propaganda campaigns and surveillance systems, paving the way to collecting and imprisoning them en masse in concentration camps.

"Concentration camps are not a relic of the past," I shared with the elderly woman. She reached for my hand, and I met it halfway to hold it. She commanded respect, as all elders do, and I lowered myself to see her face to face. Her wrinkles were at once sublime and sad, reminding me of my grandmother's brow when I embraced her as a child. I stared in her eyes and at those lines above them, scars of age that mark the wisdom and wages of past wars.

We sat and spoke in that oak pew, in front of the beautiful stained glass where I had lectured only minutes earlier. A Muslim and a Jew, reflecting on the past as we grappled with the present, in the heart of a Christian church. As it should be, and as only the Divine can make it.

Abdulla goes to bed every night dreading the devil's knock on the door. A knock he has heard in recurrent nightmares and in stories from neighbors. A knock that more than 2 million others have heard at their door, before they walked through it for the final time.

He expects it to come at any moment. He is an ethnic Uyghur and has always called Xinjiang his home. In fact, he still calls it East Turkistan in private, far from the ears of the state and the soldiers who patrol the streets. His forefathers lived and toiled on this land for centuries, land the nascent Chinese Communist government annexed in 1949.[26] Abdulla himself is a father of two, a son and a daughter, and a devout Muslim—cautiously performing his five prayers every day behind the thinning veil of secrecy that his home offers him, until the knock comes and that secrecy of home is no more.

In the past months, several of his friends and colleagues have heard that dreaded knock on their doors. And after that sound, in the quiet of the night, they have disappeared with no trace or warning. According to Darren Byler, a leading expert on China's total surveillance state, the network of concentration camps "targeted the entire Muslim population of 15 million people in Xinjiang. It precipitated a criminalization of Islamic practice and a number of Uyghur and Kazakh cultural traditions. Initially only religious leaders were sent to camps, but by 2017 the War on Terror became a program of preventing Uyghurs from being Muslim and, to a certain extent, from being Uyghur or Kazakh."[27] All of them heard that knock.

Everybody, including Abdulla, knows where they have been taken and kept. But nobody knows how long they will be held, nor do they know if they will ever come back home. Most have yet to return, and those who have returned are shells of their former selves, neighborhood ghosts. Walking cautionary tales of what looms around the corner for Uyghurs refusing to disavow Islam and submit to the unholy mandate of the state.[28]

In August 2018, a United Nations human rights panel reported that nearly 1.1 million Uyghur Muslims were being held in concentration camps in Xinjiang.[29] Gay McDougall, who sits on the UN Committee on the Elimination of Racial Discrimination, claimed that the imprisoned population could be as high as 2 million. The number could be far larger than those estimates. According to Abduresid Emin, secretary general of the International Union of East Turkistan Organizations, with whom I worked closely, the number of individuals locked away in China's concentration camps could be as high as 5 million. I met many survivors of the camps in June of 2022 in Istanbul, and in person spoke directly to wives, parents, and children of those still locked away in them. Some of them became my close friends, and others are featured on the cover of this book.

Shortly after the UN broke the news of the concentration camps, Sigal Samuel of *The Atlantic* fleshed out the hell unfolding in the camps. She reported that inmates were "forced to renounce Islam, criticize their own Islamic beliefs and those of fellow inmates, and recite Communist Party propaganda songs for hours each day."[30] Male inmates were compelled to shave their beards, which signify piety for Muslims, and others were force-fed pork and alcohol, which Muslims are categorically forbidden from consuming.[31] These force feedings were also done during Ramadan, the Islamic holy month, to shame Uyghurs and to strip them of the dignity that their faith gave them. It was clear from my conversations with survivors and the documentation of life inside the camps that China would do anything to desecrate Islam in its morbid project to uproot it from the minds, and spirits, of the Uyghur.

These concentration camps, which hold at least ten times the number of Japanese Americans the US government locked away during World War II, are where Uyghur Muslims are attempted to be remade into atheist Chinese subjects. These are horrific sites where fear and physical violence, psychological trauma, and emotional abuse are all available tools, wielded to push Uyghur inmates to renounce Islam, a faith that the state has treated as a mental illness, and to reject the distinctly Uyghur customs that are deeply intertwined with their faith.[32]

This program of brainwashing and indoctrination is not exclusive to adults. The state also operates orphanages for Uyghur Muslim children stripped from their parents, where the process of disconnecting them from their Islamic faith and ethnic heritage is deeply inculcated into their education.[33] At these orphanages, disguised as "schools," China is converting future generations of Uyghur Muslim children into loyal state subjects who embrace atheism, Communism, and Han customs. Pushing them to turn their backs on their culture and faith, and on their families, and in the direction of Beijing's vision of destroying the Uyghur Muslim people.[34]

Years have passed since the UN broke the news of China's network of concentration camps and the ancillary programs designed to purge Islam and destroy the Uyghurs, a people who cling tightly to their faith like they do to the land they defiantly still call East Turkistan.[35] Yet global outrage and political pressure have been slow to match the velocity and ferocity of China's designs to cleanse itself of a population it deems inimical to and unassimilable with its national identity.

Why? Answers can be traced to prevailing economic and geopolitical pressures; nations fear the economic hit they will likely take if they challenge or sanction China for its ethnic cleansing of the Uyghur people. China is an economic superpower, and nations across the world rely on it heavily for imports, investment, and trade. China's economic hegemony abroad has enabled it, as its stature grows, to deepen its genocidal authoritarianism at home.[36]

The economic factors deterring humanitarian intervention are accompanied by a global War on Terror landscape that opened the door for Beijing, after 9/11, to violently rev up its persecution of Uyghur Muslims behind the veneer of countering terrorism.[37] The campaign, spearheaded by the Bush administration and the United States, encouraged other nations—including China—to join in and crack down on their Muslim populations.

Islam serves as the spiritual lifeline connecting the Uyghur people to their land, their history, and one another, and the Chinese state has zeroed in on it. *If it can destroy Islam,* Beijing believes, it can destroy the Uyghurs. If it can destroy both, then it can erase the Uyghur claim to land that Beijing so desperately covets.[38] Land that is integral to China's Belt and Road Initiative, a global economic campaign that spreads China's economic might throughout Asia, Africa, Europe, and beyond. Land that is rich in resources that have become even more essential since the Russian invasion of Ukraine. As anthropologist Darren Byler notes, "The region has become the source of around 20 percent of China's oil and natural gas. It has an even higher percentage of China's coal reserves, and produces around a quarter of the world's cotton and tomatoes."[39] Xinjiang is also vital to China's soft power campaign, exemplified by the 2022 Winter Olympic Games in Beijing. Leading up to the games, which were staged against a boycott launched by various Uyghur Muslim groups, I wrote about the soft power play Beijing envisioned in Xinjiang paralleling its ongoing genocide: "In the lead up to the Olympics, there has been a concerted government push to promote Xinjiang as a snow sport destination, accelerating the removal of the indigenous Uyghur to make way for ski lifts, slopes and foreign brands ready to build showrooms atop razed mosques and bulldozed communities."[40]

Slow and silent genocide, in the form of both soft and hard power. This is precisely what China has been doing, behind a curtain of authoritarian darkness, for years. Even after the UN and foreign journalists lifted that curtain for the whole world to see, it has carried forward without pause.

The plight of Uyghur Muslims in China extends far beyond the northwest stretches of the contested territory of Xinjiang, all the way to China's coastal cities. The shadow of the camps and the perils within them also extend from the Chinese hinterland to the economic centers where Muslims, Uyghur and otherwise, live.

Yusef, a twenty-three-year-old university student living in Beijing, lamented after the crackdown on the Uyghurs, "I became lonely. Fewer Uyghurs can be seen in the streets because they're forced to learn Han culture in the camp far away in Xinjiang. Nobody has the right to decide people of which ethnicity [to] put into jail, but it's happening and it's frustrating and creepy that most Chinese people believe that it's [the] right decision [in order] to keep the whole society 'stable.'"[41]

Loneliness in a land with nearly 1.5 billion people seems impossibly absurd. Yet for Uyghur Muslims in Xinjiang and Beijing, and places between and beyond, absurdity has become lived reality. A sordid reality for an embattled people whose quest for independence, and the Islam that defines who they are, is classified as a mental infirmity that incites terrorism.[42]

Tying Islam to terror, an import from the American War on Terror, arms the government in Beijing with license to unleash genocidal terror.[43] A terror so omnipresent that the very fear of being rounded up may be even greater than the darkness of the concentration camps. The dark shadow of the "black gate," what Uyghurs often call the camps, extends deep into cities, villages, and households in Xinjiang (East Turkistan). The gates of fear are ubiquitous, blurring the line between prison and life into an unrecognizable Orwellian whole.

This fear is starkest in Xinjiang but lives among Muslims through-out China and even those who find refuge beyond its iron boundaries.[44] Fear knocks at their door wherever they are.

For Abdulla, that feared knock on the door is yet to come. It may never come, or it may come tomorrow, or the day after, or the very moment he least expects it. The fear of the unknown and the stark reality that every moment with his children, his wife, and his elderly parents could be his last, follows his every step like a shadow. He cannot escape it, and the very fear of it makes his life on the outside a prison in and of itself.

Beyond the walls of the concentration camps, Xinjiang—like Gaza—has become an open-air prison for Uyghur Muslims like Abdulla, whose every word is monitored and whose religious expression is closely policed.[45] The eyes of spies and the gaze of the state are everywhere, and most nefariously, are built into the phones and virtual behavior of every-body in China.[46] "Digital totalitarianism" is dystopian reality for Abdulla and other Uyghurs, a reality in which "the Communist Party dismantle[s] traditional domains of affiliation, identity, and social meaning—family, religion, civil society, intellectual discourse, political freedom."[47]

In China, there is no room for God, and particularly not for an Allah who inspires independence from a state that rejects Him and demands absolute reverence. The Communist regime in Beijing enshrines athe-ism and has weaponized it along with the War on Terror to bludgeon Uyghur Muslim life.[48] Allah is the enemy of the Han Communist regime, and wholly rooting him out of Uyghur life forms the marrow of its geno-cidal campaign. But for Uyghurs, Allah is the final safe haven, and Islam the last and transient liberation theology against an unholy foe.

This dialectic forms the crucible of existence for Uyghurs in China. This is life for Abdulla, or what remains of it. He only finds solace in prayer, prostrating himself before Allah, beginning in the early morning and one final time after sitting with his children at dinner. He prays five times a day and several more times—quietly, in his head—in the hours between. Abdulla also prays that the state does not take him away and destroy his family, as it has done to so many others.

Yet the paradox of prayer symbolizes the imminent perils of being Muslim in Xinjiang today. The more Uyghur Muslims are unwilling to relinquish their spiritual identity and disavow Islam, the likelier they are to be taken away and kept far from everybody they love and everything they know.

It all starts with that knock on the door, followed by a drive to a living hell that only exists to purge Uyghur Muslims of their faith, disintegrate their families, and wash away their nation. That knock has come for millions. For Abdulla, the fear of it has taken away everything that he loves. Outings with his children and wife, visits to the mosque, and the ability to be who he is, freely and outwardly, without fear of what that means for him and his loved ones. Acting Muslim invites incarceration.

Abdulla wishes for a room where the light can't find him, where he can escape his fears and shed tears alone.[49] Away from his wife and children, a room where he can find momentary release without intensifying their fears.

But in a Xinjiang ruled by China, such places do not exist. Where Orwell's dystopian 1984 situated the telescreen as the "fantastic technology of control," modern China uses fear of internment and the circuit of horrors that surround it as that all-enveloping telescreen.[50] In Orwell's fictional world, "Nothing was your own except the few cubic centimeters inside your skull"; for Abdulla and other Uyghur Muslims, that is reality.[51]

Abdulla, and the weight of his fears, were present in that Atlanta seminary. So were the fears of survivors I met in the years to come, in places like Istanbul, Belgium, Ottawa, and Washington, DC, where I interviewed concentration camp survivors, orphans, and widows of Uyghur men, who like Abdulla, lived in debilitating fear of that knock until it stole them away from everything that they loved.

The elderly Jewish woman might have known little about the Uyghur people or their plight before my lecture, but she understood Abdulla's fears because she had endured them through family.

Before I left, she stood up, straight and strong. "We have to educate our communities," she instructed me, like a mother would her son. She understood that authoritarian regimes rely on apathy and ignorance to carry forward unspeakable evils, evils like those unfolding inside those concentration camps, where darkness opens the gates to hell on earth. A hell strategically concealed from the rest of the earth.

Rwanda. East Timor. Myanmar. Nazi Germany. The world has a cruel habit of ignoring humanitarian disasters until it is too late. Old habits die hard, and the people targeted by state-led ethnic cleansing programs even harder.

But this woman wanted to turn that tide and deflate the bubbles of apathy and indifference that enable mass internment and ethnic cleansing. She felt obligated to do so for Uyghur Muslims like Abdulla and the millions locked in those concentration camps and the millions more on their way there. Her vigor inspired me inside that church as the sun began to set and darkness began to creep in.

As a child, I was taught that when elders speak, the young are ordained to listen. So she spoke, and I listened. Drawing connections between two human disasters with the hope of derailing the one unfolding right now in China. The lectures I gave after that evening in Atlanta followed her instruction, as do the very words you are reading on this page.

Righting history is more important than writing about history, that elderly Jewish woman taught me, through word and, more importantly, through action. But sometimes the two tasks are one and the same. I left that room and have not returned to it since, but the face of that woman and her words have never left me. They stand, lucidly, alongside the faces and voices of the Uyghur men and women, children and elders I have met in the months and years after leaving that church hall in Georgia.

I must uphold my ideals, for perhaps the time will come when I shall be able to carry them out.[52]

WHERE MINARETS STOOD

An animal will kill, but never to completely annihilate a race, a whole collectively. What does this make us in this world?
PHILIP GOUREVITCH, *We Wish to Inform You That Tomorrow We Will Be Killed with Our Families*

I left my father's funeral numb. He was gone, and I was still here. Driving down the same streets that I always had, seeing the same places and the same people who reminded me of him. But the world felt different. The autumn sun warmed the coldness that had overtaken me as I drove home, eastbound on Ford Road toward a new destination in life. A destination I had arrived at hundreds of times before, but that would never feel the same.

As I drove around a bend in the road, I caught sight of two minarets towering in the Michigan sky as if reaching for something above them. Reaching for light, or perhaps signaling that cruel ends may be divine guises for better beginnings. The minarets spoke, and I listened, driving down that familiar road that my father's body had traveled down one final time that day.

My mind raced through memories as I stopped at a red light. I remembered the difficult times and those joyous moments in between, like when my dad bought me that big black atlas as a child. I remember him holding it above my little body—I must have been six then—as I sat on the floor of our Beirut apartment. It was my own "world book," my private portal to learning about the world that I hoped to impact one day.[53]

Those happy moments were less frequent than the trying ones. But they become more prominent with time, and they comfort you when the pain of yesterday and the voids of today come crashing down. Providing comfort on a journey that, like all of them, must end—sort of like those minarets on Ford Road, always standing—strong and tall—to remind you that something bigger awaits after this journey. That this journey, and the intersections of pain and loss that you arrive at more frequently with age, precedes a more joyful passage.

It was a sublime sight on a somber day, reminding me that hallowed spaces remain where we can mourn and praise and contemplate journeys that come after this one. The minarets spoke, and I listened.

The minarets in Kashgar, East Turkistan, told a radically different story than the two I drove by on Ford Road. One tower was flat on the ground; the other was bent and teetering, waiting for a final gust of wind to reunite it with its counterpart.[54]

The mosque in Kashgar, topped with domes adorned with beautiful blue and yellow hues that summoned the praise of those who worshipped there, was a shattered shell, razed by a Chinese bulldozer that converted it into a morbid shrine of ethnic cleansing and the genocide waiting around the corner.[55]

"They [China] wanted to break our spirit," stated Zeinab, a Uyghur mother of two who fled Xinjiang and resettled in Australia.[56] "They destroyed so many mosques in our homeland," she continued, as tears filled her eyes. The destruction included cornerstone places of worship such as the Imam Asim Shrine and the Kargalik mosque.

When mosques fold and minarets fall upon a soil that is the only home that Uyghur Muslims have known, tears take the place of words.

Yet for Zeinab, as articulated in a poem by Paulo Coelho, "Tears are words that need to be written."[57] And these tears that spill from her eyes and inspire words that sink onto these pages, are, for her, the last line of resistance against a genocidal regime spurred on by the American War on Terror.

Five weeks after the 9/11 terror attacks, President George W. Bush landed in Beijing.[58] The global War on Terror was still in its infancy, but the American president was keen on encouraging its rapid development in China, a superpower rising to challenge unchecked American global hegemony.

Standing to the right of then President Jiang Zemin in Beijing, Bush adapted his War on Terror talk to China, declaring, "We have a common understanding of the magnitude of the threat posed by international terrorism. All civilized nations must join together to defeat this threat. And I believe the United States and China can accomplish a lot."[59]

Despite there being no proven Al-Qaeda presence throughout the Chinese mainland in 2001, President Jiang nodded.[60] However, his expressions of approval and commitment to support America's War on Terror masked a different objective, and a dramatically distinct target. The War on Terror would be the perfectly timed guise, an ideological Trojan horse, cloaking a longstanding objective in Beijing to obliterate the Uyghur and their way of life.

Al-Qaeda did not materially concern Jiang, and China's national security was not threatened by it or any other transnational terror network. There was no imminent foreign "Islamist" threat on Chinese soil, only an indigenous Muslim population in the northwest who made that land their home long before the founding of the People's Republic of China.

But 9/11 happened, creating the opening for a "final solution." Miles Maochun Yu, a researcher at Stanford University's Hoover Institution, observed, "The Chinese government took advantage of the U.S.-led Global War on Terror after the 9/11 attacks and essentially steamrolled Washington into declaring the insignificantly weak East Turkistan Independence Movement as a terrorist group. For political expediency, Washington accepted the Chinese demand with great reluctance albeit urging Beijing for restraint and religious freedom in its crackdown on these 'Uyghur terrorists' seeking independence."[61]

Thus, the War on Terror that Bush peddled in Beijing created the ideal domestic opportunity to crush, once and for all, the Uyghurs and their precarious quest for self-determination. "Beijing saw an opportunity early [after 9/11]. Millions of Uyghurs and other non-Han Chinese groups in its northwestern region of Xinjiang had been asking for greater autonomy for decades, with scores joining violent separatist movement and militias."[62]

It was open season for China to finally wage war on what had been a thorn in its side since its modern creation on October 1, 1949—a date that marks the creation of the modern Chinese state and disaster for the Uyghur people.

The War on Terror's language of "civilization against savagery" and "Islamic terrorism" provided Jiang and his more oppressive successors license to decimate the Uyghur people. In lockstep fashion, Chinese governmental leaders adopted the War on Terror parlance to impose their domestic crusade against Uyghur Muslims and to summarily brand an indigenous people seeking to realize their dreams of a free and sovereign East Turkistan as "terrorists."[63]

Virtually overnight, Bush's visit to Beijing and the War on Terror landscape converted a native population in northwest China into a satellite faction of terrorists. The lack of evidence connecting Uyghur Muslims to terror networks did not matter, nor did their justifiable grievances against Beijing. Only their faith and fight for independence mattered, and Islam was enough to mark the whole population as terrorists.

"Anti-terrorism is a fight between justice and evil, civilization and savagery," declared Chinese Foreign Minister Tang Jiaxuan, reading from a prepared statement that sounded like it had been written by a US State Department aide or a neoconservative lobbyist on K Street.[64] It was not the product of an American pen, but it did not matter, since all of the nations enlisted to fight the War on Terror spoke the same language.

The 9/11 terror attacks unfolded in Manhattan and Washington, DC. But based on the fear manufactured by Chinese leaders eager to solve their "Uyghur problem," one might have thought the Al-Qaeda terror attacks unfolded in Shanghai or Beijing.[65] But there were no such terror cells or networks in China's major cities, only a people tucked thousands and thousands of miles away, living proudly on land where minarets once stood.

The mosques razed in Xinjiang have made way for public toilets and prison camps.[66] In these camps, massive and dark structures where prayer has given way to prey, spaces where Uyghur Muslims bowed their heads in prayer have been replaced by broken limbs and broken spirits. East Turkistan, the aspirational homeland of Uyghurs, has become the site of the world's most vile strand of Islamophobia— concentration camps where up to 2 million Uyghur and ethnic Muslims find hell before they take their final breath.

However, the internment of Uyghur Muslims is only the tip of the ominous state architecture of ethnic cleansing. China's designs to crush Uyghur self-determination have mutated into a crusade to decimate an entire people.[67] Chinese Islamophobia, in short, is a state-sponsored campaign that seeks to uproot the Islam indigenous to East

Turkistan, and in its place, seed Han customs and the Communist mandate of total control.

Uyghur persecution in China is not about terrorism arising from Muslims, but about unimaginable evil coming from the corridors of power in Beijing. While it took time for the rest of the world to condemn it for what it is, 2020 ushered in rising voices calling the Uyghur Muslim crisis another ethnic cleansing, or worse. Even Donald Trump, the global figure most closely connected to Islamophobia, weighed in and accused China of waging "genocide on Uyghur Muslims."[68] In China, Islamophobia is a living system digitally designed to control, crush, and kill a people—a proud people—whose only wish is to live as they've always lived, atop a land that was always their own.

A portrait of Uyghur Muslim history and identity highlights why China, a communist nation that enshrines atheism and privileges its majority-Han ethnic population, is committed to eliminating these people. The Uyghurs are a stigmatized minority on two fronts: ethnicity and religion, and trapped in the precarious crosshairs of an Orwellian police state that views Islam as an affront to state-sponsored atheism and Uyghur identity as an obstacle to Han supremacy.

Han supremacists tend to view themselves as "white" and the Turkic Uyghur Muslims as non-white and non-Chinese.[69] Despite "Uyghur" literally meaning "civilized" in the Turkish language, Han Chinese flipped this definition on its head and marked them as racially backward and inferior. In line with this racialization, Beijing wants their land but wants to do away with the people.

However, like Kashmiris or Palestinians or First Nations in the Americas, Uyghur Muslims continue to fight for that coveted land. In addition to having a mutual religious affinity, Uyghurs share ethnic similarities with the predominantly Turkic inhabitants of their Central

Asian neighbors, such as Kyrgyzstan and Kazakhstan. Xinjiang, which means "New Frontier" in Mandarin, is romantically called East Turkistan by Uyghur Muslims, in hopes that "one day, we will be free as a nation and a people."[70]

Criminalizing and closely policing Islam, the most conspicuous and sacred identifier of Uyghur identity, is how Beijing seeks to not only stifle Uyghur aspirations for independence, but also advance a program of full-scale ethnic cleansing. In 2015, China restricted Uyghur Muslim students and teachers and other civil servants in Xinjiang from fasting during Ramadan, extending the arm of the state into family households during the holy month.[71]

This ban was accompanied, reported Human Rights Watch, by routine state vetting of Uyghur imams, close surveillance of mosques, the removal of religious teachers and students from schools, restrictions placed on Uyghur Muslims' communication with family and friends living overseas, and the screening of literature assigned to students in Xinjiang schools.[72]

"It was leaving my family and homeland, or ending up in those camps," Zeinab recalled, a choice millions of Uyghur Muslims who found themselves in Xinjiang's concentration camps never had.

The camps, called "reeducation centers" by the Chinese government, grew in size and number in 2018. Today, some estimates hold that as many as 3 million detainees may be locked away behind the impenetrable walls of 500 camps.[73] Many inside the global Uyghur movement, including Rushan Abbas of the Campaign for Uyghurs in Washington, DC, who I marched alongside in July 2022 in front of the Chinese embassy there, believes the number could be far higher. In addition to the horrors already outlined, Uyghur Muslims are forced to learn Mandarin in an effort to excise their culture and religion, and are also compelled to perform slave-like labor that reportedly pumps out products for American and European companies, including Adidas, Hugo Boss, and Apple.[74]

Old genocidal tactics are modernized to bring about a more efficient and expeditious elimination of a people, and chants of "never again" are being drowned out by cries for help. Uyghur Muslim women are being sterilized to prevent childbearing, and their heads are forcibly shaved in public.[75] The sights inside the camps of piles of Uyghur hair harken back to the "image of the glass display of mountains of hair preserved at Auschwitz" in World War II Germany.[76]

But the horror does not stop there. The China Tribunal, a human rights group that probes the harvesting of human organs, reported that "the Chinese government was taking hearts, kidneys, lungs and skin" from Uyghur Muslims. Hamid Sabi, a lawyer for the group, testified before the United Nations Human Rights Council in September 2019, "Victim for victim and death for death, cutting out the hearts and other organs from living, blameless, harmless, peaceable people constitutes one of the worst mass atrocities of this century."[77]

Locked up, uprooted from home and family, as much as 25 percent of the Uyghur Muslim population in Xinjiang is currently experiencing or has endured the horrors of the largest network of concentration camps since World War II. Those who resist while inside those walls are tortured, and deaths and disappearances reported by family members are widely documented.[78]

The majority of those placed in the camps are men, and the Chinese authorities have supplemented the disproportionate incarceration of men with a policy of forcing Uyghur Muslim women to marry (non-Muslim) Han men, further diluting the Uyghur Muslim population and sponsoring Han supremacy through compelled marriage and rape.[79]

In these concentration camps, the line between life and death often blurs. As Jean-Paul Sartre wrote in *No Exit*, "Death must enter life only to define it."[80] The camps are an entrance to a dark, evil vacuum where life and death are one and the same. There are no exits. And the prison beyond the walls is just as insufferable, where one is shackled by a paranoia that even the slightest transgression will send one back inside.

The threat of internment is a fear that hovers over Xinjiang like a black cloud and looms heavy in the mind of every Uyghur Muslim. So heavy, that for thousands of Uyghurs like Zeinab, the only relief is refuge in a foreign land. This fear is a weapon that the Chinese government has wielded to deter and intimidate Uyghurs from exercising their faith, enforced by way of a ubiquitous police presence in Uyghur Muslim communities, by tapping neighbors, classmates, and colleagues of targeted subjects as informants and spies, and perhaps most nefariously, by recruiting Uyghur children to monitor and implicate their own parents as "terrorists."[81]

Scholars have dubbed this policing that envelops Xinjiang as "preventive repression," and even "Big Brother" would be a severe understatement.[82] The gaze of the state, on the daily routine of Uyghur Muslims in Kashgar, Urumqi, and cities and villages throughout Xinjiang, is ubiquitous and incessant. It exists in the form of facial recognition cameras affixed to street poles or mobile cameras in the form of "spy doves," algorithmic vetting linked to smart cards carried by Uyghur residents, and perpetual mining and tracking of data from the very smartphones they carry everywhere they go.[83] This digital state of subjugation "bring[s] a desperate and ferocious loneliness into everyday life, tearing apart communities, turning children against their parents. It is the engineers of these systems—the algorithm tinkerers, the face recognition designers, the DNA mappers, the 'smart' pedagogists" who design the dystopian laboratory of life, or what remains of it, in Xinjiang.[84] In the camps and beyond them, Islamophobia in China is brutally engineered to destroy the Uyghur Muslim people and remove them from a land the government seeks to absorb, and remake, in the image of an atheist, Communist, and Han China.

Zeinab has two young daughters, both less than ten years old, who live with her in Australia. While speaking to her from my computer, one of them—Dara—popped her round head and wide smile onto the screen.[85] She waved and then greeted me, "asalamu alaikum," as her mother smiled behind her.

That scene would seem to be a routine one, particularly in a post-COVID-19 world. However, when juxtaposed with concurrent realities for Uyghur Muslims in Xinjiang, the scene highlights a morbid contrast. China's genocidal designs in Xinjiang have turned children against their parents, seeking to eliminate the latter and assimilate the former.

"China's crackdown has some Uyghurs in Xinjiang worried that their own children will incriminate them, whether accidentally or because teachers urge kids to spy on their parents," Sigal Samuel reported in *The Atlantic*.[86] China's project of disintegrating families, the building block of Uyghur Muslim society in and beyond Xinjiang, is achieved through the routine program of enlisting young children— like the adorable Dara—to report on the religious activities of their parents to (state-controlled) teachers.

That is only one way in which China exploits Uyghur children. Uyghur children with parents locked away in concentration camps are assigned to state-run orphanages. This is where the sons and daughters of interned Uyghurs undergo intense programs of cultural brainwashing and assimilation—concentration camps made for children.[87]

Within the walls of these orphanages, where children "between the ages of six months and 12 years are locked up like farm animals," Chinese authorities carry out what is perhaps the crux of their genocidal program: engineering an entire generation of Uyghur Muslims to turn their back on their parents, religion, and culture in favor of the atheism, Mandarin tongue, and Han customs privileged by Beijing.[88]

In the process, the Uyghur people are stripped of their very lifeline and future, their children. And a path is paved toward the elimination of 11 million Uyghur Muslims by stealing an entire generation of adolescents and children.

With a childish grin on her face, Dara popped back in front of her mother, staring into the screen. Her innocence intact, confined only by the four corners of my computer screen and her mother's loving arms, which gripped her tight as Dara sat on her lap.

Life and death are one in those camps, and exile a purgatory better than the hell of internment. Zeinab was far from her beloved homeland, but the young daughter she held close to her would not turn her in to the state for praying five times a day, or be taken from her by a government intent on brainwashing her. One day, Dara may continue the fight for self-determination from Australia, America, or perhaps the heart of Xinjiang, where minarets once stood.

Minarets that stood proudly before manifest destiny from the east landed on them. Minarets that stood defiantly when the War on Terror was imported into China by an American president only thirty-five days after the 9/11 terror attacks.

Minarets that stand unsteadily today in a land where an indigenous people are branded "foreign terrorists." Waiting to be lifted again, high and pointed toward the heavens, by the native hands of Zeinab and Dara and the millions of nameless Uyghur and ethnic Muslims locked away in those concentration camps.

As I looked at Dara, I remembered reading the account of a Uyghur mother locked alone inside a camp. "At night she kept looking at her son's picture, and crying. Since the guards could see this on the camera, they yelled at her over the speaker, 'If you look at your son's picture and cry again, we will take it away.'"[89] I wondered, and still do, how she endured. Perhaps it was faith. Perhaps it was the feeling—however fleeting—that her son will one day be seated on her lap, like young Dara sits on the lap of her loving mother, far from China and the endless gaze of the state.

"Everything in this world can be robbed and stolen, except one thing; this one thing is the love that emanates from a human being towards a solid commitment to a conviction or cause," penned Palestinian writer Ghassan Kanafani, an ode to his people that speaks directly to the plight of Uyghur Muslims, staring internment and ethnic cleansing in the face while still standing, proud and tall like minarets, atop Uyghur soil unmade by China and foreign lands far away from it.[90]

HOME IS THE OCEAN

> you broke the ocean in
> half to be here.
> only to meet nothing that wants you.
> NAYYIRAH WAHEED, "Immigrant"

What does it feel like to sail, aimlessly, alongside bodies that have been dead for days, when port after port has turned you away? Knowing that in a matter of days—or perhaps hours—those limp bodies of children you held or elders you consoled could be you?

What does it feel like, after you touch land, to shudder in fear at every glimpse of a lake or an ocean?

What does it feel like to belong to one of the "world's least wanted" people?[91] Stateless. An exile. A liminal, living in between disaster and an adopted plot on earth, among a foreign people who wish to throw you back into the very ocean that brought you?

An ocean, for Fatima, that was both home and Hades.

I had so many questions for Fatima before I met her.[92] It was late July 2020, and I had been closely following the ethnic cleansing of Rohingya Muslims—an indigenous people from the Asian nation of Myanmar—since early 2017, months after the armed forces violently cracked down on the Muslim minority group in Rakhine State.[93] The harrowing tales of children slaughtered, women raped, and 1 million Rohingya displaced from their homes and thrown into perpetual exile generated an endless list of questions I had for her.

But everything changed when Fatima sat across from me and I heard her voice. The hour between her arrival and her departure highlighted that there was an ocean between my understanding of the "Rohingya genocide"—as it has been labeled and litigated—and the experienced depths of its iniquity.[94] An ocean, like the ones Fatima crossed, affirmed that it had poured into every pore of who she is and had become her home.

"How can you be the same after you see babies being thrown into fires?" Fatima was only sixteen when she witnessed that—still a babe herself when she took in that image that consumed her and then ate away what remained of her youth.

"The cries were so loud. They sounded like screams," she recalled, looking down. "We could do nothing. If we tried, we'd end up in those fires too."

I was in Detroit conducting the interview, and Fatima in Chicago. Two Midwestern cities separated by a short drive. But the ocean between us stretched further the more that she spoke, and I felt that what she had had to endure—and would carry with her for the rest of her life—made the 280 miles between us feel like the Pacific Ocean.

Many Rohingya refugees in the United States have adopted Chicago as their new home, while others—like Fatima—are reluctant to bestow that title on their new surroundings.[95] During our discussion, she repeatedly identified elements about the Windy City—the cold weather, "strange food," and frequent stares at her hijab—that reminded her that it was not home, and far from it.[96]

But the cruelest reminder was the water and those waves of the past that haunt her present when she passes by Lake Michigan, the body of water that hugs Chicago and haunts Fatima. That lake and the city are one, and at night, Chicago's majestic skyline is mirrored beautifully by the great lake's waters.

Even when she tries to look away from the lake, the force of memory's tide pulls her toward it. Within its deep and endless blue, she can see her village being destroyed by Myanmar armed forces, she can hear babies cry while being charred in the flames lit by Buddhist extremists, and she can smell that wretched odor of death on the boat teetering on an ocean with nowhere to dock.[97]

Fatima's old home exists only in her head, and her new home is that ocean that haunts her from within and surrounds her very being. She is an exile, which Edward Said articulated is "strangely compelling to think about but terrible to experience. It is the unhealable rift forced between a human being and a native place, between the self and its true home: its essential sadness can never be surmounted."[98]

Exile is endless sadness and perpetual flux. And for Rohingya Muslims, the most intimate form of Islamophobia is exile. A state of being that is short of living, that stands on the other side of ethnic cleansing, displacement, and for too many to name and count, death.

For those who live, exile is like a tattoo. It is branded on the bodies of survivors like an unshakeable guilt, and stains their minds for as long as they walk this earth. While speaking to Fatima, I could not help but hear the haunting contralto of iconic crooner Sade Adu and recall her spellbinding lyrics about how the "scars of age" are worn like tattoos, tattoos of shame, on the faces and voices of survivors.[99]

Some, like Fatima, have crossed that ocean. They wear the war and the wages of survival on their skin, like a tattoo only visible to those who know them well, or those who must live with what they have endured, and only partly survived.

Those who were massacred, raped, or thrown into the burning fires of anti-Muslim rage yearned for but never saw those cruel waters. Tens of thousands of people were killed, and even more dubbed "missing," a strategic synonym in Myanmar for death.[100] They never saw the waters that saved Fatima and others thrown into statelessness. Instead, they saw fire. Fire ignited, in part, by a woman who refused to put it out. By a woman who marked the genocide's survivors with permanent scars of exile and tattoos of limitless pain, guilt, and the cloud of nihilism that sits between. While Fatima is in Chicago, the wars in Myanmar are still waging inside her frail body.

Aung San Suu Kyi stood before the International Court of Justice (ICJ) with a blank stare.[101] The judicial body governed by the United Nations was intimately familiar with the head of Myanmar's government, whose first act on the global stage had been celebrated by the UN and the Norwegian Nobel Peace Prize Committee.

In 1991, Suu Kyi won the Peace Prize for her nonviolent struggle for democracy and human rights. The woman who claimed that esteemed honor and declared, "It is not power that corrupts but fear," later turned her back on her humanitarian courage and those very words.[102] Three decades later, she was back in Europe defending herself, and her Buddhist populists carrying out the violent campaign against the Rohingya people, against charges of genocide.

An ocean of change can take place in thirty years, and its revealing waters can wash the reverence off of a peace icon and reveal a villain underneath. Suu Kyi stood idle and silent as her nation's armed forces ripped through Rakhine State in western Myanmar in late 2016, the beginning of an unfathomably violent onslaught on the Rohingya minority people that sought to exterminate them from the face of that land, or to push them into the ocean never to return.[103]

But the first *charge* toward genocide took place in 1982. That year, Myanmar's legislature enacted the Burmese Citizenship Law, which mandated that residents provide conclusive evidence that their parents resided in the country before it gained independence in 1948.[104] The law, many critics argued immediately after its passage, was intended to strip the Rohingya people of their citizenship status.[105] Just like the Citizenship Amendment Act in India, the law marked some people—Muslims in India and Rohingya in Myanmar—as segments of the population whose citizenship can be stripped by the state.

The events that followed confirmed their suspicion. Rohingya Muslims trace their origins in Myanmar to as far back as the eighth century, and they maintain a heavy presence in Rakhine State.[106] However, the Citizenship Law excluded the Rohingya from the classes of people that qualify for citizenship, despite meeting its requirements.

Their Muslim identity set them apart from the nation's overwhelmingly Buddhist (90 percent) majority, and the Citizenship Law converted them into stateless beings at home.[107] A small but visible minority comprising 4 percent of Myanmar's population before the violent crackdown of 2017 sliced those figures to even paltrier numbers, Rohingya have been called "illegitimate citizens" and "Bangladeshis" by the government, and after the War on Terror crept in, "terrorists"—that familiar indictment that Muslims all over the world have come to know.[108]

The War on Terror, and that inescapable label with which it branded Muslims everywhere, opened the floodgates for genocide in Myanmar. A genocide driven by an expeditious Islamophobia that, before the 9/11 terror attacks and the crusade that followed, declassified Rohingya Muslims as citizens and sought to plunge them into the ocean.

"If you call somebody a terrorist, you can do anything imaginable or unimaginable to them," shared Abed Ayoub, a Washington, DC–based immigration lawyer who has helped several Rohingya refugees resettle in the United States. "Especially in places like Myanmar, where the value of Muslim life is next to nothing."[109]

Anything. The passages of hell that comprise the Rohingya experience affirm the truth of Ayoub's words. The violence took a turn toward ethnic cleansing in late 2016, when armed forces and police descended upon Rohingya villages to rid them of the Muslim population branded "illegal" by the Citizenship Law. No means of brutality was off the table, and every weapon of violence was unleashed by the state-sponsored mobs.

Police and soldiers gang-raped Rohingya women and girls, some of them still children.[110] Private citizens joined in, ransacking Rohingya businesses and breaking into homes, where they beat up elders and shot fathers and raped mothers in front of children. The horrors did not stop there.

The United Nations collected evidence of mosques being burned to the ground. Schools were raided and razed.[111] Entire villages were flattened, and the people who called them home were sent off without any knowledge of where they would end up.

And babies, some short of their first birthdays, were thrown into burning fires while their mothers were handcuffed by thugs. The thugs laughed as the babies cried, until those flames silenced them for good and their cries were succeeded by the cries of their mothers. Cries that sounded like their souls were thrust out of their bodies forever.

Fatima saw and heard it all. You could see that guilt, although irrational, subsume her when she pieced together a story that still tore her apart. She wished she could have run between the fire and that depraved policeman, caught the baby in her young arms and then run, run anywhere, to prevent a death and preempt that emptiness that lives in her after she witnessed an act so utterly evil.[112]

But she didn't. Because she couldn't. The Buddhist mobs and the police and the soldiers were everywhere. Outnumbering the Rohingya by a ratio that spelled ethnic cleansing at first, and then genocide.

Genocide that forced one woman, Fatima, to endure life as an exile among strangers in a strange land. Genocide that pushed another woman, Aung San Suu Kyi, off the pedestal of Nobel Peace Prize winners and into the monstrous ranks of murderers, leading to global calls to strip her of that award.[113]

Two women. One Buddhist, the other Muslim. One whose name the entire world knows. The other, nameless and belonging to a people and a plight the world has turned its back on.

Fatima, whose faith was marked as "uncivilized" and "irreducibly violent" by an American War on Terror that met an existing ethnic cleansing in Myanmar and, through its weaponry of propaganda and policy, helped propel it toward genocide.[114]

Suu Kyi, who once embodied the mythic image of her religion, Buddhism, as nonviolent and supremely protective of human life.

Both are myths cultivated and curated by Western tropes and a War on Terror that reared another ugly face in Myanmar. Buddhism was manipulated and made into a death cult by Suu Kyi and her military generals, who unleashed a genocidal Islamophobia on the Rohingya people, a people native to Rakhine State.

In August 2018, the UN High Commissioner for Human Rights (UNCHR) moved that Burmese military generals should be tried for genocide. A year later, Suu Kyi stood before the ICJ in The Hague, facing those very charges. Approximately 30,000 Rohingya were killed by the state's "clearance operations" that began in 2017, and nearly 1 million were pushed out of their homes and into the ocean.[115]

Half of the refugees landed in nearby Bangladesh, a Muslim-majority state sitting on the northern extreme of the Bay of Bengal. The remaining refugees scattered to India, Thailand, Malaysia, and as far away as Europe and the United States, where Fatima lives and which she refuses to call home.[116]

Tens of thousands remain floating without a landing spot. Still trapped in the ocean with nowhere to dock.

In May 2020, three wooden boats carrying hundreds of Rohingya refugees floated between the Bay of Bengal and the Andaman Sea.[117] The refugees floated there, back and forth with the winds, during the holy month of Ramadan. Their numbers shrank after they were turned away from port after port, with scores of children, elders, and others meeting death as the boats drifted. Those boats, for tens of thousands, would become hearses for the departed. And for those still living, or barely alive, vessels where death and breath blurred into a morbid whole. For the Rohingya, one of the "world's most persecuted ethnic minorities," the tides of genocide seem to rise higher as time passes.[118]

The numbers reveal the true scale of the genocidal horror. As of 2015, the population of Rohingya Muslims in Myanmar was 1 to 1.3 million. Following the massacres and mass displacement, the figure is estimated to be 150,000 to 200,000. A staggering decline that reflects the decimation of a proud people, a people buried beneath the news headlines and lost at sea.

Mission accomplished. Today, Myanmar is building military bases where Rohingya Muslim homes and mosques once stood, the human rights organization Amnesty International claims.[119] Those Rohingya Muslims who survived the massacres and sank their feet into the soil of their homeland and refused the call of the ocean "continue to suffer the most severe" restrictions and repression.[120] Branded "illegal" by Islamophobic laws that exposed them to the very violence that claimed the lives of their loved ones and thrust others into distant corners of the globe to live—as best they could—as invisible transients and unwanted exiles.

They are liminals, trapped within that existential vacuum of blurred memories and harsh reality, fiery xenophobia and cold stares. Pushed and pulled, pulled and pushed, with no permanent place to plant their feet or dock their dreams.

Dreams that, like them, may never find a home.

"My home is not a suitcase, and I am no traveler," lamented the Palestinian poet Mahmoud Darwish, holding tight to a dream of physical return to that place his heart will always long for.[121] That place and that dream, home, which sits across an ocean that seems to widen with each passing day.

"I dream I'll go back home one day and see the village and some of the people that are still there," Fatima told me, longing for a place that does not exist as it once did before the armed forces stormed it in 2017. But we all long for home. For some of us, home remains intact, with the people and places that perpetually pull us back to it.

Prophesizing about the digitized transformation of our world and our radically mutated existence within it, American writer Shoshana Zuboff captured the essence of home, and human yearning for it. She wrote, poetically, "All creatures orient to home. It is the point of origin from which every species sets its bearings. Without our bearings, there is no way to navigate unknown territory; without our bearings, we are lost."[122]

In Chicago, Fatima leads a life without bearings. She is a castaway in a land that is not her own and which she refuses to make her home. She longs for a place that is no more and that has been replaced by a place polluted by the smell of death, where the ghosts of the past roam.

Home is no more. Home is nowhere. Home is the ocean, which stands between the homeland she longs for and the foreign city by the lake. That lake streams into the ocean she knows so well, summoning wave after wave of memories. Memories of babies burning to death, and on better days, memories of her playing with the village children before the military jeeps rolled in.

Home is the ocean. A fickle home that sometimes disturbs her with those images of genocide she yearns to forget, and hours later, streaming thoughts and memories of the fondest times in Myanmar.

Home is the ocean. A place Fatima actively seeks to avoid, but cannot. Her only familiar companion in a strange land that is hardly home. There she finds a portal to those she lost and left behind, and pours out her soul—it is like a confidante who speaks in silent waves. Sometimes Fatima hears the ocean say what she wants to hear most, in that warm whisper that summons her—momentarily—back home:

It is written. If I am really part of your dream, you'll come back one day.[123]

CHAPTER FIVE

PANDEMIC AND PLAGUE

THE FRENCH PLAGUE

> I have no idea what's awaiting me, or what will happen
> when this all ends. For the moment I know this: there are
> sick people and they need curing.
> ALBERT CAMUS, *The Plague*

"Mama, I don't want to go to school ever again," shared Farah, Ibtissam's nine-year-old daughter.[1] The coronavirus outbreak spiked in metropolitan Paris in March 2020, making France a global epicenter of the pandemic. The virus that would claim the lives of 30,000 people in France by July of that year swept everyone off the streets of Paris and the neighboring commune of Saint-Germain, where Ibtissam makes her home.[2]

"Maybe that is a good thing," Ibtissam thought about her daughter's brazen declaration. Although Saint-Germain was not Bondy, the Parisian ghetto *(banlieue)* she grew up in, where predominantly African and Arab immigrants were packed tightly into project housing *(cités)*, it was *still* France.

Ibtissam was on the other side of Paris, where policemen were more likely to wave hello than wave a baton at her Arab and Muslim sight. Only thirty miles separated her from the grime of the ghetto she revisited now and then, sifting through old memories and stopping by to see aging family members.

But the hijab she carefully wrapped around her head every morning before going out the door, and the little face that looked up at her while holding her hand, signaled that—despite her comfortable home and safer streets—this was *still* France.

The pandemic cleared everybody off of the streets, but the plague that loomed before it marred them with a virus that seeped deep into the French soul. With the hijab wrapped around her little head and a mask covering her mouth, Farah walked through the barren streets of her neighborhood with fewer faces looking in their direction, and fewer eyes scrutinizing her mother.

"Your headscarf is your crown," Ibtissam told young Farah. Words of consolation to thaw the chill of the stares tracking her little head. "Your crown."

At the age of nine, she was still too young to know what those stares meant. And too young to understand the depth of the animus that prompted them. But she would learn, with time, and that was precisely what frightened her mother, and what brought a ray of consolation to the thought of her missing school, during these dark days when a swelling pandemic converged with the longstanding French plague.

Ibtissam remembered the outbreak well. It was Tuesday, November 1, 2005, when the fires burned bright near her building in Bondy. Cars were torched, and the smell of gas seized every corner of the banlieue. Then fleets of police rushed in, and seemingly beat and battered every African and Amazigh and Arab youth they crossed paths with on the streets.[3] Many of them resembled the two Muslim boys, Zyed Benna and Bouna Traore, who were killed while hiding from Paris police.[4] The French, particularly Muslims, Blacks, and North Africans residing on the fringes of French society, deep within the banlieues, know these names well.

Benna and Traore, seventeen and fifteen years old respectively, were instantly immortalized as martyrs. And in death, inspired a resistance to French racism and Islamophobia that raged for three weeks. The hate, or *la haine,* was not new to this side of Paris, as memorialized by the 1995 classic film bearing that title, but reached furious new levels a decade later.

"The people could not take any more," Ibtissam recalled, "the death of those two boys symbolized so much pain—pain that our nationality and religion made us different. Pain that this was not really our country."

That pain exploded into nihilistic rage in Bondy, and other French ghettoes, more than a year after the passage of the nation's flagship societal law. On March 15, 2004, the French parliament enacted law number 2004-228, which restricted the wearing of "ostentatious" religious symbols in public schools. While the law's language was facially neutral, meaning it did not explicitly name Islam or the hijab itself, it sought to ban the wearing of headscarves, or hijabs, by Muslim girls and women.

The law, which came to be known universally as the Hijab Ban, solidified what the theaters of police brutality in Bondy, Clichy-sous-Bois, and other Parisian ghettos manifested a year later during the riots—that "Muslim" and "French" were clashing identities. By "taking the veil," the French state took its most strident step toward stripping its Muslims from a place in the nation.[5] More specifically, it ushered in a new order of gendered Islamophobia bent on policing Muslim women's bodies—women who were stereotyped as "powerless" beings oppressed by the "violent" Muslim males in their families. While Islamophobia imagined Muslim men as "terrorists," its feminine dimensions cast Muslim women as imminent victims of that tyranny who desperately needed to be "saved" by the French state and its law.[6]

Ibtissam was stuck in the middle. She had decided to drape the headscarf around her head a year before the enactment of the Hijab Ban. Islam became central to her life after she graduated from university, and even more so as she progressed through her career and planned to start a family of her own.

On the other hand, France was the "only home I know." It was her country of birth, the land that extended her educational opportunity and financial upward mobility, and in the years to come, the place where she would raise three young children. Two of them daughters, Muslim daughters, who would evade the poverty and violence that colored her childhood in Bondy and enjoy a better life near the center of the city, and the myriad opportunities the "real Paris" offered.

But this was still France, where Muslims remain vulnerable to the plague of Islamophobia that follows their bodies wherever they live or go. It is a nation ailed by an anti-Muslim hate that fixates intensely on the bodies of Muslim girls and women and focuses its state-sponsored Islamophobia on the heads of those who don the hijab. Policing the headscarf is a modern obsession with deep imperial roots, and the fountainhead of a gendered Islamophobia viewed as the vanguard for copycat policies across Europe, India, and North America.

The *tricolore* that waved from government buildings and hung prominently above every classroom she entered, as a student and later on as a mother, clashed with the "flag of Islam" draped around Ibtissam's head.[7]

"We are walking outcasts in our own land," and every dismissive look on the street and derogatory law that was passed deepened that feeling for Ibtissam. Her life's arc converged with the first attempt to ban headscarves in public schools, in 1989, and the emergence of the ardently Islamophobic National Rally (Rassemblement National) party in the War-on-Terror era fifteen years later.

The anti-Muslim virus that had torn up the streets of Bondy years earlier spread through France's sickened political body and popular discourse. Early on, leaders along every plot of the ideological spectrum dubbed the hijab a "marker of difference" and an "affront to civilization," sound bytes that infected the political discourse and invited bigoted extremists into French corridors of power. Fringe populist political parties were now front and center, and the explicit Islamophobic rhetoric that once conflicted with French political sensibilities was now mainstream.

"Islamic fundamentalism is attacking us at home," Marine Le Pen, head of the National Rally party and presidential hopeful, shouted. "The places of Islamic preaching will be closed and the propagators of hate will be condemned and expelled," she continued, promising to close down mosques and deport Muslims—even longstanding citizens like Ibtissam and young Farah, permanently called "immigrants" because of the religion they adhere to.[8]

The Hijab Ban was not enough. The French commitment to *laïcité*, that long-contested concept that commits the state to secularism in public life, was no longer an idea open to debate but a bludgeon used to injure. A weapon, manipulated and maneuvered in the direction of Muslims in France, in the same way that police guns and maces and batons were wielded against those African and Arab and Amazigh youth in the streets of Parisian banlieues. This time, the blows were legal and more lethal. They were inflicted within public schools "where citizens are shaped and made," and for Muslim students, assimilated or othered.[9]

Behind the veil of *laïcité*, the legal blows against Muslims kept coming. In April 2011, the French parliament enacted additional legislation making it illegal for Muslim women to wear conservative coverings, including the niqab and the burqa. Nicolas Sarkozy, president of France at the time the measure was enacted, declared, "In our country, we can't accept women prisoners behind a screen, cut off from all social life, deprived of all identity. That's not our idea of freedom."[10]

The law, driven by the belief that Muslim women were being "imprisoned" behind a "screen" by their husbands or fathers, simultaneously perpetuated two entwined gender stereotypes: that Muslim women are weak and subordinate, and that Muslim men are violent and oppressive.[11] This gendered Islamophobia reified the longstanding imperialist narrative that Muslim men were bent on war and tyranny, and that Muslim women—the immediate victims of this violence—needed saving. Writing in the *California Law Review,* Nura Sediqe and I unveil this gendered Islamophobia as a "relational dialectic that fluidly produces and reproduces how societal and state actors position Muslim masculinity as oppositional and antagonistic to Muslim womanhood; ascribe unique political meaning to Muslim male and female bodies, and normative value to identity markers associated with their respective gender expression; and enforce law distinctly across gender lines, particularly within the areas of religious exercise, counterterror policing, and immigration—legal realms where Islamophobia is pervasive and pronounced."[12]

The bodies of Muslim women, in societies where state-sponsored Islamophobia is rising or robust, are typically the first sites of state policing and legal regulation. This is vividly the case in France, starting with the Hijab Ban and expanding into other realms of feminine Islamophobia.

Therefore, like the Hijab Ban enacted seven years before it, the "Face Covering Ban" of 2011 denied women the very liberty it espoused to address: it polices Muslim women's bodies by compelling them to dress in line with specific cultural customs.[13] Those customs are French and secular, exposing the genuine objective of the 2011 act and the foundational law that preceded it: forceful assimilation and disavowal of Islamic expression, not restoration of individual liberty, was at the heart of both pieces of legislation.

"I chose to wear the hijab in my mid-twenties," Ibtissam revealed. "I knew what it meant to me and what risks it would create for me, professionally and otherwise." Her words were powerful, rebellious, and touched with the tone of Muslim feminism that moved Fatema Mernissi to ask, "Why should an unjust law be obeyed? Because men have written it?"[14] France is a European nation, and a self-proclaimed liberal republic. It is also home to the largest Muslim population in Europe, with some informal estimates holding that the faith group comprises 8 to 10 percent of the country's population.[15] These French Muslims came from Senegal and Cameroon, Tunisia and Algeria, the former colonies of France that today remain bonded to their imperial mother. It is a bond that law scholar E. Tendayi Achiume dubs "migration as decolonization," extending a right to once-colonized Muslim peoples to inhabit the land that decimated their native homes.[16] France is indelibly Muslim, by its own imperial design, and the size of the Muslim population testifies to the scale of its global plunder and modern parasitism.

However, despite the size of France's Muslim population and the towering examples of independent Muslim women in French society, like Ibtissam, the gendered stereotypes are pervasive and penetrate deep within the French cultural body. Despite what women accomplish or achieve, French Islamophobia espouses that unrelenting, violent trope: that tyrannical Muslim men lord it over their women, holding the hijab in one hand and a balled fist in the other, stripping them of their individuality and stealing their autonomy.

In essence, French Islamophobia is shaped by fears of hypermasculine and brutal Muslim men that the state longs to quell and kill, like it did in 2005, when policemen murdered Benna and Traore.[17] But it is directly enforced upon the bodies of Muslim women, whom the state polices with impunity in order to "liberate" them from the oppressive hands of their fathers and husbands. "The dominant discourse in France is that the hijab is an oppressive tool used by Muslim men to hide and silence Muslim women," writes French Muslim intellectual Rokhaya Diallo. "This is why, when French Muslim women come out and say that they choose to cover their heads in public spaces, their agency to make this decision is being questioned."[18] This French obsession with the hijab, and the female Muslim body that it adorns, has devolved into a legal psychosis hallmarked by the headscarf ban. As feminist scholar Gayatri Spivak famously stated, "White men [joined by white women] saving brown women from brown men" characterizes the logic of state-sponsored Islamophobia in France.[19]

This contradiction sits at the heart of French Islamophobia. It also justifies an onslaught of state policies that emaciate the religious liberty of French Muslim women on account of an Orientalist understanding of Muslim men as irredeemably violent and repressive. Muslim men are maimed and murdered on the streets of Bondy and other banlieues throughout the republic, and are incarcerated at clips that rival those of Black men in the United States, because of this understanding.[20]

This is how laïcité impacts French Muslims, descending on them like a disease that infects every sector of French society, and rising to the proportion of a plague in 2004 with the enactment of the Hijab Ban—a law that, arguably, stands as the world's most lucid representation of structural Islamophobia, and which has caused the passage of copycat policies in Belgium and Quebec, and a proposal in Denmark.

The Hijab Ban spurred the Face Covering Ban of 2011, and then, in 2019, another law that penetrated the private confines of Ibtissam's home. In May 2019, the French senate passed legislation banning mothers who wear the hijab, like Ibtissam, from accompanying their children during school events and trips. "The ban, proposed by the centre-right Republicans party, builds on an existing prohibition on the wearing of the garments in both primary and secondary schools."[21] The new ban brands Muslim mothers as outcasts and undesirables in the minds of their sons and daughters, like Farah, who are trapped between the deeply politicized French classroom and their Islamic households.

In France, Islamophobia is a plague that infects the paternalistic arms of the law, powers the violent hands of the police, and steers the discriminatory eyes of private citizens walking the rough concrete of Bondy or the pristine sidewalks of Saint-Germain. It is a plague that begins and ends with the classroom, that hallowed training ground that every future French citizen, regardless of race or religion, must pass through. Where they are made, and perpetually remade, to fit a national image that orients Islam as inimical and unassimilable, and where Muslims are pushed to the furthest margins and treated like outsiders.

In France, Islamophobia is a plague that forces a Muslim citizen like Ibtissam to keep her faith quarantined in the private sphere even when her body is out in public. It is a plague that instructs a young Muslim girl like Farah that for her, the cornerstone French principles of *liberty, equality, and fraternity* are reduced to an impossible ultimatum: shed your religion, and only then will these rights be yours.

In France, Islamophobia is a plague that long preceded the War on Terror. A plague that befell on Muslim women first, as the disproportionate victims, then spread onward. A plague spawned and spread by a "Muslim world" that sits at the continental footstep of Europe. Where French colonialism in African and Arab nations pulled the immigrants concentrated in the banlieues into the belly of France, and the imperial conquest of Algeria that lasted from 1830 to 1962 formed a colonial bridge that Ibtissam's parents crossed into the Paris streets that saw them as imperial subjects, not citizens, the same way France sees their children and grandchildren.[22]

French Islamophobia is a plague that preceded the coronavirus pandemic of 2020. A pandemic that enveloped the entire world with fear, claimed a frightening number of lives in France, and cleared the classrooms and streets of Paris of their familiar crowds. Despite this, it was the French plague and not the coronavirus pandemic that moved young Farah to conclude, out of fear, that she never wanted to return to those classrooms, and the French plague denied her mother the ability to join her on school outings and trips.

Farah would not return to school on that warm spring day, nor in the foreseeable future. But another student of French Islamophobia, masked at the mouth, would enter a classroom with the French flag lording over it, proselytizing about the dangers of the pandemic while peddling fears of that older longstanding plague.

French President Emmanuel Macron walked into the Pierre Ronsard Elementary School neatly dressed, with a black face mask decorated with a tiny French tricolor covering his mouth.[23]

Macron staged the event, at the height of the coronavirus pandemic, to announce that the face mask he wore was to be mandated for every resident of France moving forward. Those who violated the policy would be fined 135 euros (roughly $150) and asked to return home to collect a mask before venturing out again.

The pandemic exposed the fundamental hypocrisy of the French plague. While every citizen was ordered to cover their face, Muslim women who covered their face for religious purposes were legally reprimanded and fined 150 euros, fifteen more than the penalty for violating the new face mask mandate.[24] One face covering was legally mandated, the other legally prohibited. Even if a Muslim woman like Ibtissam wore the *very* same piece of cloth around her face as a niqab instead of a face mask, the intention of wearing it for Islamic purposes could garner punishment. It took a pandemic to expose the absurdity of this French policy and the capricious nature of a gendered Islamophobic regime that denied the free exercise of religion rights to Muslim women.

The hypocrisy at the core of French Islamophobia was on full display that day and thereafter. In the days to come, everybody on the streets of Paris covered their faces to protect themselves from the pandemic. The stares still came Ibtissam's way, and the young daughter holding Ibtissam's right hand, growing up in the dark times of overlapping pandemic and plague, would begin to understand what those stares meant.

But masks can only protect you from so much. Whether they are thin pieces of cloth covering your mouth to keep out the coronavirus, or thinly veiled principles like *laïcité,* touted to protect secularism but tilted to spread Islamophobia and infect the national body with that virus, masks eventually have to come off. And when they do, the real faces of French hypocrisy and bigotry are revealed for everyone to see and behold.

As they were on May 5, 2020, at the Pierre Ronsard Elementary School in Poissy, a banlieue four miles west of Ibtissam's home in Saint-Germain, where a French president mandated covering one's face as protection from the pandemic but restricted it as religious expression.[25] This was the French plague. No mask or face covering can protect one from this plague; the treatment is to revise what it means to be French, a definition that must be formulated free of Islamophobia and then administered in those very schools and classrooms where the virus is seeded and spread.

A treatment where *fraternity, equality, and liberty*—most vitally, *liberty*—is realized for Muslim women, the social demographic most vulnerable to this plague, and the part of the French body most policed and persecuted by its culture wars.[26]

Ibtissam has lived through the initial and darkest hours of this plague. With no vaccine for French Islamophobia in sight, she fears the worst for Farah, her daughter, who will be stripped of the liberty to cover her head and embrace both her faith and Frenchhood. Together and at once.

Like her mother, Farah loves her faith and country. And although young, she is beginning to appreciate what the French existentialist Albert Camus wrote in his timeless novel *The Plague:* "Nothing in the world is worth turning one's back on what one loves."[27]

French Islamophobia—and its deeply gendered strains—forces young Farah to turn her back on one in order to embrace the other. It is an ultimatum that has plagued her mother's life and one that, unless a vaccine is found and administered, will plague hers long after the pandemic of 2020 is cured and gone.

She is free to do what she wants, and free not to do it.[28]

THE BANLIEUE AND THE BEAST

> A burning room is a dying era
> When the Elysée-Montmartre went on fire
> I think I lived my World Trade Center
> MÉDINE, "Bataclan"

You haven't really seen Paris, and all of its lights, until you've seen them from Saint-Denis. The banlieue directly north from the center of the City of Light offers a view from the *other side* of Paris. The side, six miles from the heart of the city, where the gleam of the Eiffel Tower lights up the same sky but stands atop a radically different neighborhood.

"This is the real Paris," Malik says of his banlieue. "The one they don't want you to see."[29]

I had visited Malik's Paris before. I was welcomed by the North African faces of young men that resembled my own, and the familiar portraits of Muslim elders sitting around café tables, smoking hookahs while debating the same handful of political issues for the thousandth time.

Algerian flags and headscarves provided a distinctly Islamic tapestry to the banlieue, while the thud of drums in the background and the lyrics of Médine blasting from my friend's radio filled the air. This was the *real* Paris, or at least, the one where I felt at home.

This Parisian sound is what scholar Hisham Aidi dubbed "rebel music," the soundtrack of resistance rising from those vibrating speakers and vibrant streets, adorned by visuals of a Paris tourists would not dare step foot in.[30]

In France, "Muslim cool" takes on different colors and contours than in the United States. It attracts youth from all races and religions, even white kids, who come from the suburbs and try to be down, and get down, with the beat of the banlieue. The children of Parisian gentry on the other side of the city who, because of its perceived menace and rebelliousness, mix "asalamu alaikum" and other Islamic colloquialisms into their speech to fit into a part of Paris their parents seldom cross into, and fear.[31] That fear is shared by French politicians and scholars, who see a robust and omnipresent Islam in those French banlieues that could overtake the entire republic.[32]

Malik and I had left downtown Paris only an hour earlier, but after a short drive were submerged in a radically different world. The pristine avenues and gothic buildings were replaced with hardened streets and unsightly tenements. A world where the cold stares that locked on me, an Arab African, and my friend, an Amazigh African, were thawed by the warm embraces of those who knew us as *habibi* (beloved) and *akh* (brother) instead of as prospective terrorists. The love there thawed the cold in the center of Paris.

I saw the city's lights from its center and from the banlieue. I took in their flicker while walking down the Champs Élysées and past the Bataclan, a theater of dreams for the likes of Malik or Médine, the French Muslim rapper who rose from the belly of the banlieue and made it to that other side of Paris.[33]

I saw them for three straight nights when I stayed and slept in Saint-Denis, realizing that they glimmered the same from where I stood but meant something radically different for those who welcomed me into their world and their side of Paris.

What drew me and millions of other tourists to the City of Light cast *them* out. There were, I began to learn, *two* cities of Paris for Malik and Médine and the million other people who call the banlieues their home. From their view, those lights signaled that the beast was always watching them. While the view from the heart of Paris, where old buildings glimmered and cold stares pierced our brown skin and bearded faces, was that the banlieue was the belly of the beast, a place where terrorists dwelled, only six miles from the center of civilization and its endless source of light.

On November 13, 2015, the lights illuminating the Paris sky looked different. The view from Saint-Denis, Clichy-sous-Bois, and the string of other banlieues surrounding the city was also different. And after 9 p.m. on that evening, the state's lights would shine on the Algerian and African and Muslim inhabitants brighter than they ever had before.

A series of terror attacks ripped through downtown Paris that night, committed by ISIS sympathizers bent on fighting the civilizational crusade waged by the War on Terror.[34]

"This was our 9/11," Malik recollects, speaking to the state rage and popular Islamophobia that would come crashing down on Muslims in France, particularly those living in the Paris banlieues, in the days that followed.

That night, three teams of terrorists, acting in unison, stormed the center of the City of Light and descended on its brightest attractions. The site of the first attack was an international soccer match between the French national team and Germany at the Stade de France, which was attended by then President François Hollande.[35]

Next, the terrorists bombed the Bataclan, that theater of dreams in the heart of Paris where I first took in its magnificent lights and where Muslim rapper Médine was prevented from performing because of the religion he professed and the incisive political lyrics he delivered. The Bataclan, on that night, was a "burning room" where ninety people did not make it out alive.[36]

The terrorists did not stop there. They bombed cafés and restaurants in the heart of Paris, where the familiar lights of the city were replaced by rage that delivered 130 deaths, and for the terrorists that carried out the attacks, martyrdom and the myth of seventy-two virgins awaiting them on the other side.

This was virgin territory for the *other side* of Paris and the whole of France, which had just experienced its deadliest modern terror attack, an attack orchestrated by eleven Arab and North African men from Saint-Denis, Clichy-sous-Bois, and other banlieues on the margins of Paris and beyond. Which meant that Malik and Médine and anybody who looked the part, anybody who "looked Muslim," even tourists like myself, were presumed to be from the banlieue.[37]

We carried that mark of the alleged beast on our very skin, wherever we roamed. Spurring the suspicion of those who passed by us, and those silent stares that said so much, as we walked through the heart of Paris.

Though the 11/13 Paris attacks came on the heels of the January 7, 2015, *Charlie Hebdo* attacks, the 11/13 attacks produced tenfold more victims, leading many—like Malik of Saint-Denis—to refer to them as "France's 9/11."[38]

The banlieues, those *quartiers difficiles* where riots had erupted a decade earlier, would be the battleground for an intensified French War on Terror.[39] Those familiar theaters of riot and protest, on the *dark side* of Paris, shined a light on the city that summons 30 million tourists every year, and on 11/13, on eleven terrorists who raised hell to its streets.

In the banlieues, "There is a lot of anger and a lot of young men willing to turn themselves into soldiers for God. Most importantly, the riots, those wreckers of the banlieues, are not looking for reform or revolution. They are looking for revenge," wrote Andrew Hussey in his book *The French Intifada*.[40] While some see Muslim disaffection on the fringes of French society as "anger" and "revenge," others reimagine French

Muslims as the children of a people stripped of their lands, deity, and dignity pleading for "corrective, distributive justice" through the language of riots and rage.[41]

This is the view of the banlieues and its Muslim dwellers from the heart of Paris. Where Brown and Black skin and hijab- and kufi-clad heads are viewed in monolithic terms, all the more so after the 11/13 terror attacks—terms that see Islam, and particularly its male adherents, in the image of the eleven terrorists enlisted by ISIS to dim the lights of a city that pushed them to the margins of poverty and the fringes of citizenship.

A world of difference separates Malik and Médine from the 11/13 terrorists, despite their having walked the same hardened streets, having been raised in nearly identical tenement buildings, and having known the fixed eyes of the state and those gazing with fear from the center of Paris. "I am proud of where I come from [Saint-Denis], and love my neighborhood," Malik told me, mixing his native French with English. "But I know what I mean to them and what this place means to the police." While he did not explicitly say *that word*, thanks to our kindred circumstances in America and France, he did not have to spell it out. Malik was talking about *terrorism*, the fear conjured up in the minds of the French police and Parisians on the other side of the banlieues whenever Médine performs. As the rapper has said, "I am aware that in the eye of the average French person, I embody many fears and delusions: I am a rapper, I have Algerian roots, I am Muslim, and I grew up in housing projects."[42] Masculine Islamophobia, which stands oppositionally to how Muslim womanhood is imagined, conjures up the immediate fear of violence and rage, curated strategically by War on Terror handlers into the looming threat of the terrorist.[43]

The dreams that the City of Light inspires for those who look and believe the *right way*, the French way, become instant nightmares for those who do not. They invite fears and delusions of terrorism onto the very bodies of those who travel past the banlieues and into the heart of

Paris and who walk through the central arteries bombed on 11/13 by eleven men.

Eleven men. Not all of the 6 million Muslims who call France home. Not the nearly 2 billion Muslims around the globe who adhere to the faith in dramatically different and sometimes conflicting ways. Not the three Muslim men—Malik, Médine, and myself—whose very being seems to routinely summon looks of fear when we walk through the center of Paris, especially since 11/13. Whether we like it or not, our very bodies are associated with the terrorists. Our very beings constructed, then conflated, with crimes that we did not commit. And will never commit, despite the indictments leveled at us by French and American governments, and many more in between, because we are Muslim and Arab, Amazigh and North African men.

Arab and "North African–origin individuals are often associated with the banlieues even if they do not live there," observed Jean Beaman in *Citizen Outsider*, and they carry that distinctive mark of the beast wherever they travel.[44] This reality, for Europe's biggest Muslim population, was one that could not be dimmed. Particularly after 11/13, which seemed to confirm that ISIS and the threat of terror lurked in those banlieues, ready to attack Paris and global centers of civilization at any time.

"And because the lights of Paris epitomize cultural secularism for the world and thus 'ignorance of divine guidance' [for ISIS], they must be extinguished," Scott Atran and Nafees Hamid wrote as French police stormed the very banlieue streets that ISIS, the Islamist terror group *du jour*, had touched down in before them.[45] The other side of Paris, which the state had neglected for so long and which its laws had demonized for even longer, was fertile soil for ISIS recruitment. The disaffection and despair that riddled Saint-Denis and the other banlieues opened doors for the terror network, which was looking to make pawns out of people who were pummeled by poverty and overpoliced by the state.

"At fourteen years old, I was arrested by the police for the first time for an 'identity check.' I did nothing bad, I was five minutes from my house and going back home," Malik recalled of the perils that pounced on him minutes from the bed where he slept and the doorstep where he kissed his mother's forehead whenever he left and returned.

The banlieues were, simultaneously, places of cultural electricity and mazes of economic misery. They rang with the soulful sounds of French hip-hop and North African raï and Gnawa music. But, for many, living there sucked out the very marrow of hope that the state was unwilling to fill.

ISIS rushed to fill a void for those forlorn Muslim men, those "dangerous creations of society who [have] nothing to lose," as James Baldwin put it in 1962 when he penned *Letter from a Region in My Mind*.[46]

But this was Paris. Not Harlem. And this was a world six decades separated from the Civil Rights Movement, a world in which the War on Terror fed directly into ISIS's appetite to wage an apocalyptic war. It was the other side of the "clash of civilizations" that had been waged by the Bush administration a decade before the emergence of this ungodly terror group, reinvented in a new era in which Muslim bodies were dispensable and disposable for all parties involved.

ISIS propaganda was pumped into the banlieue streets like the sounds of Cheb Khaled and Médine, but ISIS sang a dramatically different tune. French scholar Olivier Roy has identified how Muslim youth neglected by the state become "rebels without a cause" who "find in jihad a 'noble' and global cause, and are consequently instrumentalised by a radical organization that has a strategic agenda."[47]

That agenda that uses Muslim youth as fodder in an apocalyptic war in which two fundamentalisms—the extremist Islam of ISIS and the unhinged Islamophobia of the War on Terror—collide. Similar to the way the US armed forces enlist poor American women and men, like my friend John, ISIS hovers over Muslim communities in France like a poverty pimp, exploiting economic misery and societal disaffection for morally depraved ends.

In these spaces, ISIS preys on young French men and women who see the promise of those bright Paris lights from the viewpoint of unemployment and indigence, emaciated opportunity and mounting anger. They overwhelmingly experience the state through law enforcement, by being profiled in their neighborhoods or, after 11/13, by having battalions raid their communities in search of "radicals" and "extremists."[48]

As in the United States, counter-radicalization programs disproportionately victimize poor Muslims in France.[49] Emulating the parasitic dynamic unfolding in Muslim communities and enclaves in the United States, police and Muslim informants collaborate in France in an effort to keep tabs on subjects of interest and suppress religious expression—such as the wearing of a hijab—that the state conflates with subordination and extremism.

The stated aim is to prevent the next terror attack from rising from within the belly of the banlieue, that beast looming on the periphery of Paris. A potent justification, after 11/13, that arms the state with broad latitude to profile Muslims who live there, and to expand its broader crusade of suppressing Islam.

These banlieues are where the French lights and glossy lie of colorblindness come to die. Enshrined by a 1972 law prohibiting the collection of racial and ethnic data, French colorblindness facilitates the racial and ethnic inequities in education, housing, and employment that ravage the predominantly Arab, African, and Muslim residents of the banlieues.[50] These conditions simultaneously feed anger toward the state and produce a fertile recruitment ground for ISIS. A cycle of marginalization rooted in state policy.

Race may not exist on the books in France, but its racial project is alive and well for all to see, in living color, in the streets of Saint-Denis and Bondy and banlieues beyond. Not even the bright lights from the center of the city can overshadow the pervasive racism that wears the uniform of law enforcement, or the racial inequities dwelling in the neighborhoods.

Those same Paris lights signify policies that deny their mothers and sisters the right to exercise their faith through a barrage of laws, the first inflicted when they were young boys. "I remember the law of 2004 [the Hijab Ban], when it passed, I wanted to fight on behalf of my mother," Malik stated, in a defiant retreat from his usually mild demeanor. Many young men, and women, wanted to take on the fight. But that fight did not take the form of terrorism, no matter the myths being peddled by Orientalist pundits and Islamophobic politicians.

For Malik, it meant burying his head in his books and pursuing his dream of becoming an attorney. For Médine, it meant mastering his craft as an MC and narrating the stories of triumph and despair of the banlieue as his form of rebellion. There are millions more like Malik and Médine in the belly of those French banlieues, incessantly profiled by police and castigated by the cold stares of those who pass them on the other side of Paris. They are profiled and feared and seen as everything they are not: *terrorists*.

ISIS succeeded only eleven times, and the world saw the explosive lights of that evil recruitment campaign on the night of November 13, 2015. The world does not see or hear or read about the millions of failures ISIS met inside of those banlieues, and more importantly, the failures of the state to mitigate the existential despair and disaffection that prime its soil for terror recruitment. Those Muslims failed by the French state, and that ISIS failed to recruit, are victors invisible to the world.

How can we expect them to see these statistics when they don't even see French Muslims in the banlieue as real people?

"Not all of us want to leave this place," affirms Malik. The banlieues are more than just sites of embellished terror and darkness, where "the otherness of exclusion, of the repressed, of the fearful and despised" dwells.[51]

It is not how outsiders imagine it, as the belly of the beast where terror is shaped and spawned. It is home. Home, where the terror of the state is experienced on a daily basis and the outstretched hand of ISIS is turned away far more often than it is accepted.

It is home. Where Muslim mothers adorned in hijabs can walk the streets with their daughters, hand in hand, without having to endure those endless stares of scorn.

Home. Where young boys can proudly don an Algerian soccer jersey without having to answer, "Why aren't you wearing a French shirt instead?" or be forced to respond to the ultimatum, "Which side do you really belong to?"

Home, where I was welcomed at the tables of friends who showed me the kinder side of Paris. Where I took in the City of Light from a warmer, more soulful vantage point, scored by the sounds of the call to prayer and scented with the smell of Algerian and Senegalese home cooking.

These were the Paris lights that I grew to know and love. Lights that emanated from the people and places embraced in those banlieues. People who were beautifully dissimilar, made the most of what God gave them living life on the fringes of France, and always remained proud of who they were. Characters of the brightest sort, whose light— when you saw them for who they were, up close—could not be dimmed or blurred into a murky monolith.

Lights where restaurants and cafés and souks that offered that authentic flavor of struggle that their overpriced counterparts on the other, pristine side of Paris tried to emulate but could never match.

You have not really seen Paris, and all of its lights, until you've seen them from Saint-Denis. And you have not really seen the beauty of the banlieues if you are viewing them from inside the belly of the *real* beast, six miles from Saint-Denis. A beast that only directs its light toward the banlieues when searching for "radicals" and "terrorists."

"This is where I can be me," Malik said. In Saint-Denis, Malik was just Malik. His ethnicity or beard or his religion, especially his religion, did not set him apart as somebody to fear. "This is where I feel free . . . or close to it." Or as close as somebody can get to that elusive light of freedom, being Muslim on the margins of Paris or in the heart of Detroit.

I *felt that,* wholly, during that stretch I spent in the City of Light, where the warmth of Saint-Denis pulled me in while the far more celebrated lights and towers and avenues on the other side of Paris looked upon me with scorn, suspicion, and then pushed me away. Away, into the Arab and Muslim ghettoes on the outskirts of the city, in the belly of the banlieues where I saw people who looked and believed like me and who saw me as far from the form of a terrorist. I was far from it all, in that moment in Saint-Denis, just far enough to see those Eiffel Tower lights and feel what freedom might be like in a France crusading against Islam.

A lover of Albert Camus and French existentialism, I learned about that crucible of nihilism and despair endured by the nation's Muslims through the lights of those living in the banlieue. Through Malik and Médine, who taught me that, to paraphrase Camus, the only way to deal with an unfree world is to become so absolutely free that your very existence is an act of rebellion.[52]

SECOND AND THIRD WAVES

Her wings are cut and then she is blamed for not knowing how to fly.
SIMONE DE BEAUVOIR, *The Second Sex*

I must have been fourteen years old when I could not take any more. I finally built up the nerve to stand between my father and mother, who were gradually torn apart by the trial of war in Beirut and the tribulations of poverty that awaited them, and us, in America.

My mother held on to a marriage that had died before I grew into a teenager. Grasping whatever remained of it to shield me, and my two siblings, of the permanent stigma with which the children of Muslim divorcees are branded. During the 1990s, divorce in Muslim communities, even in America, was still taboo. So she held on, and during the bleakest times, met the violent hand of my father. She veiled a broken marriage within the community and in public. But it tore her and us apart from inside.

I watched until I could not watch any more. The pain of witnessing my mother bounce from odd job to odd job, packing us time and time again from house to house while never having enough to find a real home, and the episodes of violence that unfolded inside those houses, was too much.

I was reminded of the pain that befell my mother when I met Kalsoum, a lifetime later in Wajir. Both faces, those of my mother and of the blind Somali mother, embodied the words of Egyptian feminist Nawaal El Saadawi: "Life is very hard. The only people who really live are those harder than life itself."[53] Those words scrolled across my mind again, alongside the faces of Kalsoum and El Saadawi, Ibtissam and Rokhaya Diallo, my grandmother and mother emerging prominently from a mosaic of powerful Muslim women I pictured so vividly. For reasons that are natural, my mother stood apart.

My mother, a strong Egyptian woman dealt a traumatic blow by life and its conspiring hands, was at point zero. I felt each of those blows as a young child peering from the top of the stairs, and that final time as a teenager coming between my father and mother, when I finally got up to put an end to it all.

I stood in front of my father to protect my mother, and on that day, became a man. I remember everything—from the look of surprise on his face to the alarm on my mother's—distinctly. I even remember the pungent smell from the fish market on Tireman Avenue that filled the air. Even today, the smell of fish takes me back to that day, that very moment. That moment when I rose up, and my mother realized that latching onto a marriage that only left bruises and scars hardly protected me, and my siblings, from the passing stigma of taboo or the lasting stain of trauma.

That veil she had wrapped around a fractured household would have to be lifted, permanently, in order to rebuild from the trauma it had endured for too long, and to rehabilitate herself from the pain she had suffered for even longer.

I ran through the side door of the house, dropped my books on the dining table and turned back toward the door to go meet my friends Hazem and Ali. "Where are you going, Khaled?" my mother yelled from the basement in Arabic, and then appeared at the foot of the staircase. That staircase that had witnessed so much. And on that day, it saw another unusual sight.

It was the first time I saw my mother *that* way. She looked up at me, silent, expecting a reaction of some kind. I was fourteen, and did not fully understand what it *meant* for her, and what *it* stood for and authentically represented.

A white turban tightly wrapped around her head concealed my mother's thick locks of North African, Egyptian hair. She beamed as she looked up, and I was happy to see her that way. From that day forward, that is how she presented herself when she left our house, and it was her mode of dress when she welcomed guests into it. She remade herself, and in that moment as she looked up, turned a page toward becoming the woman she wanted to be.

An unfamiliar feeling of pride took hold of me as I looked down at her from the top of that staircase. She understood what I communicated with that look, and then smiled and instructed me, "Come back home before dinner, I made *mujadara*" (lentils and rice). And that was it.

The days to come witnessed a transformation in her and in our family. My mother, always resilient, summoned renewed strength from that crown atop her head. Buoyed by it and the son who stood by her side when the blows from my father and life came, she finally filed for divorce, hardened her skin against what the community thought or said, and two years later, she finally made the pilgrimage to Mecca, fulfilling that holy mandate and returning as an esteemed member of our community.

That turban evolved into a headscarf as she aged, but remained a crown despite its changing form. I learned, each day that I lived under that roof and every day since, that the turban-turned-headscarf liberated her. And in the process, liberated us—her three children—from a rotating set of broken houses that could never be our home.

The movement to ban the hijab in France was built upon a narrative that went against everything I learned at home. Detroit was not Paris and America was not France, but the imperial tale of the headscarf as a tool of masculine Muslim oppression clashed with my mother's story, and the millions more untold.[54] Certainly, a single vignette does not set the precedent for everyone, but it was overpowering to witness my mother's strength and certitude bloom when she placed that turban on her head. Certainly, "not every Muslim women veils," but the force of gendered Islamophobia, and its feminine fronts, has levied the most disfigured stereotypes upon Muslim women who do, women like my mother.[55]

The living testimony of a Muslim woman with little education shouldering the burden of raising three children was more persuasive than the opinions of outsiders. Outsiders who typically had a vested interest in slandering Islam and painting Muslim women as hopelessly powerless and "in need of saving."[56]

Unfortunately, the French National Assembly was wholly comprised of those outsiders, and they stripped French women of the right to freely exercise their faith by a staggering 496 to 34 vote on February 10, 2004—the year after my mother made her second trip to Mecca.[57] The vote by which the Hijab Ban became law was buoyed by a state-sponsored report authored by a committee comprised entirely of non-Muslims.

This committee, called the Stasi Commission, found that "whereas the secularity of public life has long since been recognized in the religious traditions of Europe, in the Commission's view Islamic scarves express a tendency towards religious isolation. . . . As symbols of the traditional subordination of women in the Islamic world, they impede the development of girls as autonomous persons. The command to wear headscarves in public exudes from the traditional ideal of female chastity that puts women under lifelong control of men."[58]

The Hijab Ban would plague Muslim women in France for years to come. It was followed in 2011 by legislation that barred Islamic face coverings; together, the two laws formed the flagship policies of a French Islamophobia that did not stop at the borders of the secular republic. The second and third waves would break out in Quebec, Belgium, and additional European nations that enacted copycat laws based on the French Hijab Ban. Laws that stripped women of that liberty my mother took hold of when she wrapped that scarf around her head for the first time in April 1994, and every day after.

My mother did not need to be saved by an outsider. Not did she need to be liberated by legislators that did not know her; and knew her faith even less. Her saviors were present deep within her, rooted in who she was and in her faith, which governments, in France and beyond, would prohibit her from freely exercising. "My savior is Allah, and Allah alone," my mother would tell me incessantly when I was a child. Words that I did not fully absorb as a young boy and finally understand as a man, a man made with the particular touch of a single mother who found solace in the scarf she wrapped around her head with the very two hands she raised me with.

In *The Veil and the Male Elite,* the Moroccan feminist Fatema Mernissi wrote, "The veil, which was intended to protect them [Muslim women] from violence in the street, would accompany them for centuries, whatever the security situation of the city. For them, peace would never return. Muslim women were to display their hijab everywhere, the vestige of a civil war that would never come to an end."[59]

Debates about the hijab, particularly within Western political discourse, overwhelmingly fixate on trite extremes mapped at the same poles that marked the architecture of Orientalism then and Islamophobia today. These normative assessments of the headscarf as "good" or "bad," "oppressive" versus "empowering" are binaries that strip the expanse of nuance, and more importantly, deprive the very subject in question—the Muslim woman—of the agency to *choose* whether or not to cover. The matter is far too complex to be divided and debated within a binary, but ironically is an issue that comes down to a basic *singularity,* namely, a Muslim woman's individual right to dress as she pleases.

In his novel *Season of Migration to the North,* the Sudanese writer Tayeb Salih renounces the binaries that he grappled with on its pages and in his life. Through one of the story's characters, Salih provides a critical commemoration: "To those who see with one eye, speak with one tongue and see things as either black or white, either Eastern or Western."[60] It is an incisive crescendo to a marvelous book, and a command to those who read it to disavow the constrictive binaries that leave one eye, or both, blind.

This is especially true for the popular and political discourses around the hijab. Ironically, its most vehement critics have one eye, or both, veiled by a blinding Islamophobia. The very presence of Muslim women in France and "Western" nations testifies against mythic binaries that oblige them to choose between emancipation and subordination, faith and nation. The eyes of these Muslim women, whether they choose to wear the hijab or not, remain unconcealed and wide open.

At the heart of it all, again, is liberty. And the decision to cover or uncover should remain the sovereign and exclusive territory of Muslim women, not the French National Assembly, Muslim and non-Muslim men, or the realm of bodies that exist beyond the body of Muslim women. Free exercise of religion is the foundation of liberty and a principle that helped forge nations like the United States.

While *liberté* is the first of the trinity of principles that make up the French national motto, the Hijab Ban stands ominously between it—like an abusive overlord—and the millions of Muslim women in France. In March 2019, that very overlord stomped into Quebec, France's former colony in Canada, a nation widely perceived as tolerant of religious freedom, but as Palestinian Canadian law scholar Reem Bahdi reveals, houses a "deep unwillingness to challenge the stereotyping of Muslims as terrorists" that comes from the very top of the nation's legal system.[61]

"I don't care what that fucking law says," protested Lobna, a twenty-two-year-old college student on the other side of the line in Montreal.[62] I laughed at her defiance, imagining one of my nieces of the same age on the other side of the phone line, and she let out a laugh as well, while both of us quarantined inside of our homes on opposite sides of the border.

"Are you afraid of what could happen? How you could get in trouble?" I asked, a common question during the thick of the coronavirus pandemic of 2020. However, the focus of this question was Quebec's Bill 21, which wielded the French principle of *laïcité,* or secularism, to inspire the second wave of the Hijab Ban in the lone francophone province in Canada.[63]

"Nope, what are they going to do to me?" she replied, her defiance still intact. "I'm more afraid of Allah's punishment." Her faith was as firm as her voice.

Lobna's defiance conjured up the words of a luminary who had been locked up nearly fifty-seven years earlier in Birmingham, Alabama. "I would agree with St. Augustine that an unjust law is no law at all," wrote Martin Luther King Jr. in *Letter from Birmingham Jail*, affirming that an individual not only has a legal but a moral responsibility to obey just laws, but even more so, one has a moral responsibility to disobey unjust laws.[64] Lobna echoed King's very sentiment with millennial rebelliousness but the same steely conviction.

For King, jailed in Birmingham, and the young Muslima quarantined in Montreal, being answerable to the moral dictates of their God overrode the legislation drafted and enacted by men. In fact, all white men in King's case, and overwhelmingly white men in Lobna's case. Men who stood between them and their God—waving the fist of the law and its warning of earthly punishment if they violated it.

And they did. Willfully and in line with a law they both deemed more authoritative and pure.

Lobna followed in the footsteps of King and wore her hijab when she left her home. She wore it when she attended her virtual university classes, and she wore it when the first wave of the virus receded and quarantines were temporarily lifted.

Lobna refused to let a new law make her a stranger in her country. Quebec was her home, and in fact, the only home she has ever known. Lobna spoke better French than Arabic, and loved poutine as much as she did the signature Palestinian dish *makloubeh*. Months later, she introduced me to shawarma poutine, which blended both halves of her identity. French Canadian culture was ingrained in her, and in the words of Arshif, a Quebecois convert to Islam, "If you're defending your culture by taking away someone else's, then that's not much of a culture."[65]

If you enact laws that strip a citizen's ability to exercise their religion and freely *be* who they are, then a higher calling will move them to break those laws.

"This is how I want to dress, nobody can tell me different," Lobna stated, announcing that her religious and feminist liberties were joined at the hip. The second wave of French *laïcité* had no chance against Lobna, who wore her crown in Quebec with the same spirit of moral resistance as a King in Alabama.

She would stomp on that law, stomps witnessed by the other young women in her family, who looked up to her as a model. And stomps emulated from afar, in another land, where the third wave of the French plague broke out, endangering Muslim women who took *cover*.

On July 5, 2020, at the Mont des Arts Square in Brussels, over a thousand people stomped on the pavement as they protested a measure to prohibit headscarves in Belgian colleges.[66] The mass action was the largest of many that broke out in Belgium.

Signs reading "Hands off my hijab" and "Where is the freedom if I can't put on whatever I want" were hoisted up. *Signs of the times,* held by Muslim women donning their headscarves and non-Muslims marching alongside them.

In June 2019, the Belgian Constitutional Court ruled that public institutions, including colleges and universities, could prohibit the wearing of religious symbols without violating the European Convention on Human Rights (ECHR) mandate of free exercise of religion.

With the ruling, the Belgian court endorsed what the French National Assembly had established fifteen years earlier. It held that the hijab was a deviant mode of expression and a cultural practice that fell outside the bounds of religious freedom. The court, acting on a continent where nativist populism was spiking and the French plague spreading, viewed Muslim bodies—principally through the hijab—as the embodiment of a rival civilization bent on changing western Europe, and conspiring to remake it in its image.

Unlike in the United States, the ideas and imagery of the Crusades, those original holy wars that stretched from the eleventh to the fifteenth centuries, permeate the psyche of Europe. They permeate its legislative discussions and popular debates and inform academic discourse and judicial determinations throughout the continent. The imprint of the Crusades is not only prominent, but dynamic, alive, and ongoing. The Crusades stain the psyche of discourses popular and political in France, Belgium, and the rest of Europe, as prominently as the stained glass of the ancient churches that abound on the continent. Islamophobia is embedded deep into Europe's psychological fabric, and its architecture more firm and fixed than its American counterpart.

Edward Said addresses this in his landmark book *Covering Islam,* writing in 1981 that "the absence in America either of a colonial past or of a longstanding cultural attention to Islam makes the current obsession all the more peculiar, more abstract, more secondhand. . . . By comparison, in France, the country's second religion in point of numbers is Islam, which may not be more popular as a result, but is certainly more known."[67] In Europe, the Crusades are not bygone wars, but an ongoing standoff that still grips the continent.

In Europe, particularly in nations with sizable Muslim populations, the new crusades spurred on by the War on Terror are an extension of the old Crusades first waged about a thousand years ago. This, surely, is not rational. But neither is Orientalism or Islamophobia, the epistemologies that shape this distinct European view.

In Europe, and perhaps most intimately in France, Islam is far more than a novel enemy manifested in the contemporary mold of terrorism. It is a longstanding nemesis that once stretched its boundaries deep into Europe, erected mosques in the eighth century that still stand today, and injected itself deep into the loins that made Europe what it is today.

The crusade against Muslims in Belgium and France, and through much of Europe, is where the "clash of civilizations" imagery is deeply embedded and most familiar. It reaches far back into a historical memory that even ordinary citizens are familiar with, fear, and register by casting votes for populist parties and casting cold stares toward headscarved women.

American Islamophobia is more shortsighted, lacking the memory of its European parent. Cultural narratives of Islam as a tyrannical faith were imported into the United States from Europe, but damning tropes about the faith and depictions of the Prophet Muhammad as a "false prophet that could attract enough converts to enslave the nation" do not trickle down and permeate the minds of everyday Americans as potently as they do the French, Spanish, or Belgian people.[68]

Political elites in America were wary of Islam during the nation's embryonic stages, while in Europe, the history of Islamic conquest and its vestiges that remain make fear of Islam ever present and the "Islamic extremism" more layered. The anatomy of French Islamophobia is made up of this memory and a distant past that sits at the very doorstep of the present, mirroring a "Muslim world" that sits, intimately and close, across the Mediterranean.

For Europe, the "Muslim world" watches and waits from nearby and from within. It pumps waves of its "foot soldiers" across the Mediterranean, ready to fight on new fronts of the same longstanding crusade. A crusade where Muslim men are perceived as armed "jihadists," that Arabic term mangled beyond recognition, prepared to strap themselves with bombs in furtherance of the violent theater of that crusade.[69]

Meanwhile, Muslim women are the slowly plodding Trojan horse, planning and plotting, collectively conspiring to topple the secular law and the "civilization" it defends with that *flag of Islam,* that feared weapon Muslim women wear around their heads, and Muslim men brandish in their hands. Imaginations that move European states to pass law after irrational law in an attempt to remove it from existence.

"They say we are being forced to wear the hijab, and then turn around and force us to dress the way they want us to dress," wrote Zeinab, a twenty-year-old college student from Brussels who attended the July 5th march in Belgium's capital.[70]

For Belgian Muslim women like Zeinab, who attend college and plan on working for public institutions, the judicial ruling could potentially spawn the same dilemma French women like Ibtissam have faced for years. Namely, having to choose between their faith, and how they wish to exercise it, and simply *being* Belgian. Two identities that French Islamophobia, the very plague that oriented the hijab as antithetical to European civilization, carried into its neighbor to the north.

It was the third wave of that plague, and Belgian protestors donned masks as they fought back with signs in hand and hijabs on their head. Neither a pandemic enveloping the globe nor a plague from France would stop them.

They protested, and wore their headscarves, defiantly, against the fresh legal dictate. In the *Brussels Times,* Malika Hamidi observed in the days leading up to that protest in the Mont des Arts Square, "At one time, Muslim women resisted using this so-called 'symbol of oppression' as a tool of empowerment. They are doing it again today: they strongly and resolutely affirm that the headscarf can be a feminist 'statement.'"[71]

That statement was delivered, lucidly and loudly, on July 5, 2020. Muslim women did not need to be "saved" from their husbands and fathers, their governments, and definitely not their faith.[72] Instead, the march they took and the fight they waged aimed to rescue that principle of liberty endangered by the first, second, and third waves of the French plague that fed on the heads of Muslim women and the mind of Europe.

The bans inspired by the first French Hijab Ban not only strip Muslim women of the liberty to exercise their faith and govern their own bodies, but are suffocating. The hands of the law, wrapped around their necks, impose a white patriarchal or Western feminist view of the hijab. An article that is a crown for some Muslim women, a negligible piece of clothing for others, and an arcane cultural practice for some.

In line with the heterogeneity of Islamic interpretation, the hijab carries a wide range of meaning beyond the rigid assessments of the state and the cliché binaries that bind pundits and politicians; "the headscarf has no unitary meaning."[73] In response to rising Islamophobia in France and the United States, many Muslim women who previously did not veil did so as an act of political resistance. For some, spirituality or politics, or a combination of both, spurred this pivot.[74] In the case of Algerian women fighting for independence against the French, the hijab and the niqab were converted into instruments for liberation, through which armed revolutionaries safely passed military checkpoints under their anonymizing shields.[75] For others, donning the hijab is an expression of rejecting Western "normative standards of femininity" in exchange for subaltern alternatives, and so many more motives.[76]

For young girls like Farah facing French Islamophobia in Paris, or Muslima—a young Uyghur woman who survived Chinese persecution and now calls Istanbul home—the hijab is their crown. A crown that instills resolve in the face of hate, and installs strength following the crucible of ethnic cleansing.

Islamophobia removes the possibility of exploring the myriad inter-pretations of Islamic modesty and the motives that drive Muslim women to cover—*or not cover*—that are too many to count. But only Muslim women should choose. As protests in Iran and Belgium illus-trate, women are the victims of state laws that deny the Islamic and universal human right of freedom of conscience.

For Muslim women like my mother, the hijab was and remains a bridge toward emancipation, and for Lobna, it is a pathway that brings her closer to God. For some, donning the headscarf is delivery from oppres-sion, while choosing not to wear it or removing it from one's head a decision fueled by an expansive ocean of motives.

For Mernissi, a Muslim feminist proponent of "lifting the veil," the hijab was once a political necessity that mutated into a enduring tool of patriarchal control.[77] For every Ayaan Hirsi Ali who sees the hijab through the prism of oppression, there is an Ilhan Omar who wears it as a trailblazer, creating new inroads for Muslim women in an American Congress that has never seen the likes of her before.[78]

For scores of devout Muslim women, covering is a practice—whether assumed or set aside—that does not define their connection to the divine. It does not define them as a Muslim. Modesty and covering, for many Muslim women, can be performed through action, expressed through dress, or both at the same time.

For Hamidi, viewing the protests in the heart of Brussels, the head-scarf was a vivid declaration of a new wave of feminism in Belgium, a declaration by Muslim Belgian women that proclaimed the hijab a marker of empowerment, not oppression.[79]

In the end, the choice to cover or uncover should be women's, and women's alone. Not the choice of national or provincial or municipal governments, extending the oppressive arms of a thinly veiled feminism that intends to strike and suffocate, not "save" or liberate.

Muslim women—in Marseilles or Montreal, Tehran or Brussels—regardless of their individual positions on the Islamic covering or personal expressions of it, know this and *know this well*. They do not need rescuing from corridors of power that caricature them as prisoners of their faith's making.[80] Muslim women only demand from governments and the laws they draft that liberty—that long-denied liberty—to determine their lives free from the recurring blows and suffocating clutches of the law.

"Having a monolithic view of feminism is suffocating," stated Kimberlé Crenshaw.[81] And the bruises around the necks of Muslim women attest to how the state has tried, and tried a second and third and fourth time, but failed to choke their spirit and crush the savior that only comes from within them.

CHAPTER SIX

MONSTERS AND MARTYRS

UNHOLY FRIDAY

> You can be a traveler, entirely alone in a foreign land. But walk into a mosque on any Friday, and in an instant have a new community, new friends, a new family. This is the magic of being Muslim. This is the magic I experienced right now, inside the Claremont Masjid in Cape Town, this Friday.
>
> THE AUTHOR speaking in Cape Town, South Africa, August 12, 2022

It was Friday, or *jumm'ah*—Islam's holiest day of the week, when Muslims collect and convene to pray at their local mosques. A sanctified day that temporarily cures the ills of the past week and reorients one for the week ahead. For Muslims, the magic of Fridays is restorative and spiritual, bringing together believers from distinct stations of society, and disparate corners of the world.

Friday was Farid's favorite day. A day when he prayed alongside his closest friends and then afterward caught up with them about their kids, jobs, and lives in Christchurch.[1] For Farid and his wife, Husna, the Masjid Al Noor was far more than a place for worship; it was the center of the Muslim community in their New Zealand town.

Like it did every day, the Islamic call to prayer (*adhan*) rang from Husna's phone and lifted her from bed. But this was not any other day—it was Friday. She circled from her side of the bed toward the other, knowing that the task of waking her husband would be easier on this day than the six preceding it. Farid opened his eyes and embraced his wife, then sat up on the side of the bed.

Farid could not walk. His wife, Husna, was the love and the legs of his life. He waited for her patiently, excited for the day, Friday, as she walked back toward him with his wheelchair.

Farid met Husna in 1994, shortly after she moved to New Zealand from Bangladesh.[2] She had left her family and life there to start anew in Christchurch, and began her own family with Farid and their daughter Shipa. Husna filled Farid's life with the love he had always longed for, and when he could not walk anymore, drew closer to him to ease the new trials life presented. Sharing everything, including one set of legs, strengthened their bond.

Farid beamed as he looked up at the face of his wife. It was Friday, a sanctified day. The couple prepared to meet their friends, pray to their maker, and then bid farewell, as they always did. Then come back home.

But this Friday, and its customary routine and farewell, would be different. It would be final.

Husna wheeled Farid through the front door of the Masjid Al Noor.[3] She left him near the men's entrance to the prayer room, bid him farewell, then walked toward the women's entrance. Farid stared at his wife as she walked away, smiling wide, blessed to have a partner who stood by him at every turn.

This was their routine, every Friday inside the halls of that mosque. This mosque had become a home for newcomers from Somalia and Syria, Pakistan and Palestine.[4] Some of them had absolutely no family when they first arrived in Christchurch. In more ways than one, the mosque was a family. Farid and Husna's routine was a familiar one to every member of that mosque, and a consoling part of the tapestry that made it their home.

The couple assumed their places on the prayer rug. On opposing sides of the prayer hall, Farid and Husna closed their eyes and bowed their heads. They prayed to Allah for the continued health and prosperity of their daughter, Shipa.

They paid their gratitude to Allah that they had one another to love and lean on.

They prayed their thanks to Allah for the warmth of their neighbors and community in Christchurch, who embraced them and took them in as their own.

They prayed to Allah, the *same* God that Christians and Jews and other believers pray to, for the very same things members of those faiths, and more, pray for.

They prayed until fifty-one of them could pray no more.

It was Friday, Islam's holiest day of the week, but as an ungodly figure emerged from the mosque entrance at 1:40 p.m. on March 15, 2019, the unholiest of Fridays began.

The stranger walked in, and then the first gunshots came, followed by rounds and rounds and rounds more. The screams of women and children filled the air between those rounds, and then Husna gazed upon dead faces—faces of those she had spoken to just minutes earlier, faces she knew so well—before looking toward the gunman. It felt like a horror movie, except it was real life.

Husna was afraid, but she was more afraid for Farid, who sat yards away, toward the front of the prayer hall. She knew that he was vulnerable, bound to that wheelchair that required her arms and legs.

She picked herself up off the green rug now stained with red and raced toward the men's section of the hall. She ran past slain men and women and children to her wheelchair-bound husband, using her legs to serve him like when she left him at the mosque entrance.[5]

Husna was committed to reaching Farid before the gunman's bullets did, bullets that rained down on living beings as if the gunman were playing one of those modern, murderous video games. That white gunman, a terrorist with the aim of slaying as many Muslims as he could on that unholy Friday, saw them as intruders, interlopers in a land that was not theirs to live or pray in. And he assumed the *call of duty* from presidents and politicians who flagged all Muslims as "invaders."

Husna ran and the gunman aimed. Both pointing directly at Farid, waiting there, as he always did, for his wife. His love, his legs. Husna, as she had done earlier that morning and every Friday before it, returned to her husband one final time. One final Friday, on which she met the terrorist's bullets before she made it back to Farid.[6]

It was Friday, Islam's holiest day of the week, and Farid and Husna were atop the Masjid Al Noor prayer rug, like they always were at 2 p.m. on Friday. Farid sitting in that wheelchair, alone, and his beloved wife laid across it along with forty-three others murdered inside the Al Noor mosque. Farid would be wheeled out of that mosque that Friday by an unfamiliar set of hands, without the love of his life and the legs that made him complete.

It was Friday. And for Farid and Husna, their final Friday together. Husna was dead, and so was their marriage.

The terrorist then drove five kilometers across town to the Linwood Islamic Centre, killing eight more Muslims there.[7]

New Zealand is on the opposite side of the globe from Dunya's world. The twenty-two-year-old graduate student, studying social work, was on the cusp of getting engaged to her sweetheart, Hussein, and beginning a new life in their hometown of Dearborn, Michigan.[8] With roughly 70,000 adherents, Dearborn is home to more Muslims than the entire country of New Zealand, and a center of Muslim life in North America.

Muslims in New Zealand, on the other hand, comprise only 1 percent of the island nation's total population. Islam is not nearly as embedded there as in Dearborn, nor its followers as visible. However, that Friday, March 15, 2019, would make New Zealand and the city of Christchurch central in the minds of the nearly 2 billion Muslims everywhere and a capital of white terrorism moving forward.

"I [had] never heard of that city before that day, and only thought about New Zealand as this beautiful place," stated Dunya. "I didn't even know that New Zealand had a big Muslim community. But like everyone, that day, I will never forget it and what happened there."[9]

Prime Minister Jacinda Ardern called the terror attacks of that Friday "one of New Zealand's darkest days."[10] Islam's holy day was turned into the nation's most trying moment, and the hallowed halls of two mosques converted into killing rooms by a white supremacist terrorist who live-streamed the first seventeen minutes of the massacre on social media.[11]

The dark days following the attack would cast a pall on Muslims everywhere across the globe, including on young Dunya, who was beginning to plan a life with Hussein, a young man from the south side of town whom she met while substitute teaching. These dark days converged with that luminous stretch of courtship for the young couple that might ultimately lead to a bond as strong as Farid and Husna's marriage.

"I was substitute teaching when I met him," Dunya recalled. "He seemed cool and down to earth," she said of Hussein, who taught gym class and coached the basketball team at the predominantly Muslim school. He was three years her elder, and in the coming weeks, the paths of the substitute teacher and basketball coach that crossed in those school halls would align into one. Their love story was as

American as any and would be consummated in a mosque, before an imam, on the holiest day of the week, Friday. Friday, for them, would formalize their love before the eyes of Allah.

As one marriage came to a tragic end inside the Masjid Al Noor, another was being born on the opposite side of the world, in a Michigan mosque. This was *not* the natural circle of life taking its course, I thought as I spoke to young Dunya in her grandmother's living room. Husna should still have been alive, I thought, and circling back from the women's side of the prayer room toward her husband on every one of the ninety or so Fridays since she and fifty others had been gunned down in Christchurch.

I shared her story with Dunya, a young bride-to-be on the cusp of formalizing a lifelong bond with Hussein. I passed her a photo of Husna, whose big brown eyes resembled the young woman's. The bright yellow headscarf the departed wore was not unlike the hijabs Dunya wrapped around her head.[12]

Dunya paused, struggling to find words as she looked at the photo. "This is so sad, he really needed her it seemed. I pray that she's in a better place, and that somebody is taking care of him." Her remark was followed by questions about the attack, questions—and fears—shared by every Muslim entering a mosque to pray on a Friday, or like young Dunya, to trade vows with the love of their life.

These fears followed her, and young Muslims everywhere, as they tried to live as normally as one could after such a massive tragedy. However, Islam had marked Husna as an unwanted "intruder" on "white soil" in New Zealand, and Dunya lived in a concentrated Muslim enclave in the heart of the Midwest that right-winged pundits claim had been "overtaken by Sharia Law."[13] A place where the internal challenges of being a young Muslim were magnified by the new trials ushered in by Trump, and the acts of terror in New Zealand he inspired.[14]

"It's sad, because I'll always relate that day to the early days of my relationship and future marriage," Dunya stated. That sentiment, while forlorn, was hardly unique. Muslims everywhere will always remember what they were doing, who they were with, and where they prayed—indeed, especially where they prayed—that Friday. A Friday when fifty-one of their sisters and brothers were massacred in the halls of two mosques on the opposite side of the world, an attack which hit—powerfully and permanently—so close to home.

That distinct fear of the same thing happening where they prayed possessed the billions of Muslims who bowed their head hours later in various corners of the globe. Christchurch, a place the vast majority of them had not known before, consumed their minds and their prayers.

It was Friday, the holiest of days that would never be the same. Mothers kissed their sons like they might never embrace them again before parting ways. Friends hugged each other tighter. Couples, old and new, held one another longer before bidding a farewell that was supposed to be temporary but that could, in a world where unhinged Islamophobia had mutated into murderous terrorism, be their last.

That is what Christchurch seeded into their heads and what awaits them every Friday.

It was Friday, Islam's holiest day. And young Dunya traded vows with Hussein in front of the imam who blessed their union by a reading of the Qur'an. Inside that mosque in Michigan, the memory of an ungodly Friday in Christchurch and a couple torn apart loomed heavy on the bride's mind.

On that Friday, July 10, 2020, she walked out of the mosque, married before the eyes of God, with her new husband beside her. He was healthy, vibrant, with both legs under him. Dunya was overwhelmed with joy on that Friday, but I knew that Husna crossed her mind. I knew that Christchurch and its dark memory interrupted her joy, if only for seconds, and that the memory of the massacre was there with her. She knew that her faith could mark her and her new husband as targets for a new crop of terrorists who barge into mosques and massacre Muslims.

If it could happen in Christchurch, New Zealand, the next terror attack targeting Muslims could happen anywhere. Even in Dearborn, Michigan—a capital of Muslim America, where new couples beginning a life together will forever be wed to fears that will follow them, every Friday moving forward, inside the sacred halls of mosques.

Christchurch, and the carnage that unfolded in two mosques and forever tore apart a loving couple, stands as the capital of the fears racing through the minds of Muslims everywhere. Fears that will forever call to mind Husna's final walk toward her husband on that Friday, March 15.

WHITE LIKE ME

> [I am] a regular white man from a regular family . . . [who] decided to take a stand to ensure a future for my people.
> BRENTON TARRANT, *The Great Replacement*

New Zealanders, who affectionately call themselves "Kiwis," do not take kindly to being compared to their island neighbors to the northwest. The common occurrence of being conflated with the inhabitants of their far larger, more recognizable neighbor is an understandable annoyance.

This annoyance stems from the desire to be recognized for who they genuinely are. It is a universal human impulse to want to be seen as an individual, apart from the masses of stereotypes and the heavy shadow of large land masses that surround the small constellation of islands that make up New Zealand. Everybody, regardless of who they are or where they come from, yearns to be seen for who and what they are, apart from what the world has assigned them to be.

Although Australia and New Zealand are separated by the Tasman Sea and a colossal ocean of physical difference, a "regular white man" who crossed that sea in the days before March 15, 2019, would link the two nations.[15] Brenton Harrison Tarrant was an Australian, not a New Zealander, two identities commonly thought to be one. The accents are similar, but what united the two countries was a kindred colonial history in which white supremacy almost completely wiped out the indigenous populations and established two predominantly white nations in the middle of the Pacific Ocean. The two are bound by a history of dispossession and dehumanization, and in theaters distinct from the Al Noor and Linwood mosques, dark histories of state-sponsored massacres of Brown- and Black-skinned people. People like the fifty-one Muslims slain on March 15, 2019, people reduced to indistinguishable masses that needed to be exterminated to ensure the future of two new white nations.

Tarrant, the terrorist who crossed the Tasman Sea from Australia and carried out New Zealand's deadliest modern terror attack, was just another "regular white man."[16] With evil efficiency, he did what the two nations' forefathers had done to the Maoris, the Torres Strait Islanders, and the Aborigines in earlier eras. He indiscriminately murdered them, wiping them off a land that he believed was his own, not as a matter of fiat or legal status, but as a matter of blood, on account of his whiteness.[17]

Those earlier targets were not *individuals* like them, those white settlers believed. They did not deserve to be seen for who they were; only white people commanded that distinction, and the white supremacy that rang from their guns and was recorded in their laws established that, beginning on January 26, 1788, and May 7, 1856, when Australia and New Zealand were founded. And again on March 15, 2019, when whiteness was unleashed to massacre another group of nonwhites deemed "intruders" who stood in the way of imperial ambition.

First Maoris, and then Muslims. White supremacy began with the killing of indigenous Brown people, en masse, on a land that was their own, and its later chapter closed with two massacres of Brown, Black, and white citizens and immigrants inside their places of worship. Their legal or generational claim to the land, for Tarrant and his burgeoning pack of white supremacist counterparts in Australia and across the world, did not matter—only their race, and more specifically, their *nonwhiteness*.

While bestowing myriad privileges upon those who possess it, whiteness disconnects its victims from their historical claims and grievances. In addition to erasing indigenous people from their land, it erases their legal stake in the land and asserts itself, and those who possess it, as the rightful owners of the land.

Therefore, white women and men, regardless of when they arrive in lands like New Zealand and Australia, are never branded "intruders" or even "immigrants," even though an objective analysis of history affirms that they are the very essence of both. Whiteness grants them a freedom of movement, and a presumption of belonging, that is seldom extended to people of color. Although the definition of the term "immigrant" is one who comes to a nation with the intention of taking residence there but who lacks full-fledged membership (citizenship) in that nation, whiteness is hardly ever associated with that term.[18] Race, and particularly whiteness, clouds and confuses the definitions of "immigrant" and "citizen" with a range of attendant presumptions, led by popular conflations that associate belonging with whiteness and foreignness with nonwhiteness, regardless of reality.

For the settler colonists who stripped indigenous peoples in Australia and New Zealand of their lands and everything atop it, their whiteness anoints them "pioneers" and "founders." Perhaps white supremacy's most absurd lie is that Europeans "discovered" lands that had been inhabited by indigenous peoples for centuries, a lie that roots the modern entitlement of "regular white men" like Brenton Tarrant, who believes that a nation of which he is not even a citizen is "his land." This is part of the broader presumption white supremacy has created over generations, particularly in settler-colonial states like New Zealand and Australia, namely, that whiteness itself triggers the presumption of belonging and ownership. On the other hand, nonwhiteness raises the very opposite beliefs: perpetual foreignness, transience, and with regard to Muslims, danger.

In Tarrant's mind, and in the white supremacist imagination, claims to land are not a historical but a purely racial matter. This was true when English colonialists wiped out Australia and New Zealand's indigenous populations from their soil and true when Tarrant—a foreign national traveling to New Zealand—walked into the two Christchurch mosques and killed fifty-one citizens and legal residents.

Tarrant was the visitor traveling to a foreign country. Yet his whiteness enabled a fluid and invisible transition, without the markings of "foreignness" and "immigrant" ascribed to Brown Muslims, even those who are full-fledged citizens. His Muslim victims were, legally and physically, at home. However, in his mind, the only formal status that mattered was his white skin. That was his racial passport, and in his mind it made him proprietor of a foreign land. The fifty-one Muslims he gunned down, who were supremely diverse in terms of race and ethnicity, were racially flattened as nonwhite as a consequence of their Muslim identity.[19] Islam and whiteness were warring rivals, according to the old Crusades, and have been more forcefully framed as such by a white supremacist movement that integrates the civilizational tropes of the War on Terror into its worldview.

As American sociologist Erik Love has observed, "White supremacy and Islamophobia stem from the same root, and they are both burrowed into the foundations of American institutions," and indeed, are burrowed into their Australian and New Zealander counterparts, which grew from that same root.[20] This common root was the source of the absurd yet zealously held belief of one man—a foreigner, in fact—that his massacre of fifty-one Muslims in a foreign land was a defense of "his land" and "his people."

Through the terror attack in Christchurch, and the dark passages of New Zealand and Australia's colonial histories sanctified as "discovery" instead of terrorism, we learn a great deal about white supremacy. We learn that white supremacy's greatest gift is precisely the very root that gives rise to Islamophobia's greatest curse: whiteness detaches the individual from the evils of his or her racial predecessors, and affirms (and forcefully reaffirms) his or her individuality. Islamophobia, on the other hand, has the very opposite effect. It inextricably ties the misdoings of Muslim culprits to each and every Muslim, regardless of their location or citizenship.

In the white supremacist imagination, Tarrant does not represent all whites. He does not even represent the corpus of white supremacists who slay Muslims, or other nonwhite groups. He is, always, an individual. A *lone wolf* acting only for himself and nobody else.[21]

This individuality extends to other "regular white men," who have no responsibility to apologize on his behalf or condemn his terror, a recurring burden placed on the shoulders of Muslims in the aftermath of every terror attack. A permanent burden that holds them collectively culpable on account of faith.[22]

If individuality is the essence of freedom, then whiteness privileges those who are white with an ideal pathway toward freedom. Islamophobia, on the other hand, caricatures Muslims as part of an unbending, violent whole, in turn binding its followers to the misdeeds (whether real or unreal) of its bad actors. But in a world where white supremacist terror is rapidly eclipsing other forms of armed vigilante violence, there are seldom, if ever, any "lone wolves."[23]

While the War on Terror fixates wholly on "global Islamic terrorism," there is no such war against transnational white supremacy—a global movement in its own right. In fact, the new front of global populism that scapegoats Muslims for its political woes capitalizes on an explicit and unhinged white supremacy. Donald Trump, president of the nation that spawned the War on Terror and the leader who readapted its thesis by infamously declaring "I think Islam hates us," is ideological inspiration for this front.[24]

Trump, with his strategic integration of racist and anti-Muslim sloganeering, illustrated how white supremacy's modern war centered Muslims as its principal targets. Trump's potent rhetoric, and the force of his renewed War on Terror policies, which centered on closing the borders to Muslim "invaders" and guised "ISIS terrorists," directly emboldened white supremacist vigilantes like Tarrant to join this new front of the racial War on Terror.[25] Law professor Shirin Sinnar writes powerfully about "white supremacist violence [having] a complicated and historically shifting relationship to the state and state institutions."[26] With Trump holding the highest civic office in the world, white supremacists found state-sponsored fuel in the form of expressly anti-Muslim rhetoric and explicitly bigoted policy. In Trump, Tarrant found a talisman that pushed him to take up arms against a Muslim scourge that "conspired to replace" white culture.[27]

And take up arms is precisely what Tarrant did. In a seventy-four-page manifesto, Tarrant used the very language Trump had to describe Muslims, clearly outlining his belief in the supremacy of the white man and praising Trump, who he called "a symbol of renewed white identity and common purpose."[28]

However, Tarrant did not have to look to the very top of the geopolitical food chain, and the United States, for inspiration. At home in Australia, right-winged conservative senator Fraser Anning placed the blame for the act of terror on Islam, the faith of the victims. "The real cause of bloodshed on New Zealand streets today is the immigration program which allowed Muslim fanatics to migrate to New Zealand in the first place," Anning said to media only hours after the massacres. Anning then finished his absurd statement by adding untimely insult to unimaginable injury: "The truth is that Islam is not like any other faith. It is the religious equivalent of fascism. And just because the followers of this savage belief were not the killers in this instance, does not make them blameless."[29]

Anning's words reveal, in explicit and unfiltered terms, what drove his white countryman Tarrant to shoot down those fifty-one Muslims on March 15, 2019. Both believed that Muslims, by virtue of practicing a faith branded "uncivilized" and "savage" by the War on Terror, were irredeemably guilty. They were guilty of adhering to a faith oriented as antithetical to civilization and inimical to whiteness. Even when slain in one of the deadliest terror attacks in the entire region, Muslims were to blame.

White supremacists, whether holding high office or AR-15 rifles, tied the presence of Muslims with threat. Not only *terror threat*, the fundamental thread of the Islamophobia that the War on Terror spawned after 9/11; the threat of Islam, for white supremacists, sank deeper into the soil of the land they stood atop, and was a matter of race and blood and blood and soil.

To white supremacists, alt-right and old, Muslim communities represented, in Tarrant's words, "white genocide." Their very presence in the United States, for Trump and his racial War on Terror, signaled the "end of white Christian America," and their very presence in Australia and New Zealand was an offense.[30] According to law professor Darin Johnson, "White supremacist terrorism is a rising threat that has been overlooked by national security authorities as a global threat" largely because of the racial identity of the actors and the invisibility and presumption of individuality it garners them.[31] Historian Kathleen Belew traces the origins of the "modern white supremacist movement" in the United States that spawned the likes of Dylann Roof, Stephen Paddock, and Buffalo mass killer Peyton Gendron to the 1960s, when it flourished in the shadows as governments profiled and pursued immigrants, ethnic minorities, and most notably, Muslims.[32] A globalized world, fused together by digital media and social media platforms, connected the American white supremacist movement and counterpart groups in Europe, Australia, and New Zealand; these groups interact frequently, form transnational bonds and organizations, and march toward similar goals. White supremacist actors today are motivated by the same manifestos, the same figures, and as stunningly displayed on January 6, 2021, at the attack on the US Capitol, a deeply rooted refusal on the part of the governments—most notably the spearhead of the War on Terror—to combat white supremacist violence as terrorism. Full-fledged terrorism. A label that has been exclusively assigned to Arabs and Muslims for far too long.

This presumption of guilt forms the foundation of Islamophobia, globally. There was no war being waged against the uptick in white supremacist terror in New Zealand and across the world. The rising tide of populism sweeping the earth illustrated the ominous reality that white supremacists were leading this new front of Islamophobia and waging the racial crusades that enlisted the likes of Brenton Tarrant—a "regular white man" who executed fifty-one innocent people.

This was white supremacy wed to Islamophobia, a new phase of the War on Terror that past chapters of Australia's and New Zealand's colonial histories reveal is hardly novel. When asked if he felt any remorse for the murders, Tarrant said—boldly and proudly—"No, I wish I could have killed more invaders." The self-proclaimed "ethno-nationalist" soldier dutifully executed the aims of presidential dictates trumpeted from the very top of political power, and carried out the xenophobic policies of racial populists near and far. Mobilized by digital platforms like 4chan and inspired by racial populists holding the highest offices of government, white supremacist terrorism rose violently and wreaked havoc on Jews and immigrants, Black people and Muslims.[33] These platforms, along with mainstream social media outlets, enabled the peddling of "viral lies and falsehoods" about racial and religious minorities, which reached millions across national, hemispheric, and linguistic bounds,[34] in turn accelerating the formation of a transnational white supremacist movement.

"White supremacy also comes shrouded in the garb of government sanction," wrote Zak Cheney-Rice in *New York Magazine* a day after the Christchurch massacres.[35] Shrouded along with it is an unfiltered Islamophobia from these supreme rungs of entwined geopolitical and white power, which is, during a moment when the War on Terror is devolving into a race war, a deadly dialectic.

Saul was a regular white man for the first forty-one years of his life. That is, until he converted to Islam and changed his name to the *irregular* new moniker of Abdullah Ali.[36] The resident of Sydney is intimately familiar with the white supremacist movement in Australia, and he mixed with the same circles that Brenton Tarrant engaged with.

"I volunteered with a suicide telephone hotline from 2009–2011, the callers were mainly men. These experiences led me to be involved with Men's Rights as male suicide really concerned me and no one cared," Abdullah shared.

However, Abdullah gradually discovered that the men's rights movement in Australia cross-pollinated with white supremacist factions. Many of those concerned with men's rights and chauvinism, he found, were also members of white supremacist groups. Abdullah was at a pivotal fork in his life's road, personally and spiritually, but as a white man, had the ear of these elements.

"With Donald Trump running for the Republican nomination [in the United States] in 2016 it became very apparent, very quickly that the Men's Rights Movement was riddled with racists and Islamophobes. It was like a Donald Trump cult even here in Australia, because now it was really OK to call for an end to Muslim immigration, and go on about Sharia," Abdullah recollected.

Trump's anti-Muslim campaign resonated with white men in Australia, on the literal opposite side of the world. The Trump effect on white men who blamed their woes on nonwhites was global. Regular white men, like those Abdullah spoke to on a daily basis, and Brenton Tarrant, looked up to Trump as a "renewed symbol of white identity."

Abdullah, a white man mixing with white supremacists, could have walked in the same direction as Tarrant. But he did not, and by embracing Islam, did the very opposite. "[Islamophobia in Australia] led to me reverting [sic] to Islam from atheism last year. I investigated Islam more, especially after the Christchurch terrorist act."

For Abdullah, Islam filled a spiritual void and brought him the tranquility that eluded his first forty-one years on earth. The new faith he adopted was, to echo historian Juan Cole, "peaceful in character, mirroring below [on earth] the serenity in the afterlife to which [Muslims] aspired."[37]

However, as a white man whose racial identity concealed his faith, Abdullah remained privy to the unfiltered comments of white people who claimed "We are losing our Anglo Saxon way of life" or "[It's] time to vote and get back our country from these fucking Muslims." These were regular comments, from "regular" white men and women. Abdullah's white skin protected him from the stereotypes, the suspicion, and the stares that follow *visible Muslims*.[38] But, as he grew his beard, wore his thobe and "proudly walk[ed] to my local masjid," his whiteness would gradually become *cloaked* with the markers of terrorism that are assigned to the new faith he embraced after the Christchurch massacres.[39]

Whiteness, regardless of the facts at hand and the slain bodies lying before it, is utterly *disassociated* from terrorism. Despite the mass terror committed in its name in the past, or the massacres it claims today, its hands remain clean of that indictment. Neither the power of statistics nor the force of history has been able to narrow the vast ocean that separates whiteness from the phenomenon of terrorism.

In fact, the War on Terror, a child of white supremacy and its never-ending imperial ambitions, flipped the racial script. Although the American crusade claimed the lives of millions of innocents, and continues to claim bodies as you read these words, it propagated the cardinal lie that terrorism is an exclusively Muslim phenomenon. Muslims were not merely raced or stereotyped as terrorists, but the War on Terror made the two words "Muslim" and "terrorism" virtually synonymous.

This conceptual trick had destructive practical ramifications. It distanced wars waged in the name of protecting white civilization from the hellish terror unfolding in Iraq and Yemen, on one hand, and the white supremacist terror inflicted by the likes of Dylann Roof in Charleston, South Carolina—a white man who killed nine Black churchgoers inside of their church—and Brenton Tarrant in Christchurch, New Zealand.[40]

Terrorists were always Muslims, and white culprits—even after blood was spilled and racist motive established—were never terrorists. As law scholar Caroline Mala Corbin observed, there are "two common though false narratives about terrorists who attack America [and beyond]. We see them on television, in the movies, on the news, and, currently, in the Trump administration. The first is that 'terrorists are always (brown) Muslims.' The second is that 'white people are never terrorists.'"[41]

These competing racial constructions, or "racializations," are built upon the notion that whites are always innocuous and self-directed individuals.[42] Muslims, by contrast, are a faceless mass, all tied to an ominous monolith that is imagined in the form of the terror network of the day or the rival civilization that they all belong to. This image is rooted in the foundational tropes that the law, and its political and popular co-conspirators, has assigned to "whiteness" and "Islam."

The former, we know from Malcolm X, always stands for "purity" and "freedom" and "modern civilization." And the latter, as broken down by Edward Said, incessantly represents "war" and "violence" and "terrorism." Orientalism, we see through the prism of the Islamophobia that prevails in the world today, was always and remains a distinctly racial project built upon the imperial designs of white supremacists.

Therefore, Muslims are seen as terrorists even when performing acts utterly disconnected from that enterprise, while whites—like Roof and Tarrant—are overwhelmingly cast as actors behaving outside the accepted and understood boundaries of whiteness. Again, white culprits of terror are routinely called "lone wolves," that is, one-off actors whose race exempts them from the very acts of terrorism members of their ideological flock commit inside the hallowed halls of Charleston churches, Pittsburgh synagogues, and Christchurch mosques.[43] Meanwhile, the Muslims they killed yesterday are always presumed to be terrorists—a suspicion granted at birth that, in the eyes of white supremacists, whether a Trump or a Tarrant, they can never renounce or resign from.

A "lone wolf," the media has reported time and time again, a phrase reasserting the individuality of whites as the bodies of dead Blacks and Jews and Muslims lay before them and the ink of their manifestos spilled the truth of their political motives. The "lone wolf" dominating the headlines after a white terrorist attack, if you listen closely, sounds eerily similar to Tarrant's claim that he was just another "regular white man."[44]

Brenton Tarrant was just another regular white man. So regular that he believed that a country where he was not a resident or a citizen was his own.

So regular that he walked into two mosques and massacred fifty-one people. Innocent people he called "intruders" and "invaders." "Intruders" in a country that they lived in and were born in. "Invaders" in a city where they owned homes and held passports that he did not.

So regular that he believed them to be terrorists because of their faith and fashioned himself a freedom fighter "protecting" his people. "Freedom" in the figure of a foreigner toting a machine gun and recording the massacre inside two mosques that he made into morgues.

So regular that the terror he unleashed on March 15, 2019, at the Al Noor and Linwood mosques, the deadliest terrorist attack in New Zealand's modern history, resembled the very acts that gave birth to that nation and the one he hailed from.

Brenton Tarrant was just a regular white man. "White Like Me" perhaps would have been a better title for his manifesto. Tarrant, widely dubbed a lone wolf terrorist, an individual acting alone, by reporters and news headlines in the hours and days to come, and acknowledged as an individual because of the color of his skin and the supremacy that his forefathers bequeathed to him, which lawmakers today protect at all costs. While his victims, and the millions of victims that his forefathers massacred in Australia and New Zealand, were never extended the dignity of being seen, or treated, as individuals.

Just another regular white man committing the same acts of terror, modern massacres harkening back to memories of old, of the nation's founders. *Founders* that, like Tarrant, hailed from the same "Scottish, Irish and English stock" that landed in new territories and systematically eradicated their natives.[45] He was they and they were he, but the law and its collaborators in the media did not see it, and him, that way.

Although inspired by that very white supremacy, Tarrant was never associated with that history. Never connected or conflated with those pioneers of displacement and genocide that landed on two islands already inhabited by nonwhite native populations that were early erased from the earth they cultivated.

It must be good to be white. In fact, it must be divine, or very close to it. To always be seen and scrutinized as an individual, as independent. Disconnected from the vile acts of those who look like you, and disaggregated from the genocidal actors who believe like you.

Always an individual. During moments of peace and prosperity, and as illustrated after the terror attacks in Christchurch on March 15, 2019, when *regular* acts of white supremacist terror unfolded below a sun and atop a soil that recognizes it for what it is and has always been: terrorism. Terrorism that the Maori knew well long before March 15, 2019. And that New Zealand's Muslims felt, in all of its evil and ferociousness, on that ungodly Friday when fifty-one of them bowed eastward, toward Mecca's crescent, as the sun set for them one final time on earth.

One photo, captured in the aftermath of the Christchurch massacres, brought it all together, tying New Zealand's bloody beginning with its dark present. A Maori man, with a traditional face tattoo and eyes closed in mourning, locked noses with a Muslim man in the indigenous tradition called the *hongi*.[46] The Muslim man, his baseball cap tilted back, stared ahead as if piercing the face of the Maori man who knew his pain, as if he had seen it before.

The image was soul moving and embodied how indigenous Maori stood by Muslims during that nation's darkest hour. Moments when they came together as one against a white supremacist front that counts them both as inferior and expendable. There was boundless empathy, and immense power, between those two men. Power that overpowered and outsized that photo, power that almost pulls them together into a singular entity.

Power you can feel more profoundly than you can see, that fuses two Brown men—one Maori and one Muslim—against that monster of white supremacy rooted in New Zealand's history that rises again.

Turn your face toward the sun and the shadows will fall behind you.[47]

LIFE AFTER DEATH

Life doesn't really begin until you experience the death of a loved one.
MY GRANDMOTHER, Khalida Morsi

My grandmother Khalida passed away in 2003. She was the person I wanted to be before I knew my place on earth, and I orbited around her like a faithful planet rounds its sun.

The strict Egyptian matriarch who raised five children in the heart of Cairo, including my rebellious mother, was somewhat of a philosopher. I recall her sharing pearls of wisdom: "A real man does his own laundry," she would tell me, time and time again. That is only one of many gems that came from her mouth.

One day, while walking through the Jewish Quarter of Cairo, teaching me about the history of the enclave, she reflected, "Muslims can learn a great deal about Islam from our Jewish brothers." There were no more Jewish Egyptians in that neighborhood, but she was pulling on memories of the past. Perhaps she was thinking back to close friends who left Cairo but never left her.

I heard those very words again decades later when I immersed myself in Massoud Hayoun's *When We Were Arabs*, a sublime testament about the history of a Jewish family that lived in the very Egyptian streets my grandmother and I walked through.[48] I was asked to review that book, and I was honored to do so and to endorse it. Although I never shared these thoughts with the author, that book brought me closer to my own grandmother, and through its poignant nostalgia and longing, took me back to the very streets that made her.

That wonderful woman, a philosopher with a turban wrapped around her head and a sturdy cane in hand. However, my grandmother's biggest stick was always her mind. It remained sharp and steely, and did not soften as her body withered with age. She was the former head of a school in Cairo, and it was no surprise that I would try to follow in her giant footsteps, if God willed it, one day.

During my final trip to Cairo in the summer of 2004, she told me in her stern Egyptian dialect, "Life doesn't really begin until you experience the death of a loved one."

I always listened, attentively, to the words of the woman I was named after. Particularly as her life on earth reached its end, I interpreted her final words like guides, preparing me for a future that frightened me. My grandmother never said something just for the sake of saying it. Perhaps, as I reflect on those words for the thousandth time and write about them for the first, she was preparing me for the difficult *passage* to come. This passage that I write about, right now, paying homage to the gifts she unwrapped with words. Words stamped with her wit and wisdom, gifts that she gave me that live, with youthful zeal, in me and in my writing.

On February 10, 2005, I was born again. I bid my grandmother goodbye for the final time. Those final words she left me with haunted me in the days to come, and as I navigated a world where death replaced her as a companion, I finally understood what she was trying to instill in me: that death did not follow life, but was an intimate part of it.

It was fitting that we shared the same name, which derives from the Arabic word for "eternal"—Khaled, the male version of my grandmother's name, Khalida. Indeed, the memories that play through my mind, like high-definition films, live up to the measure of her name.

I see my grandmother's face every day. Her authoritative stare and high cheekbones accompany my thoughts nearly two decades after she took her last breath. She was, and remains, that tower of strength that I aspire to become and strive to honor. Indeed, her final requiem was the beginning of life anew, roaming deep in my being.

She is always there, particularly when I need guidance. Whether I'm manning the spin cycle, or making sense of the cycle of life, my grandmother's voice speaks along with every step that I take in life.

We only remember the dead persons that we know personally, or developed meaningful bonds with. Those whose words we never heard, faces we have never seen, or names we never knew, can disappear quickly into the abyss. They are dead, forever, once in life and twice in death.

Minutes after the Christchurch massacres, we knew the name of the terrorist. We knew his origins, his motives, his age, and his hateful diatribes on 8chan and other sites that gave a platform to his rage that would unravel into unimaginable violence. We also knew, in morbid detail, who his white supremacist heroes were who inspired him to walk into two mosques and indiscriminately slay fifty-one Muslims.[49]

Brenton Tarrant's life story, in a matter of minutes, claimed permanent territory in our minds. This was, after all, his aim: to become immortal in our imaginations and remain alive even after he took his last breath.

However, the bodies spread across the prayer rooms inside the Al Noor and Linwood mosques were anonymous and unknown. To the outside world, they had no names, no faces, and no individual stories before each of their lives was cut short.

They were merely "victims," sheep of the same religious flock massacred by a lone wolf who we came to know, and know very well, in the minutes that followed. While their lives in the hours that followed were vulnerable to that permanent death the media casts upon Muslims when victimized by terror.

Fifty-one Muslims died on March 15, 2019. They risked dying a second time in those fateful hours and days after the massacres.

The War on Terror, beyond the tanks and the drones, is an epistemological crusade. One that, ironically, only *humanizes* Muslims and makes them the familiar subject of news headlines when they are doing what Islamophobia warns us about: carrying out terrorism. But when Muslims die, it buries their bodies under the news coverage, deep in the abyss of forgetting, in the black hole that millions of Muslim victims gunned down by unjust wars or white supremacist terrorists are thrown into.

If there is one truth that the War on Terror has unearthed and incessantly reaffirms, it is that *Muslims are newsworthy only when villains, and seldom when victims.* The scowls of Osama Bin Laden and the faces of the nineteen 9/11 terrorists live on in our minds. While none—absolutely zero—of the nearly 13 million Muslims killed in the years before, and especially after, the War on Terror commenced claim even a small part of our memory.[50] The only Muslims we tend to remember are the culprits of violence, the craven dictators, the warmongers, and the terrorists. Most lastingly, the terrorists.

Something had to change after the horrors of March 15, 2019. This black hole Muslims were thrown into had to be filled. The lives of the fifty-one Muslims could not be buried in that permanent death that the War on Terror delivered to millions before them. That fate had to be reversed and a new precedent set.

The promise of reversal came four days after the massacres. New Zealand's prime minister, Jacinda Ardern, proclaimed before parliament, "We, in New Zealand, will give him nothing. Not even his name."[51]

That twelve-worded manifesto overpowered the seventy-four-page attempt at immortality left by the terrorist that the media, in those four days in between, meticulously analyzed and diligently decoded.[52] Ardern, poised and powerful while speaking on behalf of her tiny island nation before the world, put a halt to that.

She continued, "He sought many things from his act of terror, but one is notoriety. And that is why you will never hear me mention his name. He is a terrorist. He is a criminal. He is an extremist. But he will, when I speak, be nameless." And one without a name, in our minds today and our memories tomorrow, is dead. Dead even when still alive, poised for a lifetime sentence in prison where his scowl, his memory, and his name will rot alongside him until that irreversible end comes.[53]

Beginning with those twelve words, Ardern cut off the terrorist's lifeline to the immortality he coveted. An immortality that fed off media coverage and trending topics, one that mainstream and social media was keen on bestowing on him in the hours after the massacres. The terrorist deliberately staged the massacres for social media, as illustrated by the live-stream and the manifesto he strategically penned and left behind. As a CNN article noted the day after the massacres, it was " made for social media," the day's springboard for instant fame and lasting infamy.[54]

Ardern put a halt to these designs, deftly turning our collective sight in the other direction, moving the world to pay tribute and give life to the fifty-one victims the prevailing tide sought to bury. The Muslim victims, shot down by a white supremacist terrorist, who in those ninety-six hours after the last bullet was fired risked being buried and forgotten forever. That black hole in our memory that the War on Terror sets aside exclusively for Muslim victims, where there is no collective mourning and no elegies of respect are read, waited for them. Ardern did her part to fill that hole, stopping their fall into the forever of forgetting by doing what so many failed to do: saying their names and praising their memory.

Although inextricably tied to death, mourning is a spiritual ritual wed to life. It is, as uttered by my grandmother many years ago, an act that marks our *second* birth. And more importantly, an act that gives eternal life to those who have departed.

Ardern signaled a renewed call to give what the War on Terror had long denied Muslim victims like Mucaad Ibrahim, the youngest person murdered, and Naeem Rashid, a father who saved several lives in the Al Noor mosque before being gunned down: life after death.

The world responded. Profiles of tribute and touching commemorations were made by millions of people around the world in the days that followed. They did so on social media platforms, the modern forums of popular speech and protest, and in parks, squares, and schools. Mainstream media outlets—which had dedicated their pages to profiling the terrorist in the wake of his carnage—also turned a new page, honoring the victims and reclaiming the media terrain they had dedicated to the terrorist. Thanks to Ardern's call, faceless statistics were fleshed out into compelling elegies for readers across the world.[55]

Fifty-one lives, with each and every elegy giving life to a son or a mother, a recent immigrant or longtime citizen of New Zealand, after their bodies departed the world. Each requiem made, article written, and note of remembrance posted eroding the Islamophobic lie that Muslims are an ominous monolith, and every tribute a living rebuttal to the War on Terror baseline that Muslims are presumptively guilty and not deserving of mourning.

A grassroots battle against that vile Islamophobic baseline branded onto the bodies of the dead unfolded in the days and weeks after March 15, 2019. A battle that sought to vanquish that media canon that *Muslims were only newsworthy when villains,* and to vindicate the victims by giving them the humanity denied by the terrorist on March 15 and by mainstream media outlets in the hours that followed.

Life can change in a minute's time. At 1:45 p.m. on Friday, March 15, 2019, Naeem Rashid bowed his head in silence with brothers to his immediate left and right, and at 1:46 p.m., he was barging toward the terrorist to save their lives.[56]

Islam, for Naeem, was essentially a faith of action. It drew his deep devotion because of its emphasis on defending the oppressed, whether Muslim or non-Muslim, which took root deep within him as a child growing up in Abbotabad, Pakistan. In Pakistan, he witnessed oppression at home and in nearby Kashmir. That landscape of struggle fueled his ambition, and he ultimately climbed the ranks at Citibank and became a senior manager at its Lahore office.[57]

Individual ambition, however, was replaced by a more commanding motivation after Naeem and his wife had their first child, Talha. The money he earned in Pakistan was not enough, so in 2010, Naeem and his family left for Christchurch, New Zealand. In his new home, Naeem pursued a PhD and worked as a teacher. New Zealand quickly evolved into a home for him and his young family, which in the years to come would be expanded by two more children.[58]

As it was for thousands of newcomers before him, the first time Naeem walked into the Al Noor mosque after landing in New Zealand in 2010, it was both an old practice of faith and a bridge toward joining a new community. He walked through its doors hundreds more times in the years that followed, joined by his wife and eldest son, Talha, who often prayed to his immediate side.[59]

Then came that final Friday. A day he did not anticipate when he woke his children, carefully chose and put on his clothes, drove his family from the home they made to the mosque, cleansed his body in its bathroom, and then bowed his head and thanked his God. One last time.

One minute, everything was like it always was. The next minute came, and nothing was the same. The brothers he prayed alongside were spread across the prayer rug, with blood streaming in every direction and staining the very rug his forehead had rested on every Friday since 2010.

He stood, and time felt frozen. Then he looked around and saw what every father—every parent—could not bear to accept, could never endure. The terrorist had murdered his son Talha, only twenty-one years old.[60]

Nothing was the same. Naeem, standing in a sacred space turned into a killing field, was at that liminal impasse where life and death converge. He stood between the dead bodies, his dead son, and the terrorist. *Islam is a faith of action,* a call that Naeem heeded one final time before performing his final, and finest, act of devotion.

He lunged toward the terrorist and overpowered him in a scramble. He did not choose that fight but was commanded to it. The sordid scene, with his son lying at his foot, dead, moved him toward the terrorist.[61] Rage and desperation, fear and every emotion beyond and between, pushed him to exact justice and, perhaps unknowingly, buy time for those running toward life and away from death.

Bodies lifted from the ground and fled the mosque as Naeem fought and wrestled and clung to the shooter's body. He knew that every second meant everything.

However, the very bullets that took his son's life were embedded deep in his own body. Naeem fought the terrorist with every ounce of his faith while *dying* in that mosque. In the process, he enabled tens of his brothers and sisters—the family he had made in his new home over the past decade—to stay alive. To live onward.

He died in that very place where he prayed every Friday. Prey to a white supremacist who killed his son and killed the dreams that brought him to a country thousands of miles from his dear father, mother, and the country that mothered those dreams.

Naeem Rashid was honored as a hero by millions, including Pakistan's Prime Minister Imran Khan. That praise, however, slighted the magnitude of who he truly was and still remains. *Just a regular Muslim man, who took a stand to protect his people.* And to protect the lives of daughters and sons in the name of his lost son, Talha.

The terrorist traveled faster to the Linwood mosque across town than word of his massacre at Al Noor did. As his car speakers blared with the diatribes of white supremacist icons that fueled his frenzy, the Islamic call to prayer summoned "Sister Linda" Armstrong to the place she knew so well.[62]

Linda Armstrong, a 64-year-old white woman, grew up in Auckland, a major metropolis on New Zealand's northern island, but moved south to Christchurch and began studying Islam in her early fifties. The rising Muslim community in her adopted hometown, and the warmth of the friends she made who were part of it, inspired her to draw closer, until she too became a part of it. Linda became a Muslim as she approached the golden years of her life, and she wed Tayeb, a Malaysian man who would bring the colorful headscarves she loved from his native country.[63]

Islam's undeniable philanthropic spirit pulled Linda, a third-generation New Zealander, into the faith and community. Charity (*zakat*) is one of Islam's foundational pillars, and reading the Prophet Muhammad's declarations about the spiritual obligation to meet the needs of the hungry and underprivileged, regardless of faith, were compelling calls to action for Linda.[64]

And Linda, a Kiwi who valued action over words, stepped forward and heeded that call. In Christchurch, she volunteered at a local refugee center where families fleeing war in Syria or poverty in Somalia found sanctuary. As a Muslim who spoke their spiritual language and knew the terrain, Linda instantly became a favorite at that center, and later, at the mosque where they would worship together.

"Sister Linda," young and old Muslims from distant parts of the globe affectionately called her. And she returned that love with the service ordained by her faith, to Muslims and non-Muslims in Christchurch.[65]

Although she would not have called herself that, Linda was an activist, a title so charged in today's political discourse, so depreciated, that it is often claimed before it is earned. However, her commitment to service embodied its essential meaning, and Linda's devotion to refugees and battered women, new family and old friends, elevated her to the highest order of Christchurch's community of activists.[66]

But for Linda, the word "activist" was ultimately a synonym for Muslim. The philanthropic obligations mandated by her faith, in the country she loved, went hand in hand. Islam was not foreign to New Zealand, or antithetical to its values, and Linda's actions and very being represented that more lucidly than any manifesto could revise or deny.

"Linda had a huge heart and what little she had, she was more than happy to share with her family and Muslim community."[67] "Sister Linda," as remembered by her nephew Tony Goss, the hundreds of nephews and nieces, sisters and brothers she gained inside the refugee sanctuary where she volunteered, the women's center where she worked, and the mosque where she prayed every Friday, and where she lay—along with six other members of the family she found in her fifties—one final time.

Linda was white. Her forebears were from the very continent that had come crashing down on New Zealand and wiped out its native population hundreds of years earlier. Her skin was the same color as that of the terrorist who crashed into the Linwood mosque she attended. But those he saw as invaders, Sister Linda embraced as family, opening "her heart and home" to them.[68] And the faith the terrorist and the War on Terror marked as "savage," she clung to for salvation.

A salvation that, Linda believed with every ounce of her being and every act of service, could not be killed by drones, propaganda crusades, or fifty-one rounds of bullets. Sister Linda, and the legacy she left in Christchurch, lives on brightly within the walls of the Linwood mosque where she made her final prayer.

Death is not the end. My grandmother's words first taught me that it marks new beginnings for those that experience it. It also grants new life for those that carry the departed with them after their souls have graduated into that great mystery beyond. Indeed, we carry our loved ones with us and *within us* long after we carry their coffins to their bodies' final resting place.

The War on Terror has claimed the lives of millions of innocents whose bodies were mangled by drones and tortured into submission, bodies with no permanent resting place. We will never know the real number of those killed, their names or faces, who they loved and who they left behind, or what they dreamed of becoming in a future that was stolen from them. All of this, and every intimate detail that constructs who they were before they were permanently buried in that black abyss, will never be known.

We will never know them like we do the white supremacist terrorists who aim for immortality after their guns are emptied and their victims' bodies lie limp on church, synagogue, and mosque floors. We will never see these Muslim victims like we do the kingpins and pawns of the terrorist networks, who stay with us long after they have been slaughtered and supplanted by another terror outfit. Or, perhaps, we begin to retrench that pattern of never with a requiem of tribute, and the humanity, memory, and new life it brings.

On March 19, 2019, Jacinda Ardern stood up, and stared down the War on Terror machine that delivered permanent death to Muslim victims while extending immortality to those who mowed them down. One woman, the head of a tiny island nation shaken by its deadliest terrorist attack, uttered a twelve-word elegy that inspired millions around the world to do the same. And, as billions of eyes fixed on her capable shoulders, she set in motion the compositions and vignettes and tributes that gave life to fifty-one Muslims after death and instilled their faces and names and stories deep within us, to live on for as long as we do.

Death is not on the other side of life; they are part of an entwined whole. My grandmother shared these words with me during her final physical year on this earth, when her sturdy body grew weak and her once commanding tenor shrank to a whisper. Even after she bid farewell, that lesson came into being as she took possession of the main street of my mind, *eternally*, in the spirit of our kindred names.

Joined by the fifty-one lives that I, and the world, came to know for the first time during those transformative days that followed unspeakable terror. *They live*, along with everybody else we love, in memories that were violently aborted by the War on Terror. They live, high in the heavens and that earthly paradise of our minds, because we stood up and fought for them to claim life after death.

A fight that was chosen for us to take, much as Naeem rushed toward the terrorist to save the lives of so many. Or the fight that Linda embraced, with her heart and her hands, embracing Islam as a mandate to uplift and serve the most marginalized communities in Christchurch. Their memories live on in that terror-stricken city, forever, through the beautiful tributes that signaled the dawn of eternal life for them and the forty-nine other victims.

The dawn of a new life, of a better, purer, healthier, higher spiritual kingdom.[69]

CHAPTER SEVEN

ABLUTION AND ABOLITION

PRAYERS FOR REIGN

As Jacinda Ardern walked to the microphone, the weight of the world seemed to fall squarely on her shoulders. At thirty-seven, the youngest prime minister in New Zealand's history presided over its darkest hour. An hour when the world's expectations fell on her thin frame, and the vilest strand of the War on Terror claimed the lives of fifty-one innocents in two of her nation's mosques.

It was the Friday after that ungodly Friday that forever changed her nation. March 22, 2019, 1:40 p.m., exactly 168 hours after the Australian terrorist barged into the Masjid Al Noor, only miles from where she stood, and shot down Muslims inside a sacred space as if he were an American sniper picking off Iraqis in a war-torn nation. She approached the microphone, seven days after that event, living up to the promise on each of those days to not call the terrorist by his name.[1] And, Ardern delivered.

Many men had been in this position before her. But Jacinda Ardern was not *any man*. Apart from gender, she was different in myriad ways. If the days in the immediate aftermath of the Christchurch massacre did not solidify how far she stood apart, the words she spoke on that Friday following it did, words spoken loudly for the world to hear.

"Asalamu alaikum!" New Zealand's prime minister spoke into the microphone, uttering the universal Islamic greeting with grace and familiar lips in front of thousands of mourners in attendance and billions more glued to their television, computer, and cell phone screens.

Exactly one week after fifty-one of her fellow Kiwis were massacred by a foreign terrorist, she did not push Islam to the margins and away from the cameras like so many men before her, but deliberately chose to position it alongside her, and around her, for the whole world to see.

In that moment, as the world watched, Ardern and Islam were entwined as one. Not in the form of spiritual conversion, but in a powerful political statement that defied everything that the War on Terror zealously broadcast, by way of propaganda and policy, for two decades. She embraced Islam during an impasse when the embattled faith needed it most.

It was an overpowering symbol for Muslims standing before her and watching from home. Billions still simultaneously grieving the tragedy and fearing what monster might walk into their mosque in the days to come.

Ardern collected her breath, pausing while everybody waited for her words, and then confidently marched into uncharted territory for a "Western leader." She looked down, and then read a quote from the Prophet Muhammad, honoring him in the very tradition that Muslims do when they speak his name: "According to Prophet Muhammad— salla Allahu alayhi wa salaam (peace be upon him)—the believers in their mutual kindness, compassion and sympathy are just like one body. When any part of the body suffers, the whole body feels pain. New Zealand mourns with you, we are one."[2]

I was driven to tears, and I looked at my mother, who also had tears in her eyes. I watched this event unfold alongside my mother, on the other side of the world in a nation that elected a *leader* who was Ardern's antithesis. "Only a woman can behave like her," my mother shared, with tears in her brown eyes. "She is a mother, she understands the pain of giving life and the horror of losing children."

We, and billions around the world, were moved at how Ardern mothered a moment that no man could handle or could helm with the empathy that extended her words, and the arms in which she embraced the family of the victims tighter than the hijab she wrapped around her head in respect.

Ardern's message was clear. Islam was neither the "other" nor the "invader." Islam and New Zealand are one integrated "body," not civilizational enemies pitted against one another by a War on Terror or a white supremacist bent on mass murder. She believed that, firmly, as the weight of the world fell on her shoulders that holy Friday, a week after her nation's unholiest day.[3]

It was clear, as the Islamic call to prayer rang after Ardern spoke. Ardern not only heeded the call, but overpowered the deathly shrill of that War on Terror that invaded her nation and left fifty-one fellow Zealanders dead.

"We are one." A resounding refutation to the "with us or against us" ultimatum uttered by the first executive steward of the War on Terror, the "Islam hates us" bombshell by the latest, and the endless slurs and slights of Muslims made by male presidents and prime ministers in between.[4]

The prayers of so many Muslims for a leader who saw them as everyday people, instead of terror threats, were met by a leader who had not reached the age of forty. A politician whom many, overwhelmingly men, believed could not lead a nation before she was elected in October 2017, the first female prime minister of her country. The sexism continued after her historic win, but she strode past it, shedding it with grace.[5] And the leadership she embodied during the week after the

Christchurch massacre made history that will be remembered far beyond the boundaries of her island nation and that is embedded forever in the hearts of Muslims everywhere.

During the previous week, Ardern had donned a hijab while grieving alongside mourning families. She listened attentively while visiting the recovering mosques, and most potently, repeated and again repeated, as if it were a ritual, the names of the fifty-one Muslim victims.

Ardern refused to do what mainstream media did in the direct aftermath of the massacres. She did not utter the shooter's name once, and blocked his path toward the fame he desperately craved: "He is a terrorist. He is a criminal. He is an extremist. But he will, when I speak, be nameless."[6]

These were indictments that pundits and politicians typically reserved for Muslims. Ardern turned the War on Terror tenet that tethered terrorism to Islam on its head. And she pierced the protective shield of whiteness by calling the shooter precisely what he was, a *terrorist*.

She led in the days after that ungodly Friday in ways that nobody has, and few could, during the War on Terror's downward arc. Clad in a hijab and a traditional black gown on the Friday after it, attire that symbolized "inferiority" and "weakness" in the eyes of French legislators who voted in that country's Hijab Ban in 2004, Ardern's strength was on full display.

Her model of leadership was sublime, motherly, muscular, and unapologetic. It offered new possibilities for leadership in a world ravaged by nativist populism and unhinged Islamophobia, on a stage of tremendous magnitude. But most powerfully, Ardern was being her natural self. This was not political posturing or "woke" performance, but an organic display of who she was.[7] As a mother, a wife, a fellow citizen, and the prime minister of a nation sunk into its darkest hour.

Ardern's sincerity streamed from a place of empathy, empathy that absorbed the full violence of Islamophobia. The massacres at the Al Noor and Linwood mosques highlighted the reach and realness of that evil. They also revealed its relationship to the loaded rhetoric unleashed by divisive populists, most notably the United States' Donald Trump, France's Marine Le Pen, India's Narendra Modi, and Brazil's Jair Bolsonaro, whose brazen demonization of Islam and its adherents have armed white supremacist vigilantes to permanently ban Muslims with loaded guns instead of rhetoric.

"What the devil gave the world in Trump, God delivered [as] an angel in Jacinda Ardern," my mother stated in the colorful Arabic only her tongue could deliver. *Real recognizes real.* From the mouth of one powerful female who could see that same strength in another.

After the Christchurch massacres, it became lucidly apparent that xenophobic populism, and the Islamophobia that marches alongside it, is not empty rhetoric or a distant phenomenon. It is an enemy within.

The shock of the massacre comes at a time when Western democracies are being reshaped in line with the image of xenophobic and white supremacist populism.[8] This process has pushed for the imposition of veil and Muslim travel bans, mounting surveillance, en masse bulldozing of Muslim homes, and restrictions on public calls to prayer—all policies that the Christchurch terrorist claimed as inspirations and that the War on Terror facilitated or laid a foundation for.

On March 15, 2019, Jacinda Ardern and the world came to understand how these policies radicalize white supremacist terrorists like Tarrant. The massacres also revealed the risks of following the death spiral of hateful populism that is sinking the United States and Europe. A different course was possible, and Ardern recognized that during her nation's most fateful hours.

In the aftermath of New Zealand's deadliest terror attack, Ardern turned away from this global Islamophobic tide. Instead, she embraced everything that the War on Terror branded as "uncivilized" and embodied what it marked as terroristic: she wore the hijab, read from Islamic scripture, and paid tribute to Islam and its final messenger and prophet by reciting the ancient Arabic greeting followed by Islamic scripture. That display, in and of itself, was revolutionary, and the strides she made before and after it stand as a beacon of possibility.[9] The possibility of transformative leadership that could combat Islamophobic populism and counter the standing model of toxic control embedded by male presidents and prime ministers.

As her country stood silent and the whole world was watching a week after the terror attacks, the call to prayer reverberated as a decisive blow to the politics of Islamophobia gripping governments across the globe. This was not political gameswomanship or being swallowed by the tide of woke performative dogma.[10] It was personal. Fifty-one New Zealanders, fifty-one of Ardern's citizens, were murdered only miles away from where she donned the hijab so gracefully, quoted the prophet so eloquently, and listened to the Islamic prayer so honorably.

In the turbulence of the aftermath of the attack, Ardern was shaping a new model of engagement with Muslims that presidents before her, all men, promised but could not deliver. Whether it was Barack Obama swearing to start "a new beginning" with the "Muslim world" in Cairo but delivering more death, or Emmanuel Macron's pale commitment to integrate France's embattled Muslim population but dealing them the same familiar blows of scorn and isolation.[11]

Ardern's model of leadership did not espouse religion as a marker of divided worldviews or distinct civilizations, but instead embraced difference, as reflected in the words of Black feminist Audre Lorde, who wrote in *Our Dead behind Us*, "It is not our differences that divide us. It is our inability to recognize, accept, and celebrate those differences."[12]

Ardern honored the victims with words, and more importantly, with actions, some showcased onscreen and others not captured by the camera. It was not widely known in the aftermath of the terror attacks that Ardern authorized payment for all fifty-one funerals, regardless of the victims' citizenship status, and spearheaded a new policy that restricted the sale of the military semi-automatic weapons that led to those funerals.[13]

Ardern could not end a War on Terror started by men, or preempt the terror it incited in white supremacist vigilantes who preyed on mosques in her country and Muslims beyond it. But as prime minister of a nation that endured the lethal reckoning of the War on Terror's ugliest spawn, she could steer a new course for her nation and offer a model for others to emulate. And, in the days between those two Fridays in the middle of March in 2019, one woman did what no man dared to do.

After all, it was Khadija, a woman that first saw the beauty in Islam when the world opposed it and its first messenger, the Prophet Mohammed.[14] She was the first person to embrace Islam, and help pave a pathway for a new course. A woman first then, when the faith would face its first and formative battles. And a woman first today, when Muslims endured the latest massacre dealt by the War on Terror.

She believed in me when people rejected me.[15]

THE MESSAGE

> I know where I'm going and I know the truth and I don't have to be what you want me to be. I'm free to be what I want.
>
> MUHAMMAD ALI

It is one of history's greatest ironies that one of the world's most beloved men also belonged to its most despised religion. But for Muhammad

Ali, a fighter who scaled the tallest odds to claim victory in the "Rumble in the Jungle" in Zaire, and who had faced a more formidable foe, the American military, in the Supreme Court years earlier, what others thought seldom mattered.[16] The biblical tales of a Black David defeating one Goliath after other Goliaths won Ali the adoration of billions around the world, and after he died on July 3, 2016, made him beloved all over the world. But it was his unshakable fidelity to his convictions, political and spiritual, that made him immortal.

Ali was no politician. But everything he did, inside the ring and beyond its rope, was pointedly *political*. He was always aware of that. And just like he threw that blinding jab and signature right cross, everything he did and said was delivered with thudding *intent*.

Long before he bore the name of Islam's final prophet, the young Cassius Clay was a lightning rod. Dubbed the "Louisville Lip" for his bravado and brash talk beyond the ring, Clay emerged on the boxing scene during the golden age of its heavyweight division. The era intersected with the accelerating Civil Rights Movement, a time of radical transformation for a nation clinging desperately to its foundation of racial apartheid. It was a movement he indelibly impacted, and he emerged into one of its lasting icons.[17]

Clay not only transformed with the times, but ahead of them. Just like he did in that Miami ring on February 25, 1964, against feared knockout artist Sonny Liston, who he dethroned to become the youngest heavyweight champion in the division's history. Ali had a penchant for making history, within and especially outside of boxing's squared circle.

In Clay, the world had its youngest, brashest, and Blackest heavyweight champion, during the thick of the turbulent sixties. But for the boxing savant with the charisma of a prophet, being a sporting champion was not enough. On the day after making sports history, he took on the name of the Prophet and chose to write his own history.

Cassius Clay evolved into Muhammad Ali. And in doing so embraced a new name and an old faith, Islam, which at the time occupied the mortifying intersection of Black radicalism and foreign menace in the white imagination.[18] A white imagination that, in the 1960s, clung tight to the dying body of Jim Crow while dreaming that Joe Frazier, George Foreman, or Jerry Quarry would knock the Islam out of Ali.

But Ali defeated them all, including that *great white hope* that controlled the media outlets. That rival incessantly called him Clay, pushed him to question his defiance to American racial injustice at home and marauding war abroad, and asked him—over and over again—to renounce the religion that inspired him inside the ring, and more profoundly beyond the ropes.[19]

He did none of that. Always punching back harder than the pugilists he faced holding microphones or wearing boxing gloves. That is what made him Muhammad Ali. A man so truculent, so transcendent, so prophetic, that he was able to convert limitless scorn into undying adoration. And along with his rise, uplift a religion that he wore more proudly than any championship belt.

Muhammad Ali was no politician, but he knocked out the myth that the world of sport is segregated from the realm of politics. In doing so, Ali crushed the same limiting binaries with his fists that Edward Said did with his pen. Ultimately, he proved that two spheres believed to be diametrically opposed and segregated could be harmoniously integrated. That, more than anything, was Ali's most prophetic message.

The modern case of American football player Colin Kaepernick, who took a knee to stand up for racial justice, testifies to the indelible impact of Ali's message and to the transformative effect that sports, and athletes told to "shut up and play," can have on the world if they speak up.[20] So impactful that, during moments of profound change, sports and politics can blur into one undeniable force for progress. This force took center stage at the 2020 NBA playoffs, when a historic player-led boycott pierced the bubble that protected the athletes from a virus and the myth that racism does not penetrate into their lives.[21]

Muhammad Ali championed a new kind of athlete, athletes who were intentional about using their stage to shine light on political injustices that harmed those who looked like them or those who believed like them. He did so naturally, and not by being a politician. Rather, he remained unapologetically himself on the field of competition, and on the endless field of politics that surrounded and swallowed it.

His is a living legacy that today continues to inspire Muslim athletes performing in the face of the War on Terror and the Islamophobia it pits against them. One of these Muslim athletes shares the name of the boxing icon, and with a red shirt instead of red gloves, is leaving a mark that would make Ali proud.

The crowd of predominantly white English men, all dressed in Devil Red, met at their regular tailgating section outside Liverpool's legendary Anfield Stadium. From a distance, the group of football fanatics could be easily mistaken for one of the National Action or neo-Nazi gangs that menaced immigrants and Muslims in one of the working-class neighborhoods of Liverpool. Several could be mistaken for the anti-Muslim shooter who unloaded bullets into a hookah bar in Hanau, Germany, on February 19, 2020, killing ten innocent people the evening after Mohamed Salah and his club laced up their cleats to face Atlético Madrid.[22]

But this *gang*, punching the sky with their fists while singing in unison, were not bigots or hatemongers. One of the men, with a closely shaved head and a red Liverpool F.C. jersey with the number eleven on the back and the name M. Salah emblazoned above it, led the group in song:

Mo Salah, la, la, la, la, La, la, la, la, la, la,

If he's good enough for you,

He's good enough for me,

If he scores another few then I'll be Muslim too,

If he's good enough for you,

He's good enough for me,

Then sitting in a mosque is where I wanna be.

Everywhere Mohamed Salah played, fans like the majority-white group exploded in song in reverence of the soccer wunderkind bearing the name of Islam's final messenger and prophet.[23] It was funny, refreshing, but most of all, a new song in a league historically marred by racism and bigotry.

These white men, who would strike fear in the hearts of most Muslims and push any minority passing by them to walk on the opposite side of the street, were not conspiring to attack Muslims. In fact, they huddled around one another in reverence of the person who may well be the most famous Muslim in the world today.

Mohamed Salah thrust himself into the center of the soccer world out of relative obscurity. In 2017, Liverpool F.C.—one of the top teams in England's Premier League, and one of the most famous clubs in the world—signed the curly haired, bearded Egyptian to its roster.[24]

The deeply spiritual Salah, mild-mannered and humble off the field, was a lightning bolt on it. He quickly became the best player on his new team, and rapidly emerged into one of the world's finest footballers with his new club. During his legendary 2017 and 2018 campaigns, Salah scored an astounding forty-three goals. The mark set a new record for the club, only four goals shy of the English league's longstanding record.[25]

It was a new day, or at least it seemed like one. A man named Mohamed shattered longstanding English records, and did so with that patented smile on his face. But the feats Salah achieved with his feet were not as earth shaking as what he did after putting the ball behind the net. Immediately after scoring a goal, Salah would fall to his knees and bow his head on the field. This was no celebration. This was prayer.

Salah performed the Islamic prostration forty-three times during his inaugural season with the club, and many, many times after that, in raucous stadiums, before millions of fans in England and billions more around the world. Salah's emergence as one of the global game's most recognizable faces came at a time when Brexit emboldened xenophobes in England and Islamophobia swelled throughout the nation and Europe.[26]

The juxtaposition was surreal, and the scenes inspired by Salah were magical. In the face of these hateful currents, Salah followed in the footsteps of his boxing namesake, Muhammad Ali, and remained unapologetically Muslim. He was not as natural or adroit an activist as Ali, but his conspicuous prayers, on-the-field prostrations, and very identity on soccer's highest stages offered a vivid rebuttal to the prevailing politics of the day.

Adoring fans, the vast majority non-Muslim, emulated his prayers, wore his jersey, and chanted, "If he scores another few, than I'll be Muslim too." This impact may not have been Salah's goal, but it ranked as his greatest accomplishment.

Salah, in the world of football, was challenging the Islamophobia that encircled it and the people around it. This "Salah effect" was not just anecdotal, but measurable.[27] "Per the Stanford University Immigration Policy Lab, Salah is credited with singlehandedly reducing Islamophobia and hate crimes in Liverpool since he signed with the club in June 2017."[28]

The Stanford University study found that hate crimes in the metropolitan Liverpool area declined by 19 percent and anti-Muslim comments were down 50 percent since Salah joined Liverpool F.C. in 2017.[29] Salah's impact was quantifiable, and his on-the-field play and off-the-field presence were changing hearts and minds during an impasse when nativism was spiking upward in England and Islamophobia was proliferating across the world. In July 2020, Salah delivered Liverpool its first English title in thirty years.[30] In the process, he achieved club immortality and engraved the name Mohamed in the hearts and minds of fans.

His mark was undeniable, his impact global. Retrenching those stereotypes on the coast of Gaza, where a Palestinian child wearing the same black curly locks and kicking a ball up the beach dreams of following in a fellow Muslim's footsteps. Or atop the grassy National Mall in Washington, DC, where a white undergraduate at Georgetown University dons Salah's famous red "11" Liverpool jersey blocks away from where the War on Terror was crafted and kicks forward today.

Sports are no stranger to racism, and indeed, Islamophobia. It rears its ugly head from the stands in stadiums and sinks itself in news printed about Muslim athletes striving to be the best in their sport while remaining true to their beliefs.[31]

The world of football is marred by white supremacy, as leagues throughout Europe vividly illustrate. No matter how virulent and violent the *color of combat* is on the most celebrated pitches in England, Spain, and Italy, it is no match for the realm of boxing—as the trials of Jack Johnson, Sugar Ray Robinson, and Muhammad Ali demonstrate—and the broader world of combat sports. The "unforgivable Blackness" that Jack Johnson reckoned with, when he became the first Black world heavyweight boxing champion in 1908, enabled the unapologetic Black Muslimness of Muhammad Ali decades later.[32] While Ali's iconic rounds against bigotry are recounted again and again, racism remains a central pugilist within the rings of combat sports today.

This is particularly true in mixed martial arts (MMA), where there are no teammates to support you or bench to fall back on. Only one man or woman stands alone in that ring. Or in the case of Khabib Nurmagomedov, the mild-mannered mixed martial artist from Dagestan, inside a cage surrounded by crowds of right-winged white fans. It's a world he stepped into twenty-eight times, and on each occasion, he stepped out undefeated as a fighter and unchanged as a Muslim.

In the words of legendary fight trainer Teddy Atlas, "You don't play boxing."[33] This tenet rings especially true for MMA, its combat sports' sibling, where fighters risk their very lives every time they climb into that cage. For Khabib, the Muslim fighter known universally by one name, each one of his opponents—and the Ultimate Fighting Championship's (UFC) rapidly swelling fan base—learned, very quickly, *not to play* with his religion.

Khabib, who wears a traditional beard and prays before he enters the cage and again before he leaves it, has resurrected the spirit of Ali in the fight game. During the lead-up to his match with his nemesis and the sport's most bankable star, Conor McGregor, Khabib put his faith, Islam, on center stage along with him.

Wearing his signature Dagestani *papakha* (sheepskin hat), Khabib stepped onto the scale for the mandatory weigh-in before the bout. With Joe Rogan to his right, and thousands of fans shouting a mix of praise and expletives at the still-faced fighter, Khabib tapped his chest then nodded his head. "Not me," he whispered, and then pointed toward the sky—a quiet Islamic ritual of praise, giving all credit to God.

It was divine and defiant at the same time. It harkened back to images of Muhammad Ali praying in his corner of the ring before meeting his rival in the center. For Khabib, faith and fighting were one and the same. There was no divide.

Khabib's recognition of Allah spurred jeers and slurs from the crowd. Islamophobia, a day before the UFC's biggest fight in its twenty-five-year history, was a more menacing foe than the charismatic Irishman Khabib would trade blows with the following night.

Rogan, the renaissance podcaster who interviews thinkers by day and fighters by night, moved the microphone in front of Khabib for the ceremonial weigh-in interview. Khabib paused, and stared ahead with eyes so confident and poised.

"What will he say," I wondered, following the tense buildup for the fight. The turbulent promotion had been tainted by McGregor calling Khabib's headscarved wife a "towel" and referring to the Muslim fighter himself as a "mad backwards cunt," just two examples from the ugly litany of Islamophobic barbs he threw at the fighter and his faith before they collided in the octagon.[34] The boos and expletives in the stadium drowned out the cheers from the scattered Muslim fans in the audience, many of whom—like my friend Ahmed—remained silent because "I did not want one of those crazy white fans to hit me and my younger brother."[35]

Minutes later, Khabib would speak up on Ahmed's behalf, and on behalf of the millions of Muslims watching at home who found in him a new fighting champion, a new Ali.

"First of all, I want to say Alhamdul'llah, God give me everything!" Khabib proclaimed loudly and proudly, filling the raucous arena with the divine Arabic praise giving thanks to the Most High. The boos rained down on him, but Khabib grew more defiant in the face of opposition, like he always did. "Al-hamd-ul-llah," he again stated, breaking the word into its conjoined syllables for greater effect.[36]

He then continued, "I know that . . . I know that you guys don't like this."[37] He was calling out their Islamophobia, *directly*, on the UFC's highest stage and in front of its president, Dana White, an unabashed supporter of Donald Trump himself. It was a scene to behold, and for one Muslim fighter, a stage he did not shy away from.

Khabib seemed alone in an arena packed with Conor McGregor fans, many of whom likely shared McGregor's unsavory views of Islam and Muslims. But he did not cower in front of them or capitulate to the UFC's failure to censor the Islamophobia coming from the stands or the lips of the Irishman McGregor.[38]

In fact, Khabib, never felt alone in that stadium that Friday or in the cage on fight night. His religion and devotion to God equipped him with the might to stand strong in the face of the hate that came from the fans and the mercurial Irishman he soundly defeated.[39]

By dispatching McGregor and maintaining his perfect record, Khabib became one of world sport's most visible stars. And in the process, he became even more conscious of his role and impact as a Muslim athlete in a world marred by Islamophobia. Called the Muhammad Ali of his generation, a title he himself would not accept, Khabib confronted the challenges that came his way by remaining steadfastly himself, and steadfastly Muslim.[40]

Conscious of his unrivaled stature with Muslims and cognizant of the non-Muslim eyes that followed him, Khabib stated, "Non-Muslims don't read the Quran, they don't read the *Hadith* [the collected record of the Prophet Mohammed's deeds], they read you. So be a good ambassador of Islam."[41]

Like Ali, Khabib's greatest challenges were bouts he took on outside of the ring. Hailing from Dagestan, an embattled region of modern Russia that is overwhelmingly Muslim, Khabib walks the tightrope of representing a people bludgeoned by Soviet rule and, during the War on Terror, representing an *ummah*—the global Muslim community—that is conflated with "terrorists" and "backwardness." He hears this from his opponents and fans but never strays from his spiritual path.

He is, after all, a fighter. Doing what he does best, inside and outside of the octagon. Khabib "shook up the world" by becoming the UFC's top pound-for-pound fighter. But more importantly, like Ali, a marginalized and maligned people's champ during a moment of "civilizational war," in front of unhinged fanatics shouting slurs and toting semi-automatic weapons.

While victory against this war, and the Islamophobia it summons from each corner of that cage, seems daunting, Khabib retired with an undefeated, unblemished record. He is widely considered one of the best MMA fighters ever, and by some, the greatest ever. When he fought, he extended that elusive hand of hope to nearly 2 billion Muslims when they tune in to one of his bouts. Since he has retired, he has paved the way for the emergence of other Muslim fighters to continue his legacy, including Palestinian American Belal Mohammed, the Chechen phenom Khamzat Chimaev, and Khabib's own prodigy, Islam Makhachev in the world of MMA. And in boxing, champions like Julian Williams and Devin Haney carry Ali's torch forward, These names represent the tip of the Muslim iceberg taking MMA and boxing by storm, deepening Islam's imprint on the world of combat sports deepened by Khabib.[42]

And, for a man named Muhammad watching from on high, instills a sense of satisfaction that the work he pioneered in the world of sport, down below, is in good and able hands.

Rumble, young man, rumble.

THINGS FALL APART

> If you don't like my story, write your own.
> CHINUA ACHEBE, *Things Fall Apart*

In Boston's Waterfront Park, in the colonial city's North End, a familiar face that reigned over it and hundreds of other squares and parks all over the "civilized world" stood headless.

Christopher Columbus, or the statue erected in his glory, had been decapitated.[43] In the days to come, that headless statute and many more like it would be surrounded by a new crop of historians, who took hold of the present with the same hands that decapitated that statue. They stormed the streets of Boston, Baltimore, and other American cities near and far.

With defiance, they surrounded the statutes of Columbus, Stonewall Jackson, Robert E. Lee, and other totems of a past that excluded them from the national body. But more ambitiously, this wave aimed to cut the head off of a racist beast that had lorded it over the nation since its inception. This racist beast, like Columbus, was a seafaring one, that exported empire through wars of terror crusading as democracy.

Christopher Columbus never set foot on the American mainland, but he ruled over our imagination as the "discoverer" of a nation long inhabited by indigenous peoples, and the earliest "pioneer" of a state that built its wealth on the backs of enslaved Africans. This history was made official in the textbooks we read when inducted into the American school system, and drilled even deeper into our heads each year we celebrated Columbus Day.

One June 9, 2020, protestors chopped off the head of the Columbus statue in Boston, and in the coming days, sought to demystify the history of lies that it stood atop.[44] Columbus, like the rows of statues raised across the country, embodied an "invented past." A past, in the words of James Baldwin, an American founding father who has yet to have a statue erected in his honor, "cracks and crumbles under the pressures of life like clay in a season of drought."[45]

Following the murder of George Floyd in Minneapolis on May 25, 2020, those statues and the nation they stood atop would face that very season of drought. Those seven minutes and forty-six seconds, when an unarmed Black man's life was pressed out of his helpless body by the knee of a policeman, would inspire waves of rage that toppled statues and sprang a new season of American revolution.[46]

"A Black American Spring," as it was called by my friend and law professor Priscilla Ocen, rising a decade after that very season changed Arab nations.[47] A spring fueled by the desire to make a new nation live up to its lofty ideals by unmaking its ugly past, representations of which that still stand, like hardened and iron-fisted overseers, in parks and squares across the country—in places where Black people aspire to be free, and just aspire to *be*. "Dismantling empire is a multifaceted affair," Cornel West observed, and the music of statues crashing to the ground is the sound of revolution.[48]

I had complicated feelings about the removal of these statues and memorials. On the one hand, they stood to symbolize the tainted and racist history that made the nation, lurid reminders of that past that could activate future generations of Americans to build anew, and construct new totems of progress and possibility. On the other hand, these men—all of them white—enslaved and ethnically cleansed, raped and pillaged, slaying anyone who didn't look or believe like them en route to building a nation in their narrow, narcissistic reflection. "Thomas Jefferson owned a Qur'an?" my friend Hamza asked, picking up Denise Spellberg's book about Islam and the Founding Fathers as we sat in Haraz Coffee House in Dearborn, Michigan.[49] "Yes," I responded, "but he also owned 600 slaves."[50]

The granite of statues conceals the ugly side of "great men" who leveraged the power the law endowed them with to commit great evils, unforgivable evils that stand alongside foundational nation-making achievements.

History, at its truest, is more labyrinth than monolith. Things fall apart—both statues and history. And building new ones, more truthful versions, begins with tearing old and deceitful ones down, especially as the War on Terror continues to drone down innocent Muslim bodies in Mogadishu and police suffocate the life out of unarmed Black men in Minneapolis, blocks away from "Little Mogadishu," where Somalis resettled after the American invasion of the 1990s.

The rate of Black people killed should matter more than the fate of white statues. But in a world where the War on Terror militarizes imperialist aggression abroad and law enforcement at home, the lone effigies Black and Muslim people claim are the dead bodies of loved ones spread across distant village squares or hard urban pavements.

The sordid images of George Floyd gasping for air while calling for his dead mother were captured by a bystander recording the murder on her phone. Shortly after, the video of an innocent man's life being taken away, without remorse from the policeman, was viewed globally. Floyd's cries of "Mama! Mama, I'm through!" followed by the familiar plea "I can't breathe!" marked far more than just another police murder of an unarmed black man.[51]

Everyone saw it, all eight minutes and forty-six seconds of it.

Viewed through an international prism, Floyd's murder offered an ominous metaphor for the power inequities that exist across racial, ethnic, gender, and religious lines across the world, and it connected the killing of a Black man in Minneapolis with the unseen murders of unnamed Muslims in Kashmir, Iraq, and other places the War on Terror has turned into killing fields.

The weeks that followed the murder of Floyd on May 25, 2020, confronted the very lies that undergirded a racist underbelly that would not go away. People took to the streets, risking their lives to a pandemic that loomed above and lurked around them, and stood eye-to-eye with police while lifting up the names of Floyd, Breonna Taylor, and a seemingly endless list of Black men and women killed by police in America.[52]

These victims were gunned down on account of who they were and what they could not change. Their racial identity, *their Blackness,* marked them as presumptive criminals to the police who shot them inside their own homes or choked the last breath out of them on the street, in front of cameras, for all to see.[53]

The words of a thirteen-year-old student from Seattle, Washington, unveiled the wicked racism institutionalized within police departments across the United States, and seemingly, wherever Black lives struggle to simply *be.* "If my blackness is threatening, I will never truly be unarmed to them," stated Desi Maher, in a city where protestors took over several blocks and organized to defund the police.[54] In a city,

Seattle, where a hatemonger aimed anti-Muslim barbs at me after I presented my first book, *American Islamophobia,* in a church two years earlier.

Justin Hansford, a law professor at Howard University, observed, "Anti-Blackness is a global phenomenon; although it manifests itself differently in different countries, it is part of the same hate, and it connects people who experience it all over the world."

Hansford, who was in Ferguson, Missouri, during the first wave of the Black Lives Matter protests in 2014, noted that the protests following the killing of George Floyd were "far larger than. . . in 2014, largely because of the international solidarity infrastructure built since Mike Brown was killed."[55] In addition to international solidarity, the same surveillance mechanisms deployed against Muslims in the United States are extended to silence and prosecute BLM activists, linking these heavily policed communities in myriad ways.[56]

Although Black and Muslim identities overlap intimately in the demographics of France, the United States, and places beyond and in between, anti-Blackness and Islamophobia are distinct branches of bigotry.[57] Yet young Desi Maher's trenchant observation highlights the way in which both existences are ascribed deviance on account of their racialized identities. In the same fashion that law enforcement, and the judicial and carceral institutions that orbit and abet it, assign criminalized threat to Blackness, the War on Terror and its central purveyors assign suspicion of terrorism to Muslim bodies.

As articulated first by law scholar Natsu Saito, the 9/11 terror attacks and the policies that followed "raced" Muslims as terrorists.[58] The War on Terror and the resulting cascade of crusades examined in this book embedded this form of stereotyped threat globally, and consequently justified punitive action against Muslims by governments, vigilantes, and every societal element in between.

Being Muslim, in places like China or India, was enough to face the wrath of structural or private Islamophobia, while *acting Muslim—*

freely exercising one's faith in line with one's spiritual beliefs—invited suspicion and scorn in France and everywhere that distinctive French plague of Islamophobia was exported.[59] In New Zealand, on that unholy Friday in 2019 in Christchurch, praying before Allah invited the same murder that befell George Floyd. Fifty-one times over.

The spring of 2020 felt like a new season. A global front against anti-Black racism was galvanized, in the face of and faster than any pandemic, signifying the possibility that the slogan "Black Lives Matter" could manifest meaningful and sustainable change. Meanwhile, Muslims—Black and non-Black—envisioned that the very groundswell that marched against anti-Black racism could also, one day, be pointed in the direction of the War on Terror and the Islamophobia it spawns across the globe.

The road that the Black Lives Matter movement blazed and broadened in the spring of 2020, for marginalized people of all stripes, including Muslims, offered hope for a collateral movement against the War on Terror and the Islamophobia it fuels.

Ahmed Abuznaid, a Palestinian American lawyer and filmmaker, observed, "This is a moment where a collective growth of consciousness can be had around the Muslim Ban, headscarf bans, and war on Muslim and Arab countries. These protests can spark people to draw important connections between anti-Blackness and Islamophobia and then look to challenge the War on Terror more robustly in the days to come."[60]

Keeanga-Yamahtta Taylor drew additional connections unseen by many, observing that "the ever-expanding security state, justified by the 'War on Terror,' becomes the pretext for greater police repression at home—which, of course, disproportionately affects African Americans and Latino/as in border regions."[61]

Sometimes, the connections are so obvious that little effort is needed to make them. Five days after George Floyd was killed, an autistic

Palestinian man walking to his special-needs school in the Old City of Jerusalem was gunned down by Israeli police.

At thirty-two, Eyad Hallaq was fifteen years younger than Floyd but was profiled on account of his color and identity. Police chased the disabled man, who had routinely told his mother how much he "fear[ed] passing the police on his way to class."[62] Eyad had good reason to fear the police, the majority of them younger than him. Shaken by fear and autism, he always paced nervously past them, which a trigger-happy policeman interpreted as suspicion on the final Saturday in May.

Eyad would not make it back home to his mother on May 30, 2020. The ancient streets he walked en route to his school, and the intersections he cursed where police stood like statues, the familiar scene of his greatest fears, would be the site of his last stand.

He heard that word he had read on the news. That word levied against his uncles and cousins. That word with which every Palestinian, young or old, abled or disabled, was branded. That word, that vile lie, assigned to every Muslim walking on those biblical streets near their home or modern cities far from it, by the War on Terror and the preexisting wars it reinforced.

"*Terrorist!*" the policeman yelled, and Eyad ran. He thought of his mother while racing away from that gun, like George Floyd called his mama while being crushed by a knee. He ran toward her and away from the Israeli policeman, away from that vile lie shot in his direction. That lie that followed him because he was Palestinian, which was reason alone to stop and arrest somebody in the place he called home. He ran until he could not run any more. Until the bullet caught up with him, threw him to the ground, and stole his final breath.[63]

Eyad Hallaq was murdered for being what he was born as and could not shed. He was Palestinian. A reality he could not run from or dodge, only blocks from the only home he and his people knew.

Eyad Hallaq's death possessed me as the images of George Floyd's murder, all seven minutes and forty-six seconds of it, scrolled through my head like a horror film playing in my mind. I was en route to Atlanta from Richmond, Virginia, leaving a city that would soon be stormed by protestors and arriving in another poised to be in the eye of the new BLM storm. In a world where those three words, "Black Lives Matter," would be emblazoned on storefronts everywhere, uttered by politicians near and far, and branded on the packaging of Fortune 100 companies. It remained a sobering reality that the lives of Palestinians like Eyad Hallaq did not matter to those wielding power.[64]

I drove south to Georgia, remembering the words of Palestinian novelist Sahar Khalifeh in the classic *Wild Thorns,* when Israeli soldiers chased another Palestinian protagonist near his home: "As he disappeared into the darkness, the soldiers were already beating their rifle butts against the door below."[65] Eyad was submerged into that final darkness, from which there was no right of return. Dead, with a policeman standing over his limp body, holding his rifle to his side as its butt kissed that holy, fractured land. A portrait of murder in Old Jerusalem similar to the mise-en-scène of misery that had colored the Minneapolis streets with blood and horror only five days earlier.

"Connecting the lines" between racism in the United States and the world at large, in the words of Abuznaid, must be followed immediately by disconnecting the lies. Kindred lies that suffocated a Black man on the streets of Minneapolis and murdered a Palestinian man in the heart of the Holy Land. The War on Terror and white supremacy, unfolding in the heart of the Midwest and the center of the Mideast, tied together by lies levied against Black and Brown people that must be toppled, and toppled again, like the statues lording over our public squares and collective imaginations.

"I don't know if I can explain how it feels to know that the person holding the gun to your head sees you as a worthless animal," wrote Amer Zahr. An ode written by a Palestinian man about his people, every letter and line of which speaks to the plight of Black people in America.[66]

The racism ripping through the United States has been dubbed by many as "white supremacy's last stand."[67] A final war waged by a dying beast that sees its place in the world declining, and its numbers diminishing in an America becoming more Black and Brown.

Demographers claim that America will, in 2045, become a "majority minority" nation. This will be the first time in American history that the nation will be home to more nonwhites than whites, which leaves the "future of whiteness" in the balance as demographics shift against it.[68]

This forecast has only exacerbated that *white fragility* that stifles candid conversations about racism today, and that for centuries drove mass displacement and Manifest Destiny, mass incarceration and enslavement.[69] A fragility so precarious and potent that it also fuels imperial ambitions old and new, as evident most vividly in the War on Terror and its domestic and global crusades to maintain the demographic and political supremacy of whites—at all costs.

The indefinite future of whiteness has, in the United States and beyond, unleashed a violent underbelly of rage within the corridors of political power and on the street. This fragility, or "white anxiety," as some have called it, is why demagogues engage in fearmongering, stirring up anxiety about Mexican "illegals," Asian immigrants who take "American jobs," Muslims who are branded as terrorists, and Black men and women exercising their First Amendment rights.[70] Its power, once unclothed of its bluster and stripped down to its loins, is nothing but fear.

James Baldwin wrote, during the thick of the Civil Rights Movement,

It is now absolutely clear that white people are a minority in the world—so severe a minority that they now look rather more like an invention—and that they cannot possibly hope to rule any longer. If this is so, why is it not also possible that they achieved their original dominance by stealth and cunning and bloodshed and in opposition to the will of Heaven, and not, as they claim, by Heaven's will? And if *this* is so, then the sword they have used so long against others can now, without mercy, be used against them.[71]

The BLM protests, for whites observing from afar with fear, embodied that very sword. This is why they, and their mouthpieces in mainstream media, castigated the protesters as "looters" and "thugs" and "terrorists," seeking to strip the legitimacy of their grievances with the dulling edge of the sword they had swung for so long. But what unfolded in Minneapolis and other cities across the world was no sword seeking retribution or vengeance.

What unfolded in the summer of 2020 after Floyd's murder was indeed a new season. Whites, in fact, marched alongside protestors of all hues who were collectively conspiring to erode the most harmful invention of its era, white supremacy.[72] And once and for all, to topple it, like they did the statues erected to glorify its myth and the misery it spread.

I left Washington, DC, while the George Floyd protests were in full swing. I drove two hours south, to Richmond, on Sunday, May 31, 2020, a city that in its darker days was the seat of the Confederacy.

I walked through the city's Monument Avenue, a living shrine to white supremacist and Confederate heroes, while protests surged throughout the nation and statues fell—one by one—at the hands of protestors rewriting history on streets, in squares, and on city blocks across America and then the world. I walked by the Stonewall Jackson memorial at the intersection of Monument and Arthur Ashe Boulevard, and then walked to the head of it all.

I knew, as I stood in front of the statue of Robert E. Lee, the enigmatic Confederate general, that this too, and the avenue on which it stood, would soon face the fury of this new wave of historians who marched instead of wrote.[73] The currents of change sweeping through America's streets, with even more tides to come, gave flesh, bone, and voice to what Nigerian novelist Chinua Achebe longed for: "Until the lions have their own historians, the history of the hunt will always glorify the hunter."[74]

The lions had finally arrived, and their collective roar was heard globally.

I returned to Richmond in late August 2020, at the end of a season that fundamentally remade the city and the country.[75] I started at the head of the drag, and the head of the Confederacy, with the Robert E. Lee statue. Black Lives Matter activists had remade the statue into a colorful shrine bearing the names of those unarmed Black men and women slain by police. Lee was still there, atop his horse. But after the protestors made their mark, it was no longer *his* memorial.

I walked north, past longstanding churches and smaller monuments, finally stopping at the base where Stonewall Jackson had stood. Another Confederate general and another statue, but this one had been toppled, leaving only Jackson's title and another name spray-painted prominently below it: Jacob Blake.

Kenosha, Wisconsin, is more than 800 miles from Richmond, but its footprint was heavy in the capital of Virginia the day after the Republican National Convention. The Wisconsin city emerged as the newest site of police violence when Jacob Blake, a twenty-nine-year-old African American man, was arrested while trying to break up a fight. Police followed Blake to his automobile, and after unsuccessfully tasering him, shot him seven times in the back as he attempted to get into his car.[76]

Like the George Floyd murder, Blake's shooting was captured on video, and in line with the prevailing culture of real-time whistleblowing of police violence, disseminated broadly. Expectedly, the video *went viral* in minutes, and a new name—Jacob Blake—joined the roster of hashtags that symbolized police violence, and fueled more protests that, only months after the massive wave of actions inspired by the murders of Floyd and Breonna Taylor, only needed the slightest spark.

Five days later, on August 27, 2020, Trump issued a fiery address at the Republican National Convention in Washington, DC. He shot blame at the protestors and their "violent handlers," targeting the "socialist agenda" that "controlled the Democratic Party" for the violence ravaging American towns and cities.[77]

He fired off racially coded dog whistle after dog whistle, declaring that America's ills were not those ruptured systems that enabled police violence, the continual killing of unarmed Black people, or the vigilante violence that descended upon protestors exercising their First Amendment rights. The problem, according to Trump, was the very people being assailed, like George Floyd and Breonna Taylor; the victims left paralyzed, like Jacob Blake; and the people of all backgrounds who came together and marched because their nation was falling apart at the seams.

Things fall apart, even the world's most powerful democracies. Particularly those democracies presided over by a leadership that lords over an exhausted people demanding dignity through means enabled by the Constitution and then dehumanizes them as unruly thugs when they exercise those rights.

Some monuments of American apartheid stand defiantly, as living beings, far from Richmond's Monument Row and the former seat of the Confederacy. They stand in Washington, and in a White House, above a nation that is coming apart.

A nation that perhaps can only be saved by the protests that seek to restore dignity to a long-downtrodden people, and in turn, restore dignity to an American experiment that flouted lofty principles it consistently fell short of practicing.

If popular unrest could be mounted against white supremacy and its symbolic and systemic purveyors, then perhaps a similar front could be launched against one of its most ominous modern strains—the War on Terror. More than twenty years after its creation, it was the Black Lives Matter protests and the collateral possibilities for progress they inspired that seeded the belief that a global war that seemed never ending could be slowed, or even stopped.

After all, the War on Terror and the war on Black Americans emanated from the same corpus of lies. Lies that whites were supreme, that Christendom mandated a crusade against nonbelievers, and that the "sunbaked Hebrew who gave it [Christianity] his name" was white—merging the War on Terror, a two-decade-long campaign with far deeper roots, with the four-hundred-year war on Black women and men in America.[78]

While soldiers shot down Brown Muslim men and women from afar in war, policemen choked, shot, and murdered unarmed Black men and women on the very ground their ancestors paved.

Terror wore a rotating set of uniforms. But its unmistakable blows and strikes were one and the same. Muslims abroad and in America grew to not only understand the African American struggle more through the heavy hand of the War on Terror, but also *felt* its distinctly racist blows.

This is why the Black Lives Matter protests, in large part, resonated so deeply in Muslim-majority countries—manifested by demonstrations of solidarity in occupied Kashmir, murals memorializing George Floyd in war-torn Syria, and tributes to murdered Black women and men adorning the Israeli separation wall in the West Bank.

A wall not far from where Eyad Hallaq was gunned down and buried. A wall standing on the very soil where a Brown Jesus, who likely resembled the Muslim Hallaq more than the Ashkenazi Jewish policeman who shot him, mutated into the white totem we see in portraits across the world, and in statues erected where old and new crusades are waged in his name.

Statues, and the lies they reinforce, must be remade, or replaced with new talismans of truth. Truth that stands to give life to ignored histories and to reconstruct them in the image of those killed on the streets of American cities and violently stricken from the pages of its seminal texts.

Statues are powerful symbols. But their real value lies in their power as portals, as conveyors of grand narratives and malicious myths that are passed on from generation to generation. Howard Zinn describes this power through the figure of Christopher Columbus: "To emphasize the heroism of Columbus and his successors as navigators and discoverers, and to deemphasize their genocide, is not a technical necessity but an ideological choice. It serves—unwittingly—to justify what was done."[79] The past is built into the very core of those statues, reinforced by their clay and metal surfaces that stand, individually and ubiquitously, across and even beyond the nation.

Tearing them down offers a new symbolism and opens the door to renewed possibilities for beheading the generational lies cast against people targeted by old racisms and new crusades.

After they fall, the door is open to the more salient revolution of penning new histories. New narratives that overwrite the stacks of Orientalist and Islamophobic texts that drive the violent crusades against Muslims all over the world today.

Toppling statues is an act of abolition, and abolishing histories inked with the lies of the victor and the blood of the victimized is that first step, that first ferocious step, toward writing new ones.

Pens are the mightiest swords. And in these new crusades, where the onslaught against Muslims is inflicted as much through the fury of words as the firing of guns, a weapon that must be lifted and wielded until the War on Terror meets the same fate as that Christopher Columbus statue, standing headless, in Boston.

Writing as writing. Writing as rioting. Writing as righting. On the best days, all three.[80]

CONCLUSION

Killing an Arab

> On the horizon, a tiny steamer went by, and I made out the black dot from the corner of my eye because I hadn't stopped watching the Arab. . . . The trigger gave; I felt the smooth underside of the butt; and there, in that noise, sharp and deafening, is where it all started.
>
> ALBERT CAMUS, *The Stranger*

KILLING AN ARAB STANDS at the center of *The Stranger*. The landmark novel, set in colonial Algeria, features the forlorn protagonist Meursault—a white Frenchman who slays an Arab along the beaches of Algiers. Beaches that have cradled thousands of Algerian women and men who met death too soon. During 132 years of untold stories, these natives were buried between the pages of French imperial history and the coasts of colonial lands.[1]

The Arab of Camus's making is nameless, faceless, and referred to only as the "Arab." Millions of readers only know Meursault's victim as "the Arab." His existence is narrowed and compressed into an object—far from a living being—left for dead on the book's pages and the beaches of his colonized homeland.[2] The Arab was flatlined by Camus's pen before Meursault shot him, rendered dead by an objectification that stripped him of a name or face, a past and present, which add flesh to figures and unfold objects into individuals.

Killing an Arab is central to Camus's drama, but "the Arab" is a negligible footnote to Meursault's story. The plot proceeds to center the feelings of the white Frenchman, his travails between nihilism and numbness, and his existential vacillations between those poles and the spectrum of positions in between them. The native Arab sprawled dead on the coastline did not matter. To the story line, he only mattered as much as Meursault made him matter. The Arab was first a "black dot," then moments later, a limp carcass.[3] Then nothing more.

Only Meursault mattered. His complexity and directionless days mattered, as did the melancholy and marred relationships that formed the marrow of a life still worth making. Worth making in the motion of a man's life in a foreign land, formed into a book that stands at the epicenter of modern literature. A stranger in a French colony whose musings about life and death were an archetypal narration of French hegemony and the foreign settlers its rule made way for in Algeria, where the native laid dead—in fiction and reality.[4] Algerian blood spilled on beaches, like the endless spill of ink centering the lives and story lines of foreign strangers who walk between and on top of them.

Killing an Arab is central to the geopolitical dramas of the last two decades. It formed the mandate of the American War on Terror, which weaponized law and rhetoric to legitimize the mass execution of Arabs and Muslims and other peoples in foreign wars. In the popular imagination, "Arabs" and "Muslims" and "Middle Easterners" are one and the same, blurred together by the blinding force of Orientalism and the Islamophobia it spawned after the 9/11 terror attacks.[5]

In line with Islamophobic and literary fictions, the War on Terror crusades in India and China, Myanmar and France, in the western and eastern hemispheres have targeted the very nameless and faceless objects left for dead on Algerian beaches. They are all, and at once, "the Arabs," the "presumed terrorists," or the "black dots" seen behind the barrels of guns or the cockpits of fighter jets.[6] Killing an *Arab,* an umbrella name for Muslims and the peoples callously conflated as one, drives the mandate of the War on Terror: a crusade that unleashes Islamophobia, in distinct yet undeniably crippling forms, across the world today.

Killing an Arab is a recurring event that the world has become desensitized to. An act so common it does not bear mentioning, and for journalists curating which war victims deserve coverage, a passing occurrence for a "place . . . like Iraq or Afghanistan, that has seen conflict raging for decades."[7] The War on Terror, and the network of actual and epistemological wars that preceded it, conditioned the world not only to ignore the killing of Arabs, but to accept it.[8] Like Meursault, walking across a colonized city while his emotions whirled within, we are numb to it. Numb to the killing of Arabs, Muslims, and nonwhite peoples in lands plundered by new crusades on the margins of Europe, America, and Western citadels of "civilization."[9]

The images out of Ukraine in late February, following the Russian invasion, were harrowing. Endless crowds of people piled into makeshift bomb shelters, state and civilian buildings pummeled by relentless Russian airstrikes, and most profound among the visuals, everyday Ukrainians taking arms against one of the world's most formidable militaries to defend their land. The resistance put up by besieged Ukrainians was at once sublime and unnerving.

While Russia's advances into a country locked between European aspirations and Russian imperialism exposed the ambitions of Vladimir Putin, Western nations and their media outlets sang a common chorus. In stunning uniformity, Western halls of state and societal power condemned Russia's siege of Ukraine as "imperialism."[10] Then they praised the courage of the Ukrainian people fighting against an indomitable army and impossible odds.[11] The language of resistance and the face of anti-imperialism, which long colored campaigns old and new beyond Europe, were given a white and Western face.

Immediately, and rightfully, the world lauded Ukrainians brandishing Molotov cocktails and forming citizen-soldier legions as "freedom fighters."[12] The images of middle-aged women brandishing rifles, former heavyweight champions sacrificing luxury for love of land, and a president rebuffing offers of evacuation and proclaiming "this is the last time you might see me alive" powered a global narrative of good against evil, of David versus Goliath.[13] Ukraine was, by objective measure, no "war," but an asymmetrical clash between a people duly defending their native land and a foreign power seeking to restore its imperial reach westward.

Killing a Ukrainian, or the very thought of it, stood against the weight of the value assigned to Ukrainians' lives. This value, quantified by the scale of media coverage and global support from governments across the world, fortified worldwide solidarity with the Ukrainian people and their struggle. This solidarity was hardly isolated to politicians on the floors of state buildings or pundits speaking from their media platforms, but was also shared by everyday people. In European and American cities, villages, and towns, people hung Ukrainian flags from their homes and businesses, pinned buttons bearing the Ukrainian blue and yellow to their lapels, and placed stickers of the flag on the shells of their computers. The Ukrainian *bicolor* was more than just a flag, *far more* after the Russian siege. It became an emblem of resistance. Even more, a symbol that screamed "Ukrainian lives matter" from the collars and cars of people around the world.[14]

Killing a Ukrainian, the very horror of it, opposed the swelling tide of support rushing to that country's side. This support was, in part, the play of realpolitik, but a greater part of it reflected race and racism, and most poignantly, the entwined fervor and force of the two. An integration whereby whiteness, in the way that only whiteness can, drives the political urgency and discursive solidarity delivered to Ukraine and its soldiers and refugees, politicians and president. Whiteness is the heroism and victimhood, innocence and freedom that saturated television and handheld screens following the invasion of Ukraine.

Killing a Ukrainian is killing freedom, or in the words of a British media outlet, the siege is an "attack on civilization itself."[15] Ukraine is not merely a part of "civilization," as some see it, but a standing embodiment of it, positioned atop the very continent that birthed it, proponents proclaim, populated by a people who embody it as a standing archetype.[16] On the other side of unseeing the humanity of slain Arabs is the incessant centering and seeing of white victimhood.[17] The resonance of white Ukrainians huddled in bomb shelters, fighting in front of bombed buildings, and spread dead on the soil of their homeland was overpowering. And for gatekeepers in government and media, and billions taking in the horror, too much to bear.

Killing a Ukrainian, for those who saw themselves *in* them, shocked the conscience beyond measure. "It's very emotional for me because I see European people with blue eyes and blond hair being killed every day," shared a guest on *BBC News*—an explicit overture that did not elicit alarm but agreement from the interviewing anchor, who followed, "I understand and respect the emotion."[18] The guest, a former Ukrainian deputy general, made plain what sat quietly at the center of everyone's minds. White and especially nonwhite, intimately and painfully aware that white life and white struggle are extended an instant humanity that is foreclosed to Arabs and Muslims immersed in the very same struggles. Struggles far from Europe and America but oftentimes made by them by way of direct war, proxy war, or a War on Terror that weds both together. Struggles that Islamophobia, and its global march, rendered illegal and terroristic.

The phantasmic struggle for self-determination playing out in Ukraine is not isolated to Europe. While media coverage may make it seem as such, this is hardly the case. Ukrainian resistance, and the deeply moving images that piece it together, have been unfolding in Yemen, Palestine, Kashmir, and other Middle Eastern and Muslim-majority contexts for decades. Different theaters, indeed, with distinct shades of struggle.

Yet the essence of these quests for self-determination in the face of military actions have engendered dramatically different treatments from Western governments, and radically different coverage from media outlets.[19]

The slow and unseen quest for dignity unfolds in real time in the West Bank and Gaza. Unarmed Palestinians resisting state seizure of their homes in Sheikh Jarrah are conflated with armed militants, rendering them "terrorists."[20] The recurring killing of civilians in Gaza by Israeli airstrikes is justified by sweeping indictments that "they are Hamas" and that "Palestinian militants are using children and women as human shields," excuses adapted by Putin in his claims that the Ukrainian resistance is spearheaded by "neo-Nazis" wielding "women and children as human shields."[21] Lies at worst, and gross embellishments at best, hurled at victims to make them into monsters.

Yemen, the poorest country in the Middle East, offers another lurid illustration of the world of inconstancy between it and the Ukrainian struggle of self-determination. For nearly six years, Yemen has been relentlessly pummeled by a Saudi regime seeking to expand its regional footprint.[22] Supported by the United Arab Emirates and backed by the United States, the grossly asymmetrical "war" has sunk Yemen into emergency famine and disaster.[23] There has been no global condemnation of the war; instead, Yemenis struggling for their very survival have been met with silence, the American support of the Saudi sword, and the incessant indictment of terrorism. Fighting terrorist ghosts and the boogeyman of Iran, Saudi Arabia—armed by its close allies in Washington, DC—has license to kill Yemenis en masse. Without alarm from state actors, and without the urgency of media coverage.

The contradictions are not exclusive to the Middle East. In a display of stunning militarism, Indian forces marched into Kashmir two years ago and annexed the disputed territory.[24] Driven by an imperial mandate fueled by Hindu supremacy, Narendra Modi stewarded the legal revocation of Kashmir's longstanding autonomy, then proceeded to claim it by force.[25] Kashmiri state leaders were jailed en masse, journalists and dissidents arrested, and men, women, and youth taking up arms to protect already precarious aspirations of self-determination were wholly branded "terrorists."[26] Like its Russian counterpart, Indian imperialism swept into Kashmir with the arrogance and impunity of its leader, Modi. But unlike Russia and Putin, the world stood still and silent as India and Modi annexed Kashmir with brute military power.[27]

Palestinians, Yemenis, and Kashmiris embodied, for decades and still, the very resistance put forward by the Ukrainian people. They, too, put their lives on the line against global and regional powers. They, too, wielded makeshift weapons to protect their "land, loved ones, and way of life"—the trilogy of motivations that world leaders have cited over and again in response to the gallant Ukrainian resistance.[28] But their stories are ignored, and even worse, demonized by states, media outlets, and War on Terror discourses that bind the two.[29]

But what explains the world of difference between the Ukrainian struggles and the ongoing quests for self-determination in Muslim-majority lands? The narratives of the underdog against the superpower, the imperial bully flexing its might against its weaker neighbor, and David versus Goliath are ubiquitously clear, yet misrepresented or removed in relation to Palestine, Yemen, and Kashmir.

Within the realm of geopolitics, race, religion, and interests still matter. The three are deeply entwined, particularly in relation to the Middle East and the Muslim world, where a protracted War on Terror renders anybody Arab, Brown, or Muslim a putative terrorist, notwithstanding the righteousness of their struggle or the unhinged imperialism of their opponents.[30] The public imagining of freedom *fighter* and *terrorist*, *victim* and *villain* is intensely racial, which enables the seeing of everyday Ukrainians who take up arms and throw Molotov cocktails as heroes and powerless Muslims engaged in the very same acts, in pursuit of the same self-determination, as extremists.

Race, and the racialization of Islam as the enemy of Western civilization, has defined Western geopolitical interests over the past several decades.[31] Despite popular discourses confining American racial reckonings to the home front and internationalism plummeting among Western pundits and intellectuals, the War on Terror has shaped the global framing of Arab and Muslim quests for self-determination as terrorism. In line with this framing, the global crusade has shifted state responses against them toward draconian military measures in the lands where righteous struggles continue, and in other places where they have been summarily crushed.[32]

While foreign governments, near and far, rush to stand alongside a besieged Ukrainian people fighting for its very existence, Yemenis and Kashmiris, Palestinians and Uyghur Muslims wait. And continue waiting. Waiting on the wrong side of the racial, religious, and geopolitical divide, for a world of support that may never come.[33]

Locked between imperial interests, Ukraine occupies unenviable geography. It stands between the revitalized Russian empire and the seductive draw of Europe, pulled westward by the very affinity for democracy that spurred the Russian invasion of late February 2022, an invasion that spiraled the liminal European country into unwanted war and a fight for its existence that may very well wipe it from the map.

The narrative of the besieged Ukrainian underdog was indelible and undeniable. It shaped the chorus of Western media support for the Ukrainian resistance and the millions of refugees flooding neighboring nations and those beyond. It dissolved traditional divides on immigration across the continent and in the United States; immigration was no longer a wedge issue, at least for Ukrainians. However, it remained virulently divisive when the refugees were Arabs or Muslims, Black or

Brown immigrants washed from their homelands by Western war or economic despair.[34]

The stunning double standards were on full display in the immediate aftermath of the Russian invasion, the thick of the wartime stages that followed, and the spill of refugees across Europe. Media outlets across the United States and Europe and across their respective political spectrums humanized the plight of Ukrainians. Meticulous vignettes about real people packing their bags and fleeing their homeland powerfully connected the refugee crisis with viewing audiences worldwide. Ukrainian refugees had real names and stories, with real children and real lives left behind for an uncertain future in a foreign land far from home.

Then there were the stories, untold and unpublished, about nonwhite refugee populations. Millions of Syrian refugees remained faceless and flatly represented by media outlets, if they were covered at all, despite their massive number and harrowing struggles across countries and continents. These refugees were bereft of the humanizing tales that invite humanitarian support and the prospect of policy support; the bulk of Western media coverage devoted to Syrian refugees centered on xenophobia or the Islamophobic resistance of populist politicians and pundits.

The racial juxtaposition could not be any clearer and is often highlighted by the very media outlets that make human appeals for Ukrainian refugees. While Syrian and Afghan refugees languished between statelessness and media silence, outlets like *France 24* mentioned them only in relation to the far-right populism sweeping the nation. In the midst of the Ukrainian refugee crisis, the French news outlet finally ran a story that involved "Arab refugees." However, it did not specify which ones, nor did it extend the journalistic care or humanizing storytelling bestowed on Ukrainian refugees. Rather, it referred to them as an indistinguishable monolith, tethered to the hateful voice of far-right presidential candidate Eric Zemmour, who said, "If they [Ukrainian refugees] have ties to France, if they have family in France . . . let's give them visas."[35]

Zemmour then compared the Ukrainian refugees to "Arab or Muslim immigrants," stating, "There are people who are like us and people who [are] unlike us. Everybody now understands that Arab or Muslim immigrants are too unlike us and that it is harder and harder to integrate them."[36] For media outlets, mention of "Muslim immigrants" is relegated to the recurring theme of unassimilable aliens—not real humans in need of safe haven. They are objects all over again, like the nameless and faceless "Arab" in a landmark book who is left for dead on the beach of Algiers.[37] In reality and realpolitik, fiction and fantasy, Muslim lives take on meaning only when they're villains, not victims.

The impulse to cover and call out the racial double standard is commendable, but it is not enough. It always stops there for Arab and African, Black and Muslim refugees. There has been no shortage of stories comparing the rush of love directed at Ukrainian refugees to the xenophobia unleashed against nonwhite immigrants by European and American media outlets. However, this coverage is not followed up by what Afghan, Syrian, and Rohingya refugees need—the humanizing tales and layered storytelling that are faithfully extended to Ukrainians. Muslim refugees are objects of media coverage, not subjects of stories devoted to marking their humanity and making them whole.

The faddish race consciousness within leftist media spaces is equally confining. Too often, it raises notice of nonwhite refugees as a counterpoint to identify racism, or a reference point that stops at comparison. Nonwhite refugees do not exist simply to evidence racism in refugee resettlement and immigration. Nor are they a homogenous bloc that only warrants reference when gratifying the liberal sensibilities of journalists, or entire media outlets, keen on representing themselves as non-racists. Particularly when their media coverage, or lack thereof, shows, intentionally or disproportionately, otherwise.

The power of whiteness is most luridly on display within the media. Its gatekeepers in Western nations are overwhelmingly white, and naturally, their journalistic lens sees the world through its exclusionary contours.[38] The racism coming from the mouths of populists and pundits regarding Ukraine found unison among liberal and centrist media voices. Charlie D'Agata, of CBS News, cried on air, "[Ukraine] isn't a place, with all due respect, like Iraq or Afghanistan, that has seen conflict raging for decades. This is a relatively civilized, relatively European—I have to choose these words carefully—city, one where you wouldn't expect that, or hope that it's going to happen."[39]

His message was clear. "European" meant "white."[40] Which together stood for everything wholly and "relatively civilized."[41] Unlike Iraq or Afghanistan, the two nations decimated by two decades of American war and terror, which represented bastions of incivility, extremism, and "forever war."[42] Immigrants fleeing these nations, and refugees flung across the world, carried the threat of terror with them. Stained with this stigma and devoid of the whiteness held by Ukrainian refugees, they were cast as undesirables by the very nations that opened their borders and arms to the blue-eyed and blond-haired victims of the Russian siege. [43]

Yellow journalism has always pervaded the media. But even more distorting is the imprint of whiteness, which skews journalistic ethics and uplifts the stories of those who look like the people who hold power, believe like them, and share kindred traditions.[44] The Arab and Middle Eastern Journalist Association swiftly condemned the racism pervading media coverage of Ukraine and the neglect of nonwhite refugee populations in the days after the Russian invasion. It maintained, through a formal statement, that "newsrooms must not make comparisons that weigh the significance or imply justification of one conflict over another—civilian casualties and displacement in other countries are equally as abhorrent as they are in Ukraine."[45]

The statement brought to the fore what so many saw quietly unfolding in real time. The association questioned the ethics of media outlets that prioritized freedom fighters and refugees, resistance and war that served an existential mirror, and that served the fraternal masters of whiteness and Western interests as they stared at their reflection.

Media ethics are built on the cornerstone of fair, balanced, and objective coverage. This mission is marred by the heavy hand of whiteness within newsrooms, and more intrusively, on the very screens that breathe life into the humans conveyed within their square lines. Those within the lines are humanized and those at the margins are erased, or buried beyond the borders of the screen. This humanizing often materializes into aid that people struggling against the formidable odds of war and the even more formidable plight of statelessness need. Aid that they need in order to fight, and one day after war is over, if that day comes, to "feel free . . . and ready to live again."[46]

For Muslims who have endured these colonial and postcolonial wars and the War on Terror crusades of today, Ukraine is a painful blow. It is another reminder that their bodies, their beings, are worth less—and too often, are *worthless*. It is impossible for them, and those cognizant of the lurid and lucid double standards emanating from the conflict in Ukraine, to dream of a uniform standard applied across race, religion, and the realpolitik in between. It is impossible to imagine a world where the theaters of resistance in the Casbah or Kashmir receive the same light as the struggles in Kyiv.

Whiteness, and its disarming hue, has immense global impact. While the darker color of Islamophobia, and the peoples it marks as terrorists until proven otherwise, scoffs at the flags of Muslim struggles for self-determination, and denies the dignity that comes before.

For me, as a young boy living in Beirut, the ten-minute trek from school to our family apartment was a mise-en-scène of war's indignities. It was the late 1980s, and Lebanon was gripped by the final stages of an existential unmaking. It would never be the same, and the war that shattered its people forged its new fractured national identity. An identity that had disintegrated from within, and which mirrored the decimated buildings and broken souls limping on the outside.

One afternoon in March, I saw an old man with gray hair. The man stood horizontally, as only he could. He had no legs, but two muscular arms and a torso tied to a beige skateboard that moved him about. He was a man, but at that moment, he was a metaphor for a nation stripped of its limbs and a people making do and moving about with whatever they had left. Whatever they could scramble together on that stage of war and the soil that it left barren.

I was young, and the first feelings his image spurred were sadness and pity. I did not yet read the works of Camus or Jean-Paul Sartre, or those of the great novelists of the Arab world who wrote about native trials in my native tongue. But as a wartime child, I could feel the force of the nihilism that surrounded my world, the "days of dust" and their irremovable residue that clouds Lebanon, and the weight of the existential absurdity only war could inscribe in me and around me.[47] I *felt* that and much more, and my eyes moved onto the man. The more closely I watched him, the more I understood him and the war that had made and unmade him. I absorbed the depth of the creases across his brow, the shine of the brown glowing from his skin, the strong gray locks above his crown, and the might of the will that moved him forward, then rolled him onward.

He was a man. A man first. Not an Arab or a Muslim. Not a Muslim or a Christian, a Sunni or a Shiite. Not a cripple or a casualty. But a man, and that mattered before any other fact or footnote did. And it mattered more as I took the time to scrutinize his story and soak in the nuances of his personhood as I stood there, twenty yards away, on the opposite side of age. The lens of my young eyes, perhaps too young to appreciate the travails of his world, could still see the trace of his scars and the depth of his wrinkles. He was a man, with a story made up of a real place and a rich plot, a bountiful past and a broken future. A future that he rolled into, every day along those accosted Beirut avenues and backways, with a gallant stride that no man's pity or child's sorrow could undo.

He survived. Against the odds of war and the crushing angst of life that met him on the other side, the side of death that could not claim him. He lived, in a nation where killing an Arab was everyday theater. Where pity for "the nation" and its fragmented peoples rounded up "as Arabs" was a scarce export.[48] Where millions of Arabs like him, in Lebanon and the entire region beyond, were "black dots" in the eyes of strangers but real human beings, scarred with depth of life's beauty and tragedy, to those who took the time to *see* them.[49] For every nameless Arab killed in a French novel and every Muslim maimed in the novel narratives of these new crusades, millions of children and elders, women and men—like the man in front of my young eyes—lived. He was, against the odds and between the bombs and beaches in Beirut, still alive.

Alive to me, but killed by the denial and dehumanization of media coverage while they still walked the earth. Only to be killed again, in that barren chamber of silence and anonymity, by a Chinese prison guard or an American drone strike, a strike that fell from a sky that showered fatal rain and foreign reign. Killed, for the billionth time, on the beaches of Algiers, in the alleys of Srinagar, or in the back ways of Beirut, a city where my dead father once held my hand as I tried to look away. But couldn't. Instead, I learned to look forward.

Forward. Past the standing mirage of imperial myths. Forward. Toward a sublime future where words, penned in the present, mend the wounds of crusades old and new.

Forward. Running as wildly and as freely in the world as you do in your dreams.

You have to decide who you are and force the world to deal with you, not with its idea of you.[50]

EPILOGUE

I RETURNED TO ISTANBUL in June 2022, deepening my ties with the displaced Uyghur community in the Turkish metropolis. The process of writing about their struggle opened paths toward new friendships and lifelong ties, propelling me into the very center of their movement for dignity and self-determination. Following fundraising efforts for widows and orphans in the community, Uyghur diaspora leaders invited me to speak at the East Turkistan World Symposium, a historic convening that brought together religious, civic, and intellectual figures from Muslim-majority nations to build global solidarity for their struggle. I met survivors of concentration camps and family of the dead and missing who were attending to tell their stories. Family members like Muslima, a seventeen-year-old student who lives with her younger sister and mother in Turkey, yearning for the return of her father. Her eyes and words were piercing when she spoke, and Muslima's visage left an imprint that evolved into the cover of this book. Muslim governments had turned their backs on Muslima and the Uyghur Muslim struggle, with many even siding with China on account of economic interests or realpolitik.[1] This conference sought to turn the tide, or at minimum, to foster support among leaders of Muslim societies around the world who could help, we hoped, turn the tide.

Istanbul was an ideal site for the meeting. Standing at the crossroads of Europe and Asia, it is logical terrain for emerging

Uyghur organizing and leadership in exile, and is, as I gradually discovered, a meeting space for stateless Muslim populations pushed to Turkey because of war, statelessness, and in the case of the Uyghurs, genocide. On June 13, 2022, I met with Uyghur leaders Rushan Abbas and her husband Abdulhakim Idris, of the Campaign for Uyghurs organization, to strategize about educating Muslim American communities about the plight of the Uyghurs. Later that evening, I sat with leading figures of the Kashmiri struggle for self-determination outside of Sultanahmet, the historic Istanbul enclave. Tourists flocked to the historic mosques and venerable sites that surrounded us while I met with political dissidents to strategize about making a better tomorrow for their people. It felt surreal, sitting among and between the very Uyghur and Kashmiri leaders I had written about as a scholar and author, and even more so, being honored as a *member* of their struggles. But the experience was real, and as clear a reality as the call to prayer that rang out of the Blue Mosque standing in the center of our sublime backdrop.

It would have been impossible to meet these figures, all at once and in a span of hours, in London, or Washington, DC, or any other Western metropolis of that stature. They found safe haven, for however long it lasted, in Istanbul—a politically imperfect place that, at minimum, provided religious refuge from the panopticon of all-seeing surveillance in Xinjiang and the Hindutva imperialism in Kashmir. All of us—Kashmiris, Uyghurs, and one American—were far from home. But we felt right at home, with one another, in Istanbul that night.

"Turkey is where we can be Muslim and politically free," shared my guide Abduresid Emin, the young Uyghur dynamo behind the landmark symposium and the philanthropic effort to support Uyghur orphans and widows that had brought me to Istanbul the month before. Abduresid, not yet thirty years old, serves as the secretary general of the International Union of East Turkistan Organizations. He toted my first book, *American Islamophobia,* with him, which I had brought as a gift for his wife. Over the years, he has become not just a good friend, but a brother. Abduresid was always smiling, always on the move, always strategizing for the sake of his people. Abduresid and the other young Kashmiris we sat near in a terrace restaurant in Istanbul were laughing, planning, and dreaming, freely. For them, Istanbul offered freedom, or a semblance of it that they had never known before.

Our meeting, and its sublime locale, was a rebellion itself against the western and eastern conduits of Islamophobia that spurred our convening. In "Algeria Unveiled," postcolonial giant Frantz Fanon wrote, "[It is] the plans of the occupier that determine the centres of resistance around which a people's will to survive become organized."[2] Not on this night in Istanbul, which provided intellectual oasis and physical exodus from the Islamophobic hegemony that trapped us.

It was at once an inspiring and absurd scene. A Muslim American academic sitting between Kashmiris and Uyghurs in exile, discussing the bulldozing of Indian Muslim homes by the Modi regime amid the picturesque backdrop of the Bosporus, landmark mosques in every direction, and minarets that reached high into the Turkish sky. But again, it was real, and a reality stitched together by an Islamophobia that reached into every corner of the globe. Pushing us toward Istanbul for refuge or research, safe haven and service, held together by a commitment to fight for disparate struggles rooted in that global crusade that marked our faith, Islam, as the enemy.

Istanbul was indeed a crossroads. A new crossroads of possibility for peoples stripped of their land, and a revolutionary cosmopolitanism that revitalized movements flattened by authoritarian hegemons and imperial bigots. The city spawned institutions like ILKE and Kashmir House, established to reclaim the narrative of the people and the future trajectory of their movement. It birthed the network of civic, educational, and media organizations that held the Uyghur people together against ethnic cleansing and genocide. I left the city with an optimism that had eluded me for a long time, widened by the smiles of young Kashmiri and Uyghur women and men, like Abduresid, who wore smiles on their faces while fighting against seemingly impossible odds and indomitable foes. "How could he smile?" I thought, knowing his father is in a prison camp, and after his people have endured so much? Faith, I concluded, was the only answer. And a faith greater than mine, which I admired and envied all at once, hardened by a genocidal campaign that had marked it as a "mental illness" and marred a proud Uyghur people for far too long.[3]

These Muslim exiles in Istanbul exist on the fringes of a foreign land where a government's warm welcome could be chilled by winds of change that can, in an instant, send them packing. They exist at the intersection of world history where their homelands are sites of new imperial conquests spearheaded not by European, American, or white supremacist crusades, but Islamophobia of a different color. They exist to struggle, and it is only because of that struggle that their history, traditions, and dreams for a better tomorrow still exist. That fight, for my Kashmiri and Uyghur friends, is not a matter of volition but an act as natural as breathing, so we spoke, broke bread, and breathed in the Istanbul air that brought us together that warm summer evening.

Their fight is why I write. Each word is a blow against an Islamophobia that despite stripping them of loved ones, land, and dignity, seemed to only make them stronger. This global crusade that fuels wars against Muslims in China and India, France and Myanmar, and places beyond and in between, rages on, spawning new fronts that will unfold after the final words of this book are written. But the people who inspired this book are more important than the contents of its pages. For the fallen victims, there are victors who rise to write, then fight. The survivors of global Islamophobia will live on—and fight on—to give voice and flesh to new chapters that will take place after this book's final word is written and read.

Istanbul, Turkey
June 13, 2022

Acknowledgments

"WRITING IS, AT BEST, a lonely life," reflected Ernest Hemingway, a conclusion made even truer by the pandemic that set in and reset our normality, or what remained of it, in March of 2020. Hemingway continued, "For [the writer] does his work alone and if he is a good enough writer he must face eternity, or the lack of it, each day."

The second part of this observation has been illustrated by the emergence of virtual technologies that simultaneously draw us closer and keep us isolated. Physical isolation has become even more of a reality, for the writer and everybody else in society. Yet the bridges that technology can build, if used adeptly, allow us to reach a range of individuals and rich experiences that the pandemic, with its physical restrictions, would have made impossible when Hemingway penned those words. While working on this book I was oftentimes alone in body, but I was always accompanied by the faces and ideas, reflections, and voices of so many. In many respects, the faces and voices of those people kept me going, driving me to piece together their experiences in the form of this book.

A mosaic of inspirations contributed to this book. Above all, the individuals I encountered and interviewed comprise its very heart; their contributions gave distant ideas and events voice, flesh, and bone. It was humbling to learn about their struggles, and I felt empowered to write after every conversation, interview, and virtual exchange. Writing a book encompasses a constellation of smaller, unseen tasks, including scribbles in notepads, reminders on sticky notes, and quotations typed into digital files.

I take great pride in being an author, but in my daily routine I'm a law professor first. I am blessed to have the support of many within the legal academic and advocacy worlds. Dean Richard Bierschbach of the Wayne State University School of Law believed strongly in my work and provided vital support for this book. Deans Stacy Leeds, an inspiration of mine, and Margaret McCabe at the University of Arkansas School of Law were also instrumental in the development of this book, and beyond that, in my development as a thinker. I am immensely grateful to them and to the colleagues and friends I have made at both institutions. Dean Reem Bahdi, the first Palestinian dean of a North American law school, at Windsor Law, is a hero and friend.

Beyond legal academe, the Open Society Foundation's support of my public advocacy and intellectualism has been a blessing. I am particularly indebted to Alvin Starks, a dear friend, for making Islamophobia a cornerstone racial justice concern within the institution, and by extension, nationally. Perhaps one of the brightest developments in the thick of the Islamophobic fervor that has gripped the United States over the past decade has been seeing the fight against it rise as a primary social justice mandate, and the leadership of Alvin Starks is a central ingredient in that development.

I draw so much strength and balance from family and friends. First and foremost, I am grateful to my mother Fikrieh, who sacrificed so much so that I could even dream of doing what I do today. She is my first hero, who raised me and my siblings as best as she could, working odd jobs in one of the United States' most economically deprived cities, as an immigrant woman far from family and support. My siblings, Khalida and Mohammed, and my many nieces and nephews bring joy to my life whenever they are near. While too many to name, friends I have had for years and those I have met more recently bless me with levity and community, and in some respects, extended family. I thank those whose insight and intellect fueled me while writing this book, most notably Bernadette Atuahene, Amer Zahr, Ahmed Al-Rumaihi, Abed Ayoub, Nadim Hallal, Adham Kassem, Steve Jenkins, Suhaib Al-Hanooti, Ahmed Abuznaid, Hamada Zahawi, Erin Durrah, Reshaan Dollie, Rizqah Dollie, Shakirah Thebus, Sajjad Shah, Hamza Nassar, Miguel Duarte, Sergio Perez, Eyvin Hernandez, Abduresid Emin, George Naggiar, as well as others whose names appear in its pages. I owe immense gratitude to Zamzam Saleh, who supported my work with care and compassion. She provided me with love and enriched my writing. I will always be indebted to her for this, and so much more.

I am especially grateful to my writing workshop community at Harvard University, a wonderful group that inspired me to find dimensions of myself as a writer that I could not chart before. I am also blessed to have the support of the Damon J. Keith Center for Civil Rights, led by my colleague Peter Hammer, the Langston Mercer Black Law Professors' community, and my colleagues at the Desmond Tutu Centre for Religion and Social Justice at the University of the Western Cape in Cape Town, South Africa. Moreover, I am especially blessed to work with charities including Baitulmaal, Droplets of Mercy, Muslims of the World, and Penny Appeal Canada, which provide key pathways to help many of the Muslim populations I write about in this book, and I am proud that we have raised millions of dollars together to provide direct aid.

One of my grandest fortunes is having crossed paths with Naomi Schneider years ago, during the early stages of my public intellectual work. That encounter built a bridge toward working with the University of California Press, which I consider as much of an intellectual home as the law schools where I teach and have taught. I have become friends with many members of the UC Press community who have helped enrich my writing and advance my work to audiences near and far.

Finally, I am forever thankful for Allah's known and guised blessings. Through personal struggle, pandemics, and trials lodged between, the strength and knowing I draw from Him affirm, time and time again, that I am walking my purpose with the time that I have here on earth.

Notes

INTRODUCTION: TWO TUESDAYS

1. These were the rumors circulating in the immediate aftermath of the explosion, according to a text message I received from my sister, Khalida, August 4, 2020.

2. Austin Ramzy and Elian Peltier, "What We Know and Don't Know about the Beirut Explosions," *New York Times*, August 5, 2020.

3. Robert Fisk, *Pity the Nation: The Abduction of Lebanon* (PublicAffairs, 2002).

4. Erik Love, *Islamophobia and Racism in America* (NYU Press, 2017).

5. Sahar Aziz, *The Racial Muslim: When Racism Quashes Religious Freedom* (University of California Press, 2021).

6. "Racialization" is defined as "an unstable and de-centered complex of social meanings constantly being transformed by political struggle" assigned to identities in society. Michael Omi and Howard Winant, *Racial Formation in the United States: From the 1960s to the 1990s*, 2nd ed. (Routledge, 1994), 55. Also see Leti Volpp, "The Citizen and the Terrorist," *UCLA Law Review* 49 (2002): 1586, who wrote in the

wake of the 9/11 terror attacks, "We are witnessing the redeployment of old Orientalist tropes. Historically, Asia and the Middle East have functioned as phantasmic sites on which the U.S. nation projects a series of anxieties regarding internal and external threats to the coherence of the national body."

7. Deepa Kumar, *Islamophobia and the Politics of Empire: Twenty Years after 9/11* (Verso, 2021).

8. "The central argument of this book is that anti-Muslim racism is best understood, in its myriad and ever-changing manifestations, as rooted in empire. Thus, Muslim inclusion within an imperial system that presides over war, genocide, and torture does little to dent racism." Ibid., 8.

9. Khaled A. Beydoun and Nura Sediqe, "Unveiling," *California Law Review* 111 (forthcoming 2023). Gendered Islamophobia theory holds that state and societal tropes ascribed to Muslim women are oppositional to those assigned to Muslim men. It elucidates how prevailing ideas of "submissiveness" and "subordination" attached to Muslim womanhood, and the grand aim of "liberating Muslim women" that follows, are rooted in an imperial epistemology that caricatures Muslim men as "violent," "oppressive," and "tyrannical."

10. Kumar, *supra* note 7, at 20.

11. Ibid.

12. Fatema Mernissi, *Scheherazade Goes West: Different Cultures, Different Harems* (Washington Square Press, 2001), 11.

13. E. Tendayi Achiume, "Migration as Decolonization," *Stanford Law Review* 71 (2019): 1541.

14. Jean-Paul Sartre, *Being and Nothingness* (Routledge, 1943).

15. See Marianna Spring, "Beirut Explosion: How Conspiracy Theories Spread on Social Media," *BBC News*, August 5, 2020.

16. Fisk, *supra* note 3.

17. Maria Abi-Habib and Ben Hubbard, "U.S. Contractor Knew of Explosive Material in Beirut Since at Least 2017," *New York Times*, August 10, 2020.

18. Kumar, *supra* note 7, at 17–20.

19. The bibliographic essay at the end of this book offers a detailed overview of my data and sources.

20. Edward Said, *Out of Place: A Memoir* (Granta, 1999).

21. Kumar, *supra* note 7, at 21.

22. Volpp, *supra* note 6, at 1486.

23. Kenneth R. Bazinet, "A Fight vs. Evil, Bush and Cabinet Tell U.S.," *Daily News*, September 17, 2001.

24. Samuel P. Huntington, *The Clash of Civilizations and the Remaking of World Order* (Simon and Schuster, 1996).

25. Here, I am using the descriptors fashioned by Edward Said in *Orientalism*.

26. Mahmoud Darwish, *Unfortunately, It Was Paradise: Selected Poems* (University of California Press, 2003).

27. Here, I am paying homage to the title of Edward Said's memoir, *Out of Place* (1999), where he articulates that grand sense of feeling perpetually alienated on account of his identity as a Palestinian child, and later, a world-renowned scholar and public intellectual.

28. Khaled A. Beydoun, "Exporting Islamophobia in the Global 'War on Terror,'" *New York University Law Review* 95 (2020).

29. Ibid., 84.

30. Kumar, *supra* note 7, at 20.

31. "I define structural Islamophobia as the fear and suspicion of Muslims on the part of institutions—most notably government agencies—that is manifested through the enactment and advancement of policies. These policies are built upon the presumption that Muslim identity is associated with a national security threat." Khaled A. Beydoun, "Islamophobia: Toward a Legal Definition and Framework," *Columbia Law Review Online* 16 (2015).

32. Yasmeen Serhan, "The Trump-Modi Playbook," *The Atlantic*, February 25, 2020.

33. During Ramadan (Arabic), Muslims fast from sunup to sundown, abstaining from eating, drinking, and other prohibited activities for thirty days.

34. Maryam Mafi and Azima Melita Kolin, *Rumi: Gardens of the Beloved* (Element, 2004).

CHAPTER 1. FOREVER TURNED AROUND

1. "Jihad" means "struggle" in Arabic; it also means "striving." But in mainstream political parlance, the word has become tightly connected to terrorism, and thus far removed from its recognized formal denotations.

2. Khaled Hosseini, *The Kite Runner* (Riverhead Books, 2013), 352.

3. See "Kenya: Suspected Al-Shabaab Militants Attack Police Post in Wajir County," *Crisis24*, May 16, 2020.

4. James Baldwin, *The Fire Next Time* (Dial Press, 1963).

5. Keren Weitzberg, *We Do Not Have Borders: Greater Somalia and the Predicaments of Belonging in Kenya* (Ohio University Press, 2017).

6. The opening passage, and prayer, in the Holy Qur'an.

7. Nawaal El Saadawi, *Woman at Point Zero* (Zed, 1983).

8. James Baldwin, "Of the Sorrow Songs: The Cross of Redemption," in *The Cross of Redemption: Uncollected Writings* (Vintage, 2011), 145, 147.

9. Those words, in varying forms and sequences, were echoed by scores of patients I spoke to during my two days at the hospital.

10. Michael T. Flynn, *The Field of Fight* (St. Martin's, 2016), 2.

11. Eyder Peralta, "In Kenya, a Rise in Attacks by Islamist Al-Shabab Insurgents," NPR, February 16, 2020.

12. "At Least 10 Killed in Kenya Bus Attack Claimed by Al-Shabab," *Al Jazeera English*, December 7, 2019.

13. "Wajir county is 99% Muslim, but Kenya as a whole is over 80% Christian." "Al Shabaab Militants Single Out and Kill Eight Christians and Three Other Non-Muslims in Bus Attack," Barnabas Fund, December 12, 2019.

14. Mitchell D. Silber and Arvin Bhatt, *Radicalization in the West: The Homegrown Threat* (New York City Police Department, Intelligence Division, 2007), 5–10.

15. Khaled A. Beydoun, "Trump's Counterterror Program," *Al Jazeera English,* January 25, 2017.

16. "Orientalists divided human societies into civilizations that have a core set of values that drive their progress (or lack thereof). The people who inhabit these civilizations were said to have a cultural 'essence' that explains who they are across time. Essentialism of this sort is one of the pillars of race making." Deepa Kumar, *Islamophobia and the Politics of Empire: 20 Years after 9/11* (Verso, 2021), 19.

17. Ibid., 42.

18. George W. Bush, "Text: George W. Bush Addresses the Nation," *Washington Post,* September 20, 2001.

19. Kenneth Roth, "The Law of War in the War on Terror," *Foreign Affairs,* January/February 2004.

20. Michael Lipka and Conrad Hackett, "Why Muslims Are the World's Fastest Growing Religion," Pew Research Center, April 6, 2017.

21. See Khaled A. Beydoun, "Exporting Islamophobia in the Global 'War on Terror,'" *New York University Law Review Online* 95 (2020).

22. Darren Byler, *In the Camps: China's High-Tech Penal Colony* (Columbia Global Reports, 2021).

23. Khaled A. Beydoun, "The World of Inconsistencies between Ukraine, the Middle East and Beyond" (Opinion), *Washington Post,* March 7, 2022.

24. Donny Hathaway, "Someday We'll All Be Free," *Extension of a Man* (Atco Records, 1973).

25. Mos Def, "Love," *Black on Both Sides* (Rawkus and Priority Records, 1999).

CHAPTER 2. WAR AND TERROR

Epigraphs: James Baldwin, *The Price of the Ticket: Collected Nonfiction, 1948–1985* (Beacon Press, 2021), 101; Edward Said, "Blind Imperial Arrogance," *Los Angeles Times,* July 20, 2003; George Orwell, "Politics and the English Language" (1948), www.orwell.ru/library/essays/politics/english/e_polit/.

1. Interview with John on June 28, 2020—name changed to protect his anonymity.

2. Sarah Kendzior, *The View from Flyover Country: Dispatches from the Forgotten America* (Flatiron Books, 2018).

3. David R. Roediger, *Working toward Whiteness: How America's Immigrants Became White* (Basic Books, 2005).

4. Henry A. Giroux, "Totalitarian Paranoia in the Post-Orwellian Surveillance State," *Truthout,* February 10, 2014.

5. J. D. Vance, *Hillbilly Elegy: A Memoir of a Family and Culture in Crisis* (Harper, 2016), 52.

6. Evelyn Alsultany, *Arabs and Muslims in the Media: Race and Representation after 9/11* (NYU Press, 2012), 9.

7. Steve Beynon, "After Years of Failure to End the Crisis, Veteran Suicide Takes Center Stage on Capitol Hill," *Stars and Stripes,* March 5, 2020.

8. Jean-Paul Sartre, *The Devil and the Good Lord and Two Other Plays* (Knopf, 1960), 69.

9. Ali Harb, "From War to Poverty: Refugees' Endless Struggle," *The Arab American News,* June 6, 2016.

10. Alexia Fernandez Campbell and *National Journal,* "Detroit Is a Dream Come True for Iraqi Refugees," *The Atlantic,* March 18, 2015.

11. Najam Haider, *Shi'a Islam: An Introduction* (Cambridge University Press, 2014).

12. Khaled A. Beydoun, "Bisecting American Islam? Divide, Conquer, and Counter-Radicalization," *Hastings Law Journal* 69 (2018): 432–33.

13. "Dearborn Rejoices as Saddam Statue Falls," *ABC News,* January 6, 2006.

14. "Iraqi Americans Celebrate Hussein's Execution," *NBC News,* December 29, 2006.

15. Lesley Hazleton, *After the Prophet: The Epic Story of the Shia-Sunni Split* (Anchor Books, 2009), 194–98.

16. Interview with Hussein on June 2, 2020—name changed to protect his anonymity.

17. *Insh'Allah* means "God willing" in Arabic. It is a common phrase used not only by Muslims but also Arabs of other faiths.

18. See Lesley Hazleton, *After the Prophet: The Epic Story of the Shia-Sunni Split* (Anchor Books, 2009).

19. Howard Zinn, *Terrorism and War* (Seven Stories Press, 2002).

20. Khaled A. Beydoun, "Fred Korematsu: An Unsung 'Muslim American' Civil Rights Hero," *The Islamic Monthly,* February 2, 2015.

21. "September 11 Attacks," *History,* August 25, 2018.

22. Ganesh Sitaraman, "Counterinsurgency, the War on Terror, and the Laws of War," *Virginia Law Review* 95 (2009): 1745.

23. Hamid Algar, *Wahhabism: A Critical Essay* (Islamic Publications International, 2002).

24. Farah Pandith, "Extremism Is Riyadh's Top Export," *Foreign Policy,* March 24, 2019.

25. Evelyn Alsultany, *Arabs and Muslims in the Media: Race and Representation after 9/11* (NYU Press, 2012), 2–7.

26. Richard Delgado and Jean Stefancic, *Critical Race Theory: An Introduction* (NYU Press, 2001).

27. Ian Haney Lopez, *White by Law: The Legal Construction of Race* (NYU Press, 1996), 28.

28. Cheryl Harris, "Whiteness as Property," *Harvard Law Review* 106 (1993): 1716.

29. Edward J. Blum and Paul Harvey, *The Color of Christ: The Son of God and the Saga of Race in America* (University of North Carolina Press, 2012), 8.

30. Ibid.

31. Roediger, *supra* note 3, at 7.

32. See the US Supreme Court decision Plessy v. Ferguson, 163 U.S. 537 (1896).

33. See the Supreme Court decision Dred Scott v. Sandford, 60 U.S. 393 (1857).

34. Ibram X. Kendi, *Stamped from the Beginning* (Hachette, 2016), 31–46.

35. Haney Lopez, *supra* note 27, at 13.

36. See Deepa Kumar, *Islamophobia and the Politics of Empire: 20 Years after 9/11* (Verso, 2021).

37. Khaled A. Beydoun, "Antebellum Islam," *Howard Law Journal* 58 (2015). Also see Sylviane A. Diouf, *Servants of Allah: African Muslims Enslaved in the Americas* (NYU Press, 2013).

38. Richard Reeves, *Infamy: The Shocking Story of the Japanese American Internment in World War II* (Picador, 2016).

39. Natsu Taylor Saito, "Symbolism under Siege: Japanese American Redress and 'Racing' of Arab Americans as 'Terrorists,'" *Asian Law Journal* 8 (2001): 12.

40. Korematsu v. United States, 323 U.S. 214, 217–18 (1944). "[W]e are unable to conclude that it was beyond the war power of Congress and the Executive to exclude those of Japanese ancestry from the West Coast war area at the time they did."

41. Trump v. Hawaii, 585 U.S. 1 (2018). Justice Roberts delivered the majority opinion holding that it is within the president's Article II authority to limit the entry of aliens, if admitting them "would be detrimental to the interests of the United States." See also Shoba Sivaprasas Wadhia, *Banned: Immigration Enforcement in the Time of Trump* (NYU Press, 2019).

42. Isolating a class of people, oftentimes on account of race, national origin, religion, or a combination of these identities, law scholar Mark Tushnet argues, "is the central issue in thinking about civil liberties in wartime." Therefore, "otherization" is the process whereby state policy identifies a class of people as disloyal or subversive, threatening or warmongering during time of war. Mark Tushnet, "Defending Korematsu? Reflections on Civil Liberties in Wartime," *Wisconsin Law Review* (2003): 278.

43. Khaled A. Beydoun, *American Islamophobia: Understanding the Roots and Rise of Fear* (University of California Press, 2018), 76–78.

44. Edward Said, "The Essential Terrorist," in *Blaming the Victims: Spurious Scholarship and the Palestinian Question,* ed. Edward Said and Christopher Hitchens (Verso, 2001), 149.

45. George W. Bush, "Text: George W. Bush Addresses the Nation," *Washington Post,* September 20, 2001 (hereinafter War on Terror speech).

46. Samuel P. Huntington, "The Clash of Civilizations?," *Foreign Affairs,* Summer 1993.

47. Samuel P. Huntington, *Who Are We? The Challenges to America's National Identity* (Simon and Schuster, 2004), 24.

48. Beydoun, *supra* note 43, at 78–83.

49. "Warfare with other societies helped create the modern state as an entity separate from civil society and with the organizational means of supervising the population of a given territory." David Lyon, *The Electronic Eye* (University of Minnesota Press, 1994), 28.

50. Sarah Kendzior, *The View from Flyover Country: Dispatches from the Forgotten America* (Flatiron Books, 2018).

51. Ben Rhodes, "The 9/11 Era Is Over," *The Atlantic,* April 6, 2020.

52. Mark Danner, *Spiral: Trapped in the Forever War* (Simon and Schuster, 2016).

53. H. G. Wells, *The History of Mr. Polly* (1910).

54. Kimberlé Crenshaw, "Mapping the Margins: Intersectionality, Identity Politics, and Violence against Women of Color," *Stanford Law Review* 43 (1991): 1241.

55. Susan M. Akram and Kevin R. Johnson, "Race, Civil Rights, and Immigration Law after September 11, 2001: The Targeting of Arabs and Muslims," *NYU Annual Survey of American Law* (2002): 334. Marjorie Cohn, comparing the modern American surveillance state to the fictional land of Oceania in George Orwell's *1984*, observed, "Orwell never could have imagined that the National Security Agency (NSA) would amass metadata on billions of our phone calls and 200 million of our text messages every day. Orwell could not have foreseen that our government would read the content of our emails, file transfers, and live chats from the social media we use." Marjorie Cohn, "Beyond Orwell's Worst Nightmare," blog post, January 31, 2014.

56. Giroux, *supra* note 4. "Under the rubric of battling terrorism, the US government has waged a war on civil liberties, privacy and democracy."

57. Mahmood Mamdani, *Good Muslim, Bad Muslim: America, the Cold War, and the Roots of Terror* (Pantheon, 2004) (examining the genesis of the good-bad Muslim binary and its global application).

58. See Karen Engle, "Constructing Good Aliens and Good Citizens: Legitimizing the War on Terror(ism)," *University of Colorado Law Review* (2004): 59.

59. Nazita Lajevardi, *Outsiders at Home: The Politics of American Islamophobia* (Cambridge University Press, 2020), 30.

60. Vali Nasr, *The Shia Revival: How Conflicts within Islam Will Shape the Future* (W. W. Norton, 2007), 227.

61. Crenshaw, *supra* note 54, at 1241, 1244.

62. Linda Bosniak, *The Citizen and the Alien: Dilemmas of Contemporary Membership* (Princeton University Press, 2008), 30–31. "[Muslim Americans] may now enjoy nominal citizenship status, but their members are, in fact, afforded less in the way of substantive citizenship than others in society" (30).

63. Khaled A. Beydoun, "Between Muslim and White: The Legal Construction of Arab American Identity," *NYU Annual Survey of American Law* 69 (2013): 29.

64. Beydoun, *supra* note 43, at 76–78.

65. Edward W. Said, *Representations of the Intellectual* (Pantheon, 1994), 31.

66. Bush, War on Terror speech, *supra* note 45.

67. See Mamdani, *supra* note 57.

68. Asma T. Uddin, *When Islam Is Not a Religion* (Pegasus, 2019), 27–34.

69. Edward W. Said, *Orientalism* (Vintage, 1979), 9.

70. George Orwell, *1984* (Secker & Warburg, 1949), 319.

71. Hamid Dabashi, *Brown Skin, White Masks* (Pluto Press, 2011), 12.

72. Said, *supra* note 69.

73. Abed Ayoub and Khaled A. Beydoun, "Hollywood Shoots Arabs: The Movie," *Al Jazeera English*, January 25, 2015.

74. Leti Volpp, "The Citizen and the Terrorist," *UCLA Law Review* 49 (2002): 1586.

75. Said, *supra* note 65, at xii.

76. James Baldwin, *The Fire Next Time* (Dial Press, 1963), 81.

77. Stephennie Mulder, "History Shows What's Wrong with the Idea That War Is 'Normal' in the Middle East," *Time* (January 14, 2020).

78. Jack Shaheen, *Reel Bad Arabs: How Hollywood Vilifies a People* (Olive Branch Press, 2012).

79. Bush, War on Terror speech, *supra* note 45.

80. *"Shock and Awe" Campaign Underway in Iraq,* CNN (March 22, 2003).

81. Bush, War on Terror speech, *supra* note 45.

82. Ibid.

83. Orwell, *supra* note 70, at 89.

84. Akram and Johnson, *supra* note 55.

85. Andrew Selth, "Burma's Muslims and the War on Terror," *Studies in Conflict and Terrorism* 27 (2004): 107.

86. Leti Volpp, "Citizenship Undone," *Fordham Law Review* (2007): 2579, 2580.

87. Khaled A. Beydoun, "'Un-Mosquing' Obama's First US Mosque Visit," *Al Jazeera English,* February 4, 2016.

88. Barack Obama, "A New Beginning" speech, June 4, 2009.

89. Ibid.

90. Trevor McCrisken, "Ten Years On: Obama's War on Terrorism in Rhetoric and Practice," *Journal of International Affairs* 81 (July, 2011): 781.

91. Micah Zenko, "Obama's Final Drone Strike Data," Council on Foreign Relations blog post, January 20, 2017.

92. Rosa Brooks, "Drones and the International Rule of Law," *Journal of Ethics and International Affairs* 28 (2014).

93. "Obama Signs Executive Order on Gitmo," *New York Times,* January 24, 2009.

94. Sahar Aziz, "Policing Terrorists in the Community," *Harvard National Security Law Journal* 5 (2014): 147.

95. Khaled A. Beydoun, "'Muslim Bans' and the (Re)Making of Political Islamophobia," *Illinois Law Review* (2017).

96. Chauncey Devega, "From 9/11 to 11/9: Is Donald Trump's Election Collateral Damage from the 'War on Terror'?," *Salon,* November 16, 2016.

97. Jenna Johnson and Abigail Hauslohner, "'I Think Islam Hates Us': A Timeline of Trump's Comments about Islam and Muslims," *Washington Post,* May 20, 2017.

98. Jack Shafer, "Donald Trump Could Write the Book on Talking Like a Demagogue," *Politico,* June 1, 2020.

99. Edward Said, "Blind Imperial Arrogance," *Los Angeles Times,* July 20, 2003.

100. Ayaan Hirsi Ali, *Infidel: My Life* (Atria, 2008).

101. Thomas Kidd, *American Christians and Islam: Evangelical Culture and Muslims from the Colonial Period to the Age of Terrorism* (Princeton University Press, 2009), 145.

102. Sam Harris, "Lifting the 'Veil of Islamophobia': A Conversation with Ayaan Hirsi Ali," blog post, May 8, 2014.

103. Jordan Peterson, "A Message to Muslims," The Daily Wire, July 13, 2022.

104. Christopher Hitchens, *God Is Not Great: How Religion Poisons Everything* (Twelve, 2007).

105. Daniel Oppenheimer, "Christopher Hitchens' Last Years: Islam, the Iraq War, and How a Man of the Left Found His Moment by Breaking with the Left," *Salon,* February 14, 2016.

106. Hamid Dabashi, "The Liberal Roots of Islamophobia" (Opinion), *Al Jazeera English,* March 3, 2017.

107. Hitchens, *supra* note 104.

108. Khaled A. Beydoun, "US Liberal Islamophobia Is Rising—And More Insidious than Rightwing Bigotry" (Opinion), *The Guardian,* May 26, 2018.

109. Frantz Fanon, *Black Skin, White Masks* (Pluto Press, 1986), 38.

110. "Hunger Strike," *Temple of the Dog* (A&M, 1991).

111. Interview with Jihan on July 10, 2019—name changed for anonymity.

112. Saba Aziz, "'Totally Destroyed': East Aleppo a Year after Battle," *Al Jazeera English,* November 17, 2017.

113. Harper Neidig, "Trump Warns against Syrian Refugees: 'A Lot of These People Are ISIS,'" *The Hill,* June 29, 2016.

114. Khaled A. Beydoun, "The Ban and the Borderlands Within: The Travel Ban as a Domestic War on Terror Tool," *Stanford Law Review* 71 (2019): 251.

115. Beydoun, *supra* note 43, at 40–44.

116. Margaret Talbot, "The Story of a Hate Crime," *The New Yorker,* June 15, 2015.

117. That is, anti-Muslim animus or violence inflicted by individual bigots or actors not tied to the state; versus "structural Islamophobia," such as law, policy, and action taken by a state agency or actor.

118. Basit Mahmood, "Is Islamophobia the 'Last Acceptable Form of Prejudice'?," *Newsweek,* September 11, 2020.

119. Mathis Bitton, "France's Failed Colorblindness Experiment," *The National Review,* July 17, 2020.

120. Nick Cumming-Bruce, "'No Such Thing': China Denied U.N. Reports on Uyghur Detention Camps," *New York Times,* August 13, 2018.

121. Albert Memmi, *The Colonizer and the Colonized* (Beacon Press, 1957).

122. Jonathan A. C. Brown, *Misquoting Muhammad: The Challenge and Choices of Interpreting the Prophet's Legacy* (Oneworld, 2015).

123. Albert Camus, *The Stranger* (Knopf, 1988), 12.

124. Baldwin, *supra* note 76, at 24.

125. Wael B. Hallaq, *An Introduction to Islamic Law* (Cambridge University Press, 2012).

126. Baldwin, *supra* note 76, at 70.

127. Edward Bulwer-Lytton, *Richelieu; Or the Conspiracy* (1839).

CHAPTER 3. BLOOD AND SOIL

Epigraphs: Salman Rushdie, *The Satanic Verses* (Penguin, 1988), 185; Rana Ayyub on Twitter, March 16, 2020.

1. Interview with Mrinal on March 10, 2017—name changed to protect her anonymity.

2. Kim Severson, Matthew Haag, and Julie Moskin, "Anthony Bourdain, Renegade Chef Who Reported from the World Tables, Dies at 61," *New York Times,* June 8, 2018.

3. Max Fisher, "Everything You Need to Know about Narendra Modi's 2014 Rise," *Vox,* May 14, 2015.

4. *Anthony Bourdain: No Reservations,* season 2, episode 5, "India (Rajasthan)."

5. James Traub, "Is Modi's India Safe for Muslims," *Foreign Policy,* June 26, 2015.

6. Imran Kazmi, "Anthony Bourdain: Celebrity Chef Who 'Humanised' Palestinians," *Express Tribune,* June 8, 2018.

7. Aatish Taseer, "India Is No Longer India," *The Atlantic,* May 15, 2020.

8. Lindsay Maizland, "India's Muslims: An Increasingly Marginalized Population," Council on Foreign Relations, August 20, 2020.

9. Narendra Jadjav, *Untouchables: My family's Triumphant Journey out of the Caste System in Modern India* (Scribner, 2005).

10. Kingshuk Nag, *The Saffron Tide: The Rise of the BJP* (Rupa Publications, 2014).

11. Rana Ayyub, *Gujarat Files: Anatomy of a Cover Up* (Rana Ayyub, 2016).

12. See Vinay Pitapati, *India before Modi: How the BJP Came to Power* (Hurst and Company, 2021).

13. Rupam Jain Nair, "New Recruits to Hindu Cause Hear Anti-Muslim Message," Reuters, October 12, 2015.

14. Audrey Truschke on Twitter, May 30, 2019. See Audrey Truschke, *Aurangzeb: The Man and the Myth* (Penguin, 2017).

15. Prashant Waikar, "Reading Islamophobia in Hindutva: An Analysis of Narendra Modi's Political Discourse," *Islamophobia Studies Journal* 4 (2018): 161.

16. Vinayak Damodar Savarkar, *Hindutva: Who Is a Hindu?* (2017).

17. Devjyot Ghoshal, "Amit Shah Vows to Throw Illegal Immigrants into Bay of Bengal," Reuters, April 12, 2019.

18. Interview with Mrinal on January 10, 2020.

19. Amrit Dhillon, "'If They Kill One, We Will Kill 100': How Can This Man Lead India's Biggest State?," *Sydney Morning Herald,* March 31, 2017.

20. Dexter Filkins, "Blood and Soil in Narendra Modi's India," *The New Yorker,* December 2, 2019.

21. Interview with Syed Mohd Gulam Baquer on February 11, 2020.

22. Interview with Jaiwanth Reddy on February 15, 2020.

23. Samanth Subramanian, "How Hindu Supremacists Are Tearing India Apart," *The Guardian,* February 20, 2020.

24. Interview with Dr. Sharath R. on February 21, 2020—name abridged in line with interviewee's wishes.

25. Khaled A. Beydoun, "Exporting Islamophobia in the Global 'War on Terror,'" *New York University Law Review* 95 (2020): 96.

26. Interview with Shivansh Umatt of New Delhi on February 27, 2020.

27. Jean-Paul Sartre, *No Exit and Three Other Plays* (Random House, 1976).

28. Ibid.

29. Conrad Hackett, "By 2050, India to Have Largest Populations of Hindus and Muslims," Pew Research Center, April 21, 2015.

30. Filkins, *supra* note 20.

31. Interview with Mrinal, *supra* note 1.

32. "Citizenship (Amendment) Act of 2019: What Is It and Why Is It Seen as a Problem," *Economic Times,* December 31, 2019.

33. Sameer Yasir and Billy Perrigo, "'The Police Did Nothing': Students in India Are Protesting after a Masked Mob Violently Attacked a Top Delhi University," *Time,* January 7, 2020.

34. Ayyub, *supra* note 11, at 67.

35. "Renowned Chef Anthony Bourdain Commits Suicide in Hotel Room," *The Telegraph,* June 8, 2018.

36. "The idea of India was a historical recognition that over time—and not always peacefully—a great diversity had collected on the Indian subcontinent. The modern republic, as a reflection of that history, would belong not to any one group, but to all groups in equal measure." Taseer, *supra* note 7, at 4.

37. Ibid.

38. James Baldwin, *The Fire Next Time* (Dial Press, 1963).

39. Interview with Abdul R. on October 1, 2019—name changed to protect his anonymity.

40. Poorna Swami, "A Template for Violence," *The Caravan,* September 17, 2019.

41. Ayyub, *supra* note 11, at 81–82.

42. Kamal Mitra Chenoy, S. P. Shukla, K. S. Subramanian, and Achin Vanaik, "Gujarat Carnage 2002," *Outlook India,* April 11, 2002.

43. This was the slogan pushed by Donald Trump as he campaigned for the American presidency in 2016, illustrated most vividly by the red hats his supporters wore at campaign rallies and beyond. The hat emerged into a political statement that superseded its electoral purpose and maintained its resonance after Trump was voted out of office in 2020.

44. Rebecca Ratcliffe, "Howdy Modi: Indian PM Appears with Trump at Texas Rally," *The Guardian,* September 23, 2019.

45. Ayyub, *supra* note 11, at 80.

46. Khaled A. Beydoun, "Modi's Crusade: Citizenship Amendment Bill Paves the Way for an India without Islam," *The New Arab,* December 13, 2019.

47. Ibid.

48. Ibid.

49. Sabrina Siddiqi, "Trump and a Muslim Registry: Does He Want One—And Is It Even Possible?," *The Guardian,* November 27, 2016.

50. Interview with Mohammed Asif Khan on March 8, 2020.

51. Bernadette Atuahene, *We Want What's Ours: Learning from South Africa's Restitution Program* (Oxford University Press, 2014).

52. Interview with Shoaib Hussein on March 2, 2020—name changed to protect his anonymity.

53. Bibhudatta Pradhan, "Millions in India Could End Up in Modi's Detention Camps," *Bloomberg,* Febuary 25, 2020.

54. Guarav C. Savant, "America Loves India, America Respects India: Donald Trump," *India Today,* February 25, 2020.

55. Ayyub, *supra* note 11, at 80.

56. Joanna Slater and Nina Masih, "Death Toll Passes 30 in Delhi Violence as Modi Issues Plea for Calm," *Washington Post,* February 26, 2020.

57. CJ Werleman, "A Short History of India's Anti-Muslim Pogroms," March 12, 2020.

58. Priyanka Bansal, "Trump Is Enabling Modi's Islamophobia in India. But So Are Many Indian Americans," *Yahoo.com,* February 28, 2020.

59. Beydoun, *supra* note 25, at 96–98.

60. Wire Staff, "Delhi Riots Death Toll at 53, Here Are the Names of 51 of the Victims," *The Wire,* March 6, 2020.

61. Mira Kamdar, "What Happened in Delhi Was a Pogrom," *The Atlantic,* February 28, 2020.

62. Mobashara Tazamal, "COVID19 Is Exacerbating Islamophobia in India," The Bridge Initiative, Georgetown University, May 14, 2020.

63. Sameer Yasir, "India Is Scapegoating Muslims for the Spread of the Coronavirus," *Foreign Policy,* April 22, 2020.

64. "Tablighi Jamaat: The Group Blamed for New COVID-19 Outbreak in India," *BBC News,* April 2, 2020.

65. Niharika Sharma, "The Nizamuddin Meet Wasn't the Only Instance of Callousness amid the COVID-19 Scare in India," *Quartz India,* April 2, 2020.

66. "Tablighi Jamaat: The Group Blamed for New COVID-19 Outbreak in India," *BBC News,* April 2, 2020.

67. Baldwin, *supra* note 38, at 56.

68. Sameer Yasir, "Indian Muslims Attacked over Coronavirus," *Foreign Policy,* April 22, 2020.

69. Jeffrey Gettleman, Kai Schultz, and Suhasini Raj, "In India, Coronavirus Fans Religious Hatred," *New York Times,* April 12, 2020.

70. Ibid.

71. Interview with Abdullah on June 25, 2020—name changed to protect his anonymity.

72. Zach Schonbrun, "Tarnished by Charlottesville, Tiki Torch Company Tries to Move On," *New York Times,* August 20, 2017.

73. Interview with Yusuf, 35, on April 15, 2020.

74. Beydoun, *supra* note 46.

75. Mo Abbas, Bill Neely, and Alexander Smith, "Trump Heaps Praise on India's Modi in Packed Stadium," *NBC News,* February 24, 2020.

76. "Delhi Riots: Victims Struggle to Rebuild Their Lives," DW, March 20, 2020.

77. Naomi Barton, "Delhi Riots: Mosque Set on Fire in Ashok Nagar, Hanuman Flag Placed on Minaret," *The Wire,* February 25, 2020.

78. Snighda Pooman, "The 3 Most Polarizing Words in India," *Foreign Policy,* February 13, 2020.

79. Arabic.

80. Leti Volpp, "Citizenship Undone," *Fordham Law Review* 75 (2007): 2579, 2584.

81. Ibid.

82. Ayyub, *supra* note 11, at 14.

83. "India Court Upholds Ban on Hijab in Schools and Colleges," NPR, March 15, 2022.

84. "Looking at Kashmir through 2020 Pulitzer Prize–Winning Photos," *US News,* May 6, 2020.

85. Hannah Ellis-Peterson, "India Strips Kashmir of Special Status and Divides It into Two," *The Guardian,* October 31, 2019.

86. "Photo of Toddler Sitting on His Grandfather's Body Angers Kashmir," *Al Jazeera English,* July 2, 2020.

87. "Security Forces Save a Three-Year-Old Child from Being Killed by Terrorists in Kashmir. Watch as Cops Take Him to His Mother," *Op India,* July 1, 2020.

88. Ibid.

89. Ibid.

90. Ashraf Wani, "Kashmir: Heartbreaking Images Show 3-Year-Old Crying over Body of Grandfather Killed in Cross-Firing," *India Today,* July 1, 2020.

91. Taseer, *supra* note 7, at 4.

92. Ellis-Peterson, *supra* note 85.

93. Interview with Yusra on January 19, 2020—name changed to protect her anonymity.

94. Goldie Osuri, "Imperialism, Colonialism and Sovereignty in the (Post) Colony: India and Kashmir," *Third World Quarterly* 38 (2017).

95. Interview with Roya, 25, on April 15, 2020—name changed to protect her anonymity.

96. Arshad R. Zargar, "After Record-Long Blackout, India Restores Full Internet Access in Kashmir—For Now," *CBS News,* March 4, 2020.

97. Sanjay Kumar, "Kashmir's Communication Blackout Is a 'Devastating Blow' for Academics, Researchers Say," *Science Magazine,* August 19, 2019.

98. "Amid Curfew and Communication Blackout, Over 100 Political Leaders, Activists Arrested in Kashmir," *Outlook,* August 7, 2019.

99. Zargar, *supra* note 96.

100. "Limited Internet Restored in Kashmir, No Access to Social Media," *Al Jazeera English,* January 25, 2020.

101. Kai Schultz and Sameer Yasir, "India Restores Some Internet Access in Kashmir after Long Shutdown," *New York Times,* January 26, 2020.

102. Interview with Ali Hussain Mir on March 2, 2020.

103. Meeting with Kashmiri leaders and the founders of Kashmir House, Istanbul, June 12, 2022.

104. Navnita Chadha Behera, "Terror Trail Leads from Kabul to Kashmir," Brookings Institute, May 25, 2002.

105. Bhavna Vij-Aurora, "Allahabad to Prayagraj: The Politics of Name Change," *Outlook India Magazine,* November 26, 2018.

106. Junaid Kathju, "As Civilian Is Killed in Encounter, Police Place Kashmiri Child at Centre of Propaganda War," *The Wire,* July 1, 2020.

107. "Russell Tribunal Triggers Debate on Kashmir Crisis," World Kashmir Awareness Forum, December 22, 2021.

108. John Muir, *Wilderness Essays* (Martino Fine Books, 2018), 78.

CHAPTER 4. INTERNMENT AND EXILE

Epigraphs: Aldous Huxley, *Brave New World* (Chatto and Windus, 1932), 112; Philip Gourevitch, *We Wish to Inform You That Tomorrow We Will Be Killed with

Our Families (Farrar, Straus and Giroux, 1998), 67; Nayyirah Waheed, "Immigrant," in *Salt* (CreateSpace, 2013), 5.

1. Julia van den Muijsenberg, "Uyghur Camp Survivor: 'The Chinese Guards Laughed, Checking Our Naked Bodies. We Couldn't Even Cry,'" *The International Angle,* January 9, 2020.

2. "U.N. Panel Confronts China over Reports That It Holds a Million Uighurs in Camps," *New York Times,* August 10, 2018. The number of Uyghur and ethnic Muslims imprisoned in Chinese camps could be as high as 2 million. Lindsay Maizland, "China's Repression of Uyghurs in China," Council on Foreign Relations, June 30, 2020. The number of concentration camps was sourced from Sheena Chestnut Greitens, Myunghee Lee, and Emir Yazici, "Counterterrorism and Preventive Repression: China's Changing Strategy in Xinjiang," *International Security* 44 (2019): 9, 10.

3. Van den Muijsenberg, *supra* note 1, at 2.

4. See Bernadette Atuahene, "Dignity Takings and Dignity Restoration: Creating a New Theoretical Framework for Understanding Involuntary Property Loss and the Remedies Required," *Law and Social Inquiry* 41 (2016): 796, 817, where the author defines a "dignity taking" as the stripping of humanity that accompanies the taking of property.

5. Van den Muijsenberg, *supra* note 1, at 4.

6. David Stavrou, "A Million People Are Jailed at China's Gulags. I Managed to Escape. Here's What Really Goes On Inside," *Haaretz,* October 17, 2019.

7. Adrian Zenz, "'Wash Brains, Cleanse Hearts': Evidence from Chinese Government Documents about the Nature and Extent of Xinjiang's Extrajudicial Internment Campaign," *Journal of Political Risk* 7 (2019).

8. Sigal Samuel, "China Is Treating Islam Like a Mental Illness," *The Atlantic,* August 28, 2018.

9. Staff, "'Eradicating Ideological Viruses': China's Campaign of Repression against Xinjiang's Muslims," Human Rights Watch, September 9, 2018. Xinjiang is also referred to as the Xinjiang Uyghur Autonomous Region. For purposes of brevity, I sometimes refer to the disputed territory as Xinjiang and East Turkistan. For a comprehensive history of the territory, see James Millward, *Eurasian Crossroads: A History of Xinjiang* (Hurst and Company, 2007).

10. Jean Seaton, "Why Orwell's 1984 Could Be about Now," BBC Culture, May 7, 2018.

11. See Khaled A. Beydoun, "Exporting Islamophobia in the Global 'War on Terror,'" *New York University Law Review* 95 (2020): 81, 93–96, for an examination of how the American War on Terror facilitated the Chinese regime's crackdown on the Uyghur under the banner of counterterror.

12. Van den Muijsenberg, *supra* note 1.

13. The Han are the largest ethnic group in China, comprising roughly 91 percent of the population. Staff, "Who Is Chinese? The Upper Han," *The Economist*, November 19, 2016.

14. Michel Foucault, *Discipline and Punish: The Birth of the Prison* (Penguin, 1975), 205. A panopticon is a form of prison designed to maintain continual surveillance of the captives. Jeremy Bentham, *Panopticon* (1791). See also Ross Anderson, "The Panopticon Is Already Here," *The Atlantic*, September 2020, examining President Xi Jinping's use of artificial intelligence to police and subdue Xinjiang's Uyghur.

15. Law scholar Chaz Arnett defines "e-carceration" as "electronic correctional surveillance, such as electronic ankle monitors . . . which seeks to encapsulate the outsourcing of aspects of prison into communities under the guise of carceral humanism: the repackaging and rebranding of corrections and correctional programming as caring and supportive, while still clinging to punitive culture." "From Decarceration to E-Carceration," *Cardozo Law Review* 41 (2019): 641, 645.

16. China has an estimated 200 million surveillance cameras throughout its territory, "four times as many as the United States." Paul Mozur, "Inside China's Dystopian Dreams: A.I., Shame and Lots of Cameras," *New York Times*, July 8, 2018.

17. See generally Shoshana Zuboff, *The Age of Surveillance Capitalism: The Fight for a Human Future at the New Frontier of Power* (PublicAffairs, 2019).

18. Eurasia Group, "The Digital Silk Road: Expanding China's Digital Footprint," April 9, 2020.

19. Khaled A. Beydoun, "The New State of Surveillance: Societies of Subjugation," *Washington and Lee Law Review* 79 (2022).

20. Khaled A. Beydoun, "For China, Islam Is a 'Mental Illness' That Needs to Be Cured," *Al Jazeera English*, November 28, 2018.

21. Ibid.

22. For an accessible account of the establishment and expansion of the Chinese surveillance state across the country, see generally Kai

Strittmatter, *We Have Been Harmonized: Life in China's Surveillance State* (Custom House, 2020).

23. Raul Hilberg, *The Destruction of the European Jews* (Holmes and Meier, 1985).

24. Kate Cronin-Furman, "China Has Chosen Cultural Genocide in Xinjiang—For Now," *Foreign Policy,* September 19, 2018.

25. "Data Leak Reveals How China 'Brainwashes' Uighurs in Prison Camps," *BBC News,* November 24, 2019.

26. "Why Is There Tension between China and the Uighurs?," *BBC News,* September 26, 2014.

27. Darren Byler, *Inside the Camps: Life in China's High-Tech Penal Colony* (Columbia Global Reports, 2021), 18–19.

28. Aidan North, "The Ominous Metaphors of China's Uighur Concentration Camps," *The Conversation,* January 19, 2020.

29. "Committee on the Elimination of Racial Discrimination Reviews the Report on China," United Nations Human Rights, Office of the High Commissioner, press release, August 10, 2018.

30. Samuel, *supra* note 8.

31. Jon Sharman, "China 'Forcing Muslims to Eat Pork and Drink Alcohol' for Lunar New Year Festival," *The Independent,* February 7, 2019.

32. Samuel, *supra* note 8.

33. Nicole Bozorgmir and Isobel Yeung, "Uighur Parents Say China Is Ripping Their Children Away and Brainwashing Them," *Vice News,* July 1, 2019.

34. "Document: What Chinese Officials Told Children Whose Families Were Put in Camps," *New York Times,* November 16, 2019.

35. This was emphatically stressed during my interview with Julie Millsap, the communication director of the Washington, DC–based advocacy group Campaign for Uyghurs, on August 17, 2020.

36. "China's Global Power Damps Criticism of Uighur Crackdown," *Financial Times,* December 22, 2019.

37. Beydoun, *supra* note 11, at 93–96.

38. Joseph Grieboski, "Tension, Repression, and Discrimination: China's Uyghurs under Threat," *Georgetown Journal of International Affairs,* September 23, 2014.

39. Byler, *supra* note 27, at 14.

40. Khaled A. Beydoun, "The Long Jump over Xinjiang: Digging for Gold at China's Genocide Olympics," Al Araby, February 3, 2022.

41. Interview with Yusef via completed questionnaire, March 3, 2020.

42. Samuel, *supra* note 8.

43. Beydoun, *supra* note 11, at 93–96.

44. Jianli Yang and Lianchao Han, "Beyond Xinjiang's Camps, China Threatens Uighurs Globally," *The Hill*, June 5, 2020.

45. "China Has Turned Xinjiang into a Police State Like No Other," *The Economist*, May 31, 2018.

46. Chris Buckley and Paul Mozur, "How China Uses High-Tech Surveillance to Subdue Minorities," *New York Times*, May 22, 2019.

47. Zuboff, *supra* note 17, at 389.

48. Eleanor Albert, "The State Religion of China," Council on Foreign Relations, October 11, 2018.

49. Tears for Fears, "Everybody Wants to Rule the World," *Songs from the Big Chair* (Phonogram and Mercury, 1985).

50. Lawrence Lessig, "On the Internet and the Benign Invasions of Nineteen Eighty-Four," in On *"Nineteen Eighty-Four,"* ed. A. Gleason, J. Goldsmith, and M. Nussbaum (Princeton University Press, 2010), 213.

51. George Orwell, *1984* (Secker & Warburg, 1949), 26.

52. Anne Frank, *The Diary of a Young Girl* (Bantam, 1993).

53. David Mann, "The *World Book,*" in *Evocative Objects: Things We Think With*, ed. Sherry Turkle (MIT Press, 2007).

54. Amy Gunia, "China Destroyed Mosques and Other Religious Sites in Xinjiang, Report Says," *Time*, May 7, 2019.

55. Ibid.

56. Interview with Zeinab on January 9, 2020—name changed to protect her anonymity.

57. Paulo Coelho.

58. Robin Wright and Edwin Chen, "Bush Says China Backs War on Terror," *Los Angeles Times*, October 18, 2001.

59. Ibid.

60. Speculation about China becoming the next "Al Qaeda haven" continued in the years that followed, a ploy drummed up by Washington and Beijing to justify the extension of the American War on Terror into China. See

Andrew Chang, "Could China Be the Next Al Qaeda Haven?," *ABC News*, January 6, 2006.

61. Miles Maochun Yu, "China's Final Solution in Xinjiang," *The Caravan* (Hoover Institution), October 9, 2018.

62. Akbar Shahid Ahmed, "China Is Using U.S. 'War on Terror' Rhetoric to Justify Detaining 1 Million People," *Huffington Post*, December 2, 2018.

63. Yu, *supra* note 61.

64. Wright and Chen, *supra* note 58.

65. Jacques Neriah, "The Chinese Approach to Uyghur Separatism," *The Caravan* (Hoover Institution), October 2, 2018.

66. ANI, "Public Washroom Constructed on Razed Mosque Site in China's Xinjiang," *The New Indian Express*, August 17, 2020.

67. Yu, *supra* note 61.

68. Daniel Lippman and Nahal Toosi, "Trump Administration Weighs Accusing China of 'Genocide' over Uighurs," *Politico*, August 2, 2020.

69. James Fallows, "On Uighurs, Han, and General Racial Attitudes in China," *The Atlantic*, July 13, 2009.

70. Interview with Zeinab, *supra* note 56.

71. Aftab Ali, "China Bans Muslims from Fasting during Ramadan, Says Uighur Community," *The Independent*, June 17, 2015.

72. "China: Religious Repression of Uighur Muslims," Human Rights Watch, April 12, 2005.

73. Alexandra Ma, "Maps Show 500 Suspected Camps, Prisons China Uses to Detain Uighurs," *Business Insider*, November 25, 2019.

74. Simina Mistreanu, "Study Links Nike, Adidas and Apple to Forced Uighur Labor," *Forbes*, March 2, 2020.

75. Adrian Zenz, "China's Own Documents Show Potentially Genocidal Sterilization Plans in Xinjiang," *Foreign Policy*, July 1, 2020.

76. Rayhan Asat and Yonah Diamond, "The World's Most Technologically Sophisticated Genocide Is Happening in Xinjiang," *Foreign Policy*, July 15, 2020.

77. Will Martin, "China Is Harvesting Thousands of Human Organs from Its Uighur Muslim Minority, UN Human-Rights Body Hears," *Business Insider*, September 25, 2019.

78. Rob Schmitz, "Families of the Disappeared: A Search for Loved Ones Held in China's Xinjiang Region," NPR, November 12, 2018.

79. "Xinjiang Authorities Push Uyghurs to Marry Han Chinese," Radio Free Asia, www.rfa.org/english/news/special/uyghur-oppression/ChenPolicy2.html.

80. Jean-Paul Sartre, *No Exit and Three Other Plays* (Random House, 1976), 31.

81. Greitens, Lee, and Yazici, *supra* note 2, at 9.

82. Ibid.

83. Beydoun, *supra* note 19. "Spy doves" are drones designed to look like real birds. These mobile surveillance devices are used by the Chinese state to track and spy on Uyghurs and the general population. See www.siliconrepublic.com/machines/china-spying-doves-iot.

84. Byler, *supra* note 27, at 121.

85. Name changed to protect the anonymity of the child.

86. Sigal Samuel, "China's Jaw-Dropping Family Separation Policy," *The Atlantic,* September 4, 2018.

87. Bozorgmir and Yeung, *supra* note 33.

88. "Xinjiang: Children of Uyghur Deportees Locked in Orphanages," Asia News, July 3, 2018.

89. Darren Byler, *In the Camps: China's High-Tech Penal Colony* (Columbia Global Reports, 2021), 31.

90. Raffaele Morgantini, "Ghassan Kanafani: Revolutionary Writer and Journalist," *Investig'Action,* July 21, 2017.

91. "The Rohingya: World's Least-Wanted People," Radio Free Asia (collection of articles and images), September 1, 2020.

92. Interview with Fatima R. on July 20, 2020—name changed to protect her anonymity.

93. Azeem Ibrahim, *The Rohingyas: Inside Myanmar's Hidden Genocide* (Hurst and Company, 2016).

94. Reed Brody, "International Court of Justice Orders Burmese Authorities to Protect Rohingya Muslims from Genocide," Human Rights Watch, January 27, 2020.

95. Emily Fishbein, "A Place I Can Call Home," *Chicago Reader,* July 3, 2019.

96. "Rohingya Refugees Rebuilding Their Lives in Chicago," *Al Jazeera English,* January 24, 2019.

97. "Rohingya Survivor: The Army Threw My Baby into a Fire," *Al Jazeera English,* October 13, 2017.

98. Edward Said, "Reflections on Exile," *Granta Magazine,* September 1, 1984.

99. Sade, "Like a Tattoo," *Love Deluxe* (Epic, 1992).

100. Laignee Barron, "Rohingya Crisis: Report Says 43,000 Missing, Presumed Dead," *Time,* March 8, 2018.

101. "Myanmar: Aung San Suu Kyi Appears before ICJ in Genocide Case," Amnesty International, December 10, 2019.

102. Bernard Kouchner, "Free Aung San Suu Kyi," *New York Times,* June 12, 2019.

103. Brody, *supra* note 94.

104. "Discrimination in Arakan," Human Rights Watch, 2002.

105. Moshe Yegar, *Between Integration and Secession: The Muslim Communities in the Southern Philippines, Southern Thailand, and Western Burma/Myanmar* (Lexington, 2002).

106. Katie Hunt, "Rohingya Crisis: How We Got Here," CNN, November 12, 2017.

107. "Buddhism in Myanmar," Religious Literacy Project, Harvard School of Divinity.

108. David Steinberg, "'Legitimacy' in Burma/Myanmar: Concepts and Implications," in *Myanmar: State, Society, and Ethnicity,* ed. N. Ganesan and Kyaw Yin Hlaing (ISEAS, 2007), 109–42.

109. Interview with Ayoub, Legal Director of the American Arab Anti-Discrimination Committee and immigration law expert, on April 2, 2020.

110. Shoon Naing, "Hundreds Rally against Myanmar Police over Child Rape Cases," Reuters, December 23, 2019.

111. "Mosques, Madrasas to Be Razed in Myanmar's Rakhine State," Voice of America, September 21, 2016.

112. I cross-checked this testimony with several sources, including this article published by the *New York Times,* which illustrated that the throwing of babies into fires was, horrifically, a common occurrence in Rakhine State during the violent crackdown in 2017: Jeffrey Gettleman, "Rohingya Recount Atrocities: 'They Threw My Baby Into a Fire,'" *New York Times,* October 11, 2017.

113. George Mobniot, "Take Away Aung San Suu Kyi's Nobel Prize. She No Longer Deserves It," *The Guardian,* September 5, 2017.

114. Beydoun, *supra* note 11, at 82–84.

115. UN High Commissioner for Refugees (UNHCR), https://www.reuters.com/article/myanmar-rohingya-un/myanmar-generals-had-genocidal-intent-against-rohingya-must-face-justice-un-idUSL8N1VH04R.

116. "Myanmar Rohingya: What You Need to Know about the Crisis," *BBC News*, January 23, 2020.

117. Hannah Beech, "Hundreds of Rohingya Refugees Stuck at Sea with 'Zero Hope,'" *New York Times*, May 1, 2020.

118. Joanna Tan, "From Stateless to Displaced, the Rohingya Are Still Searching for Hope Years after Fleeing Myanmar," CNBC, July 3, 2020.

119. "Timeline: How the Crackdown on Myanmar's Rohingya Unfolded," *Al Jazeera English*, December 9, 2019.

120. Ibid.

121. Mahmoud Darwish, "Diary of a Palestinian Wound" (1971).

122. Zuboff, *supra* note 17, at 5.

123. Paulo Coelho, *The Alchemist* (Harper One, 1993), 86.

CHAPTER 5. PANDEMIC AND PLAGUE

Epigraphs: Albert Camus, *The Plague* (Vintage, 1991); Médine, "Bataclan," *Storyteller* (DiN Records, 2018); Simone de Beauvoir, *The Second Sex* (Vintage, 2011), 312.

1. Names of the mother and daughter have been changed in line with the wishes of the subjects.

2. "Death Toll from Virus Exceeds 30,000," *France 24 News*, July 10, 2020.

3. The Amazigh people, popularly referred to as Berbers, are a culturally heterogeneous people indigenous to northern Africa. Many French people, particularly in the banlieues, trace their origin to Amazigh nations in Africa and identify as Amazigh. Bruce Maddy-Weitzman, *The Berber Identity Movement and the Challenge to North African States* (University of Texas Press, 2011), 143–46.

4. Thomas Crampton, "Behind the Furor, the Last Moments of Two Youths," *New York Times*, November 7, 2005.

5. Jane Kramer, "Taking the Veil: How France's Public Schools Became the Battleground in a Culture War," *The New Yorker*, November 15, 2004.

6. Khaled A. Beydoun and Nura Sediqe, "Unveiling," *California Law Review* 111 (forthcoming 2023).

7. The headscarf, or hijab, is commonly referred to as the "flag of Islam." It is perceived by many to be a quintessential symbol of Islam that conjures up stereotypes of Muslim women as subordinate, passive, and confined. These tropes conflict with the images of women promoted by Abercrombie and Fitch, a popular clothing company that promotes a wholesome, all-American lifestyle to college-aged teens and young adults. Ann Taylor, Sanaa Ayoub, and Fatima Moussa, "The Hijab in Public Schools," *Religion in Education* 41 (2013): 8.

8. Chloe Farand, "Marine Le Pen Launches Presidential Campaign with Hardline Speech," *The Independent,* Feburary 5, 2017.

9. Khaled A. Beydoun, "Laïcité, Liberalism and the Headscarf," *Journal of Islamic Law and Culture* 10 (2008): 204.

10. Angelique Chrisafis, "Nicolas Sarkozy Says Islamic Veils Are Not Welcome in France," *The Guardian,* June 22, 2009.

11. Ibid.

12. Beydoun and Sediqe, *supra* note 6.

13. Bronywn Winter, *Hijab and the Republic: Uncovering the French Headscarf Debate* (Syracuse University Press, 2008).

14. Fatema Mernissi, *Scheherazade Goes West: Different Cultures, Different Harems* (Washington Square Press, 2001), 58.

15. Conrad Hackett, "5 Facts about the Muslim Population in Europe," Pew Research Center, November 29, 2017.

16. E. Tendayi Achiume, "Migration as Decolonization," *Stanford Law Review* 71 (2019): 1509.

17. Mehammad Amadeus Mack, *Sexagon: Muslims, France, and the Sexualization of National Culture* (Fordham University Press, 2017), 35–78.

18. Rokhaya Diallo, "Hijab: A Very French Obsession" (Opinion), *Al Jazeera English,* April 4, 2018.

19. Gayatri Spivak, "Can the Subaltern Speak? Speculations on Widow Sacrifice," *Wedge* 7 (1985): 120.

20. Christopher de Bellaigue, "In France, Muslims Face Mass Incarceration," Pulitzer Center, April 8, 2016.

21. Jon Stone, "French Senate Votes to Ban Mothers Who Wear Headscarves from Accompanying Children on School Trips," *The Independent,* May 17, 2019.

22. Jennifer E. Sessions, *By Sword and Plow: France and the Conquest of Algeria* (Cornell University Press, 2014).

23. Bill Bostock, "France Has Made Wearing Face Masks Compulsory in Public, While Maintaining a Controversial Ban on Burqas and Niqabs," *Business Insider,* May 11, 2020.

24. Jason Silverstein, "France Will Still Ban Islamic Face Covering Even after Making Masks Mandatory," *CBS News,* May 12, 2020.

25. Bostock, *supra* note 23, at 1.

26. Adrien K. Wing and Monica Nigh Smith, "Critical Race Feminism Lifts the Veil? Muslim Women, France, and the Headscarf Ban," *University of California Davis Law Review* 39 (2008): 743.

27. Albert Camus, *The Plague* (Vintage, 1991), 102.

28. Nawaal El Saadawi, *Woman at Point Zero* (Zed, 2007), 63.

29. Interview with Malik on March 3, 2020—name changed to protect his anonymity.

30. Hisham D. Aidi, *Rebel Music: Race, Empire, and the New Muslim Youth Culture* (Vintage, 2014).

31. Su'ad Abdul Kabeer, *Muslim Cool* (NYU Press, 2017).

32. Giles Kepel, *Les Banlieues de l'Islam: Naissance d'une Religion en France* (Points, 2015).

33. Elian Peltier, "Médine: The Pugnacious French Rapper Who Hits Back at Critics," *New York Times,* November 18, 2018.

34. Khaled A. Beydoun, "Beyond the Paris Attacks: Unveiling the War within French Counterterror Policy," *American University Law Review* 65 (2016): 1276.

35. "Paris Attacks: What Happened on the Night?," *BBC News,* December 9, 2015.

36. Rokhaya Diallo, "Can a Muslim Perform at the Bataclan in Paris?," *Al Jazeera English,* June 21, 2018.

37. Erik Love, *Islamophobia and Racism in America* (NYU Press, 2017), 2–3.

38. Beydoun, *supra* note 34.

39. Jean Marie Beamen, "Identity, Marginalization, and Parisian Banlieues," *Research in Urban Sociology* 10 (2010): 153.

40. Andrew Hussey, *The French Intifada: The Long War between France and Its Arabs* (Farrar, Straus and Giroux, 2014), 404.

41. Achiume, *supra* note 16, at 1553.

42. Peltier, *supra* note 33, at 2.

43. Beydoun and Sediqe, *supra* note 6.

44. Jean Beamen, *Citizen Outsider: Children of North African Immigrants in France* (University of California Press, 2017), 56.

45. Scott Atran and Nafees Hamid, "Paris: The War ISIS Wants," *Foreign Policy*, January 7, 2016.

46. James Baldwin, "Letter from a Region in My Mind," *New Yorker*, November 17, 1962.

47. Olivier Roy, "What Is the Driving Force behind Jihadist Terrorism? A Scientific Perspective on the Causes/Circumstances of Joining the Scene," BKA Autumn Conference, November 18, 2015.

48. Beydoun, *supra* note 34, at 1304–14.

49. Khaled A. Beydoun, "Between Islamophobia, Indigence, and Erasure: Poor and Muslim in 'War on Terror America,'" *California Law Review* 104 (2016).

50. Beamen, *supra* note 39, at 9.

51. Hussey, *supra* note 40, at 404.

52. Albert Camus, *The Rebel: An Essay on Man in Revolt* (Vintage, 1991).

53. El Saadawi, *supra* note 28.

54. Beydoun, *supra* note 34, at 1301.

55. Beydoun and Sediqe, *supra* note 6, at 31.

56. Lila Abu-Lighud, *Do Muslim Women Need Saving?* (Harvard University Press, 2015).

57. Elaine Sciolino, "French Assembly Votes to Ban Religious Symbols in Schools," *New York Times*, February 11, 2004.

58. Beydoun, *supra* note 9, at 204.

59. Fatima Mernissi, *The Veil and the Male Elite* (Perseus Books, 1991).

60. Tayeb Salih, *Season of Migration to the North* (Heinemann, 1969), 151.

61. Reem Bahdi, "Narrating Dignity: Islamophobia, Racial Profiling, and National Security," *Osgoode Hall Law Journal* 55 (2018): 557.

62. Interview with Lubna on April 18, 2020—name changed to protect her anonymity.

63. "Bill 21: The Law against Religious Freedom," Canadian Civil Liberties Association, 2020.

64. Martin Luther King Jr., *Letter from Birmingham Jail* (American Friends Service Committee, April 16, 1963).

65. Christopher Curtis, "'Crushing' Debate over Bill 21 Also Affects Muslims Who Don't Wear the Hijab," *Montreal Gazette*, June 22, 2019.

66. "Brussels Students Protest Headscarf Ban in Education," *Brussels Times*, July 5, 2020.

67. Edward Said, *Covering Islam: How the Media and the Experts Determine How We See the Rest of the World* (Pantheon, 1981), 13.

68. Robert Allison, *The Crescent Obscured: The United States and the Muslim World, 1776–1815* (Oxford University Press, 1995), 37.

69. Marc Sageman, *Understanding Terror Networks* (University of Pennsylvania Press, 2004), 1–60 (for an analysis of the terms "jihad" and "jihadist" as applied and misapplied within American halls of power).

70. Email exchange with Zeinab B. on July 16, 2020—name changed to protect the anonymity of the subject.

71. Malika Hamidi, "Headscarf Ban: Belgian Muslim Women Are Resisting in Order to Free Themselves," *Brussels Times*, July 1, 2020.

72. Abu-Lighud, *supra* note 56.

73. See Adrien Katherine Wing and Monica Nigh Smith, "Critical Race Feminism Lifts the Veil? Muslim Women, France, and the Headscarf Ban," University of Iowa Legal Studies Research Paper No. 08-23, *UC Davis Law Review* 39:743, no. 3 (2005).

74. For an account of the political motives for donning the veil, see Elham Manea, "The Veil as a Political Act," E-International Relations, February 7, 2018. See also Khaled A. Beydoun, "Acting Muslim," *Harvard Civil Rights and Civil Liberties Law Review* 53 (2018), for a theoretical analysis of how Muslim men and women outwardly perform their identities in line with suspicion and stigma.

75. See the movie *The Battle of Algiers* (1966).

76. Jasmin Zine, "Unveiled Sentiments: Gendered Islamophobia and Experiences of Veiling among Muslim Girls in a Canadian Islamic School," *Equity & Excellence in Education* 39(3) (September 2006): 239, 240.

77. Mernissi, *supra* note 59, at 11.

78. David Smith, "'My Choice': Ilhan Omar Becomes First to Wear Hijab in Congress," *The Guardian*, January 3, 2019.

79. Hamidi, *supra* note 71.

80. Abu-Lighud, *supra* note 56.

81. Homa Khaleeli, "#SayHerName: Why Kimberlé Crenshaw Is Fighting for Forgotten Women," *The Guardian*, May 30, 2016.

CHAPTER 6. MONSTERS AND MARTYRS

Epigraphs: Pre-Khutbah given on August 12, 2022, at the Claremont Main Road Masjid in Cape Town, South Africa, alongside Imam Dr. A. Rashied Omar; Brenton Tarrant, "The Great Replacement," online manifesto, March 15, 2019.

1. "New Zealand Mosque Attack: Who Were the Victims," *Al Jazeera English*, March 22, 2019.

2. Charlotte Greenfield and Tom Westbrook, "'I Am Your Mother Now': New Zealand Mosque Shootings Hit Tight-Knit Bangladesh Community Hard," Reuters, March 19, 2019.

3. Farid Ahmed, *Husna's Story: My Wife, the Christchurch Massacre and My Journey to Forgiveness* (Allen and Unwin, 2020).

4. Megan Specia, "The New Zealand Shooting Victims Spanned Generations and Nationalities," *New York Times*, March 19, 2019.

5. Ibid.

6. Niloy Alam, "Bangladeshi Woman Dies Trying to Save Husband from NZ Terrorist," *Dhaka Tribune*, March 15, 2019.

7. "Timeline of New Zealand Terror Attack," DW, March 15, 2019.

8. Names changed to protect the anonymity of the subjects.

9. Interview with Dunya on June 21, 2020—name changed to protect the anonymity of the subject.

10. "One of New Zealand's Darkest Days," *BBC News*, March 15, 2019.

11. "Christchurch Shootings: 49 Dead in New Zealand Mosque Attacks," *BBC News*, March 15, 2019.

12. Alam, *supra* note 6.

13. Abby Ohlheiser, "No, Dearborn, Michigan Is Not under Sharia Law," *The Atlantic*, October 13, 2013.

14. Zareena Grewal, *Islam Is a Foreign Country: American Muslims and the Global Crisis of Authority* (NYU Press, 2013).

15. "'I Decided to Take a Stand'—Suspected Mosque Shooter Brenton Tarrant Says Attack Inspired by Anders Breivik," *Independent,* March 15, 2019.

16. Ibid.

17. Kaz Ross, "How Believers in 'White Genocide' Are Spreading Their Hate-Filled Message in Australia," *The Conversation,* November 29, 2018.

18. Linda Bosniak, *The Citizen and the Alien: Dilemmas of Contemporary Membership* (Princeton University Press, 2008), 1–5.

19. Khaled A. Beydoun, "Faith in Whiteness: Free Exericise of Religion as Racial Expression," *Iowa Law Review* 105 (2020).

20. Erik Love, *Islamophobia and Racism in America* (NYU Press, 2017), 4.

21. Khaled A. Beydoun, "'Lone Wolf': Our Stunning Double Standard When It Comes to Race and Religion," *Washington Post,* October 2, 2017.

22. Todd H. Green, *Presumed Guilty: Why We Shouldn't Ask Muslims to Condemn Terrorism* (Fortress Press, 2018).

23. Kathleen Belew, "There Are No Lone Wolves: The White Power Movement at War," in *A Field Guide to White Supremacy,* ed. Kathleen Belew and Ramón A. Gutiérrez (University of California Press, 2021).

24. Theodore Schleifer, "Donald Trump: 'I Think Islam Hates Us,'" CNN, March 10, 2016.

25. Arsalan Iftikhar, "Trump Sees Immigrants as Invaders. White-Nationalist Terrorists Do, Too," *Washington Post,* March 17, 2019.

26. Shirin Sinnar, "Hate Crimes, Terrorism, and the Framing of White Supremacist Violence," *California Law Review* 110 (2022): 7.

27. Renaud Camus, *You Will Not Replace Us!* (self published, 2018). The title of this manifesto has been adopted as the slogan of disparate white supremacist groups, in the US and globally, who believe that the "white race" is being endangered by the rise of communities of color.

28. "New Zealand Shooter Praised Trump, White Terrorist Breivik in Manifesto," *Telesur English,* March 15, 2019.

29. Claire Lampen, "Senator Fraser Anning Blames Mosque Massacre on Islam," *The Cut,* March 15, 2019.

30. Robert P. Jones, *The End of White Christian America* (Simon and Schuster, 2016).

31. Darin E. W. Johnson, "Homegrown and Global: The Rising Terror Movement," *Houston Law Review* 58 (2021): 1059.

32. Kathleen Belew, *Bring the War Home: The White Power Movement and Paramilitary America* (Harvard University Press, 2018).

33. Johnson, *supra* note 31, at 1073.

34. Cass R. Sunstein, *Liars: Falsehoods and Free Speech in an Age of Deception* (Oxford University Press, 2021), 41.

35. Zak Cheney-Rice, "The Endgame of White Supremacy Is Always Death," *New York Magazine*, March 16, 2019.

36. Interview with Abdullah Ali via completed questionnaire, March 21, 2020.

37. Juan Cole, *Muhammad: Prophet of Peace amid the Clash of Empires* (Nation Books, 2018), 54.

38. Muslims who express their religious identity through visible symbols, e.g., the hijab, traditional clothing, or grooming customs associated with the faith.

39. Khaled A. Beydoun, "Acting Muslim," *Harvard Civil Rights and Civil Liberties Law Review* 53 (2018).

40. Jason Horowitz, Nick Corasiniti, and Ashley Southall, "Nine Killed in Shooting at Black Church in Charleston," *New York Times,* June 17, 2015.

41. Caroline Mala Corbin, "Terrorists Are Always Muslim, but Never White: At the Intersection of Critical Race Theory and Propaganda," *Fordham Law Review* 86 (2017).

42. Race is the product of racial formation, commonly referred to as "racialization." Racialization is defined "as an unstable and 'de-centered' complex of social meanings constantly being transformed by political struggle." Michael Omi and Howard Winant, *Racial Formation in the United States: From the 1960s to the 1990s,* 2nd ed. (Routledge, 1994), 55. Racialization is a fluid and never-ending process, steered by a (changing) set of criteria that includes physical complexion, geographic origins, ancestry, biology, political or social stimuli, and variably, religion. See ibid., 71.

43. Khaled A. Beydoun, "Lone Wolf Terrorism: Types, Stripes and Double Standards," *Northwestern University Law Review* 112 (2018): 1213.

44. Ivan Strenski, "The Myth of the 'Lone Wolf' Shooter Blinds Us to the Reality of White Supremacy," https://rewirenewsgroup.com/2019/08/14/the-myth-of-the-lone-wolf-blinds-us-to-the-reality-of-white-supremacy/ (August 14, 2019).

45. Lisa Martin and Ben Smee, "What Do We Know about the Christchurch Attack Suspect," *The Guardian,* March 15, 2019.

46. Jerome Taylor, "The Incredible Kindness of Beings," *The Correspondent,* April 16, 2019 (the photo was also taken by the author, Jerome Taylor).

47. Maori proverb.

48. Massoud Hayoun, *When We Were Arabs: A Jewish Family's Forgotten History* (New Press, 2019).

49. "'The Great Replacement'—Decoding the Christchurch Terrorist Manifesto," Centre for Analysis of the Radical Right, March 18, 2019.

50. Anadolu Agency, "At Least 12.5M Muslims Died in Wars in Past 25 Years, Expert Says," *Daily Sabah,* April 21, 2018.

51. Annalisa Merelli, "New Zealand Prime Minister's Brave Lesson on How to Deny Terrorist's Fame," *Quartz,* March 19, 2019.

52. "'The Great Replacement,'" *supra* note 49.

53. "Christchurch Mosque Attack: Brenton Tarrant Sentenced to Life without Parole," *BBC News,* August 27, 2020.

54. Jenna Marsh and Tara Mulholland, "How the Christchurch Terrorist Attack Was Made for Social Media," CNN, March 16, 2019.

55. Khaled A. Beydoun, "'In New Zealand We Will Give Him Nothing—Not Even His Name,'" (Opinion), CNN, March 19, 2019.

56. "Teacher, Taxi Driver among Brave Men Who Risked Their Lives," *Strait Times,* March 17, 2019.

57. Specia, *supra* note 4.

58. Ellyn Santiago, "Naeem Rashid: A Tribute to the Christchurch Attack Hero," *Heavy,* March 15, 2019.

59. "Teacher, Taxi Driver among Brave Men," *supra* note 56.

60. Ibid.

61. Santiago, *supra* note 58.

62. Mike McRoberts, "Family of Mosque Shooting Victim Linda Armstrong Says She'd Be at Peace," *Newshub,* March 14, 2020.

63. Anneke Smith, "Christchurch Mosque Attacks: Linda Armstrong Remembered as Kind, Loving Person," Radio New Zealand, March 20, 2019.

64. Chelsea Boyd, "Christchurch Mosque Shootings: Honouring the Dead—Linda Armstrong, 65," *New Zealand Herald,* March 18, 2019.

65. McRoberts, *supra* note 62.

66. Boyd, *supra* note 64.

67. Specia, *supra* note 4.

68. Boyd, *supra* note 64.

69. Ameen Rihani, *The Book of Khalid* (Melville House, 2012), 218.

CHAPTER 7. ABLUTION AND ABOLITION

Epigraphs: Muhammad Ali, "Clay Discusses His Future, Liston and Black Muslims," *New York Times,* February 27, 1964; Chinua Achebe, *Things Fall Apart* (Anchor Books, 1994), 19.

1. Richard Gonzalez, "New Zealand Listens to Muslim Prayers a Week after Mosque Shootings," NPR, March 21, 2019.

2. Khaled A. Beydoun, "Today, I'm a New Zealander," *Al Jazeera English,* March 23, 2019.

3. Ibid.

4. For an analysis of the impact racial and Islamophobic slurs have had on Muslims in the decade after the 9/11 terror attacks, see Sahar F. Aziz, "Sticks and Stones, the Words That Hurt: Entrenched Stereotypes Eight Years after 9/11," *CUNY Law Review* 13 (2009): 33.

5. "Jacinda Ardern: New Zealand's Labor Leader Faces Sexism after Winning," *Washington Post,* August 2, 2017.

6. Beydoun, *supra* note 2.

7. "Woke" is a term that refers to remaining politically conscious and, specifically, supportive of issues aligned with left-leaning views.

8. Benjamin Moffitt, *The Global Rise of Populism: Performance, Political Style, and Representation* (Stanford University Press, 2017).

9. Beydoun, *supra* note 2.

10. Kelly Luo and Jenny M. Gray, "Performing Wokeness," *The Crimson,* October 1, 2018.

11. Lorenzo Vidino, "Emmanuel Macron's War on Islamism Is Europe's Future," *Foreign Policy,* February 24, 2020.

12. Audre Lorde, *Our Dead behind Us* (W. W. Norton, 1986).

13. Daniel Garrand, "New Zealand Helping to Pay Christchurch Shooting Victims' Funerals, Regardless of Immigration Status," *CBS News,* March 17, 2019.

14. Reşit Haylamaz, *Khadija: The First Muslim and the Wife of the Prophet* (The Light, 2007).

15. Prophet Muhammed.

16. Andres F. Quintana, "Muhammad Ali: The Greatest in Court," *Marquette Sports Law Review* 18 (2007): 171.

17. Jess Staufenberg, "Muhammad Ali: A Symbol of the Civil Rights Movement," *The Independent*, June 4, 2016.

18. Victor Mather, "In the Ring He Was Ali, But in the Newspapers He Was Still Clay," *New York Times*, June 9, 2016.

19. Dave Zirin, *What's My Name, Fool? Sports and Resistance in the United States* (Haymarket, 2005).

20. "Colin Kaepernick Protests Anthem over Treatment of Minorities," *The Undefeated*, August 27, 2016.

21. "What We Know and Don't Know about the Boycott That Stopped Sports," ESPN, August 26, 2020.

22. "Germany Shooting: 'Far-Right Extremist' Carried Out Shisha Bar Attacks," *BBC News*, February 20, 2020.

23. Thomas Bristow and James Rodger, "The Mo Salah 'I'll Be a Muslim Too' Chant: The Lyrics, Story, and What the Star Had to Say," *Birmingham Live*, May 14, 2018.

24. Mathew Treadwell, "Liverpool Complete £34.3m Signing of Mohamed Salah on Five-Year Deal," *Sky Sports*, June 23, 2017.

25. Nick Miller, "Liverpool's Mohamed Salah: How Many Goal-Scoring Records Could He Break?," ESPN, May 4, 2018.

26. Josh Gabbatis, "Brexit Strongly Linked to Xenophobia, Scientists Conclude," *The Independent*, November 27, 2017.

27. Mei-Lan Steimle, "The Salah Effect," *Stanford Magazine*, September 2019.

28. Adam Wells, "Study: Mo Salah's Popularity Has Reduced Islamophobia, Hate Crimes in Liverpool," *Bleacher Report*, June 4, 2019.

29. Ala' Alrababa'h, William Marble, Salma Mousa, and Alexandra Siegel, "Can Exposure to Celebrities Reduce Prejudice? The Effect of Mohamed Salah on Islamophobic Attitudes and Behaviors," Stanford Immigration Policy Lab, May 2020.

30. Khaled A. Beydoun, "Salaam, Liverpool: Salah and Mane, the Muslims Who Saved a Club," *The New Arab*, July 3, 2020.

31. Khaled A. Beydoun, "The Vilification of Muslims in World Sport," *Al Jazeera English*, September 2, 2015.

32. Geoffrey C. Ward, *Unforgivable Blackness: The Rise and Fall of Jack Johnson* (Vintage, 2004).

33. Teddy Atlas, *Atlas, from the Streets to the Ring: A Son's Struggle to Become a Man* (Harper, 2006).

34. Khaled A. Beydoun, "Bigotry Fueled the Conor McGregor–Khabib Nurmagomedov Brawl after UFC 229," *The Undefeated*, October 8, 2018.

35. Interview with Ahmed on May 21, 2020.

36. Khabib Studios, "Alhamdulillah—Khabib Nurmagomedov," YouTube, October 7, 2018.

37. Ibid.

38. Khaled A. Beydoun, "Bigotry Fueled the Conor McGregor–Khabib Nurmagomedov Brawl after UFC 229," Andscape, October 8, 2018.

39. Lance Pugmire, "Faith Comes before Fists for Khabib Nurmagomedov," *Los Angeles Times*, April 5, 2018.

40. Abdul Rahman Sidduqui, "Before Khabib, Muhammad Ali Was Told to Put Up with Bigotry," *Medium*, October 8, 2018.

41. See https://islamic-quotes.com/post/647671055032385536/non-muslims-dont-read-the-quran-they-dont-read.

42. Khaled Beydoun, "Khabib, Islam, and the Making of a UFC Champion," TRT World, August 4, 2021.

43. "Beheaded Columbus Statue in Boston Will Be Removed from North End Park," CBS Boston, June 10, 2020.

44. Theresa Machemer, "Christopher Columbus Statues Beheaded, Pulled Down across America," *Smithsonian Magazine*, June 12, 2020.

45. James Baldwin, *The Fire Next Time* (Dial Press, 1963), 81.

46. Paul Walsh, "7 Minutes, 46 Seconds: Error in George Floyd Killing Timeline Won't Affect Changes, County Says," *Star Tribune*, June 18, 2020.

47. Priscilla Ocen and Khaled A. Beydoun, "Are We Witnessing the Emergence of a Black Spring?," *Ebony*, May 5, 2015.

48. Cornel West, *Democracy Matters: Winning the Fight against Imperialism* (Penguin, 2004), 141.

49. Denise A. Spellberg, *Thomas Jefferson's Qur'an: Islam and the Founders* (Knopf, 2013).

50. Henry Wiencek, "The Dark Side of Thomas Jefferson," *Smithsonian Magazine*, October 2012.

51. Richard A. Oppel Jr. and Kim Barker, "New Transcripts Detail Last Moments for George Floyd," *New York Times*, July 8, 2020.

52. Bridget Reed, "Breonna Taylor Shot by Police in Her Own Home: What We Know," *The Cut*, June 5, 2020.

53. Paul Butler, *Chokehold: Policing Black Men* (New Press, 2017).

54. Tweet from Dahlia Bazzaz, staff and education reporter for the *Seattle Times*, June 13, 2020.

55. Interview with Justin Hansford on June 24, 2020.

56. Khaled A. Beydoun and Justin Hansford, "The F.B.I.'s Dangerous Crackdown on 'Black Identity Extremists,'" *New York Times*, November 15, 2017.

57. Donna Auston, "Mapping the Intersections of Islamophobia and #Black-LivesMatter: Unearthing Black Muslim Life and Activism in the Policing Crisis," *Sapelo Square*, August 30, 2016.

58. Natsu Taylor Saito, "Symbolism under Siege: Japanese American Redress and the 'Racing' of Arab Americans as 'Terrorists,'" *Asian American Law Journal* 8 (2001).

59. Khaled A. Beydoun, "Acting Muslim," *Harvard Civil Rights and Civil Liberties Law Review* 53 (2018).

60. Interview with Ahmed Abuznaid on June 25, 2020.

61. Keeanga-Yamahtta Taylor, *From #BlackLivesMatter to Black Liberation* (Haymarket, 2016), 187.

62. "Israeli Police Killing of Palestinian Leads to Apologies and Echoes of the U.S.," NPR, June 5, 2020.

63. Nir Hasson, Jack Khoury, and Josh Breiner, "Israeli Police Officers Shoot and Kill Disabled Palestinian Man in Jerusalem," *Haaretz*, May 30, 2020.

64. "How Black Lives Matter Went Mainstream after Floyd's Death," *Washington Post*, June 9, 2020.

65. Sahar Khalifeh, *Wild Thorns* (Olive Branch Press, 1991), 201.

66. Amer Zahr, *Being Palestinian Makes Me Smile* (Simsim, 2014), 89.

67. Paul Holston, "Experts Say White Supremacists See Trump as 'Last Stand,'" PBS, August 11, 2016.

68. Linda Martin Alcoff, *The Future of Whiteness* (Polity, 2015), 3.

69. Robin J. DiAngelo, *White Fragility: Why It's So Hard for White People to Talk about Racism* (Beacon Press, 2020).

70. Erika Lee, *America for Americans: A History of Xenophobia in the United States* (Basic Books, 2019), 251–58 (for an analysis of the slur "illegal" and its modern origins in American immigration).

71. Baldwin, *supra* note 45, at 70.

72. Amy Harmon and Sabrina Tavernise, "One Big Difference about George Floyd Protests: Many White Faces," *New York Times,* June 17, 2020.

73. Sarah McCammon, "In Richmond, Va., Protestors Transform a Confederate Statue," NPR, June 12, 2020.

74. Interview with Jeremy Brooks, "Chinua Achebe, the Art of Fiction No. 139," *The Paris Review,* Winter 1994.

75. Khaled A. Beydoun, "Trump's Portrait of America Is a Monument to Its Racist Past," *The New Arab,* August 31, 2020.

76. "Jacob Blake: What We Know about Wisconsin Police Shooting," *BBC News,* August 31, 2020.

77. Adrian Morrow, "Trump Blames Democrats for Violence during Final Night of Republican National Convention," *The Globe and Mail,* August 28, 2020.

78. Baldwin, *supra* note 45, at 44.

79. Howard Zinn, *A People's History of the United States* (Harper, 1980), 182.

80. Teju Cole on Twitter, April 11, 2014, https://twitter.com/tejucole/status/454646310994710528?lang=en.

CONCLUSION: KILLING AN ARAB

Epigraph: Albert Camus, *The Stranger* (Vintage, 1989), 58–59.

1. See Jennifer E. Sessions, *By Sword and Plow: The French Conquest of Algeria* (Cornell University Press, 2014), for a critical and comprehensive history of French colonial rule of the North African nation.

2. Ibid., 59.

3. Albert Camus, *The Stranger* (Vintage, 1989), 58.

4. See James McDougall, *A History of Algeria* (Cambridge University Press, 2017), 86–129, for an analysis of the colonial laws enforced by the French to seize Algerian lands, and a history of the war crimes committed against Algerians.

5. See Khaled A. Beydoun, "Between Muslim and White: The Legal Construction of Arab American Identity," *NYU Annual Survey of American Law* 69 (2013): 29, examining how civil courts presiding over the naturalization claims of Arab immigrants cast Islam as nonwhite until 1944, and in turn conflated Arab with Muslim identity.

6. Camus, *supra* note 3, at 58.

7. "CBS: Ukraine Is 'Civilized,' Unlike Iraq and Afghanistan," YouTube, February 26, 2022.

8. Said theorized this master discourse as a process whereby the West, or the "Occident," defined itself as the mirror image of the Muslim world, which comprised a segment of the "Orient." See generally Edward Said, *Orientalism* (Vintage, 1979).

9. "[Ukraine] isn't a place, with all due respect, like Iraq or Afghanistan, that has seen conflict raging for decades. This is a relatively civilized, relatively European—I have to choose these words carefully—city, one where you wouldn't expect that, or hope that it's going to happen." Charlie D'Agata, CBS foreign correspondent, "CBS: Ukraine Is 'Civilized,'" *supra* note 7.

10. Khaled A. Beydoun, "The World of Inconsistencies between Ukraine, the Middle East and Beyond" (Opinion), *Washington Post*, March 7, 2022.

11. Ibid.

12. Ibid.

13. Barak Ravid, "Zelensky to EU Leaders: 'This Might Be the Last Time You See Me Alive,'" *Axios*, February 25, 2022.

14. Elissaveta M. Brandon, "In a Visual Rebuke to Putin, Ukraine's Colors Are Being Displayed in Protest All Over the World," *Fast Company*, March 17, 2022.

15. Harry Bruinius, "'They Seem So Like Us': How Bias Creeps into War Reporting," *Christian Science Monitor*, March 4, 2022.

16. Ukraine is 99 percent white. Char Adams, Zinhle Essamuah, Shamar Walter, and Rima Abdelkader, "'Open the Door or We Die': African Students Report Racism and Hostility Trying to Flee Ukraine," *NBC News*, March 1, 2022.

17. See Cheryl I. Harris, "Whiteness as Property," *Harvard Law Review* 106 (1993): 1707 (discussing the property value attached to whiteness and the legal and de facto values attached to it).

18. "'Europeans with Blue Eyes, Blonde Hair Being Killed': Media Coverage of Ukraine Criticised for Racism," *Newslaundry*, February 28, 2022.

19. See Beydoun, *supra* note 10.

20. See generally Noura Erakat, *Justice for Some: Law and the Question of Palestine* (Stanford University Press, 2019), for an examination of human rights challenges confronted by the Palestinian people living in the West Bank, Gaza, and within the boundaries of Israel.

21. Adam Taylor, "Civilians in Ukraine Are Being Asked to Fight Russia However They Can," *Washington Post*, February 25, 2022.

22. See Helen Lackner, *Yemen in Crisis: The Road to War* (Verso, 2019), for an accessible history of the Saudi-led war on Yemen and its people.

23. Lisa Schlein, "Conflict and Economic Collapse in War-Torn Yemen Worsening Hunger Crisis," *VOA News*, July 28, 2021.

24. For historical background on Kashmir and its precarious position, see Jasjit Singh, "Kashmir, Pakistan, and the War on Terror," *Small Wars and Insurgencies* 13, no. 2 (2002): 81.

25. Anchal Vohra, "Modi Took Complete Control of Kashmir Two Years Ago—And Got Away with It," *Foreign Policy*, August 3, 2021.

26. See Devjyot Ghoshal, "Thousands Detained in Indian Kashmir Crackdown, Official Data Reveals," Reuters, September 12, 2019, for a review of the mass arrests made after India's military takeover of Kashmir in September 2019.

27. See Vohra, *supra* note 25.

28. See Beydoun, *supra* note 10.

29. "Islamophobia is also a systematic, fluid, and deeply politicized dialectic between the state and its polity: a dialectic whereby the former shapes, reshapes, and confirms popular views or attitudes about Islam and Muslim subjects inside and outside of American borders." Khaled A. Beydoun, "Islamophobia: Toward a Legal Definition and Framework," *Columbia Law Review Online* 16 (2015): 119.

30. See Khaled A. Beydoun, *American Islamophobia: Understanding the Roots and Rise of Fear* (University of California Press, 2018), which theorizes how expressions of Muslim identity raise the presumption of terror suspicion.

31. "The September 11 terrorist attacks [and the War on Terror that followed] finalized a transformation of Muslim identity that had been in the making for decades and was grounded in European Orientalism." Sahar Aziz, *The*

Racial Muslim: When Racism Quashes Religious Freedom (University of California Press, 2022), 6.

32. Khaled A. Beydoun, "Exporting Islamophobia in the Global 'War on Terror,'" *New York University Law Review* 95 (2020): 81.

33. Beydoun, *supra* note 10, at 4.

34. Frank Langfitt and Eleanor Beardsley, "African Students Say They're Facing Discrimination as They Try to Leave Ukraine," NPR, March 3, 2022.

35. "French Far-Right Candidate Zemmour Says Ukrainians Welcome, but Not Arab Refugees," *France 24*, March 9, 2022.

36. Ibid.

37. Camus, *supra* note 3, at 59.

38. This is especially the case in the US, for the entire ecosystem of news media that converges and interacts with mainstream news media outlets. See Gabe Schneider, "U.S. Newsrooms Are Very White. So Are the Critics and the Journalists That Cover Them," *Poynter,* December 4, 2020.

39. "CBS: Ukraine Is 'Civilized,'" *supra* note 7.

40. "'European' has become a code word for white and a justification of the primary reason that people should care about the conflict, displacement, and killing. Bloody conflicts in Syria, Somalia, and other places have not received the wide-reaching international media coverage—or urgent international government action—that the invasion of Ukraine has inspired." Rashawn Ray, "The Russian Invasion of Ukraine Shows Racism Has No Boundaries," *Brookings,* March 3, 2022.

41. "CBS: Ukraine Is 'Civilized,'" *supra* note 7.

42. For a critique of this Orientalist trope in relation to Afghanistan, see Steven A. Cook, "End the 'Forever War' Cliché," *Foreign Policy,* April 22, 2021.

43. See Ray, *supra* note 40.

44. Ibid.

45. See "The Arab and Middle Eastern Journalist Association (AMEJA) Statement in Response to Coverage of the Ukraine Crisis," AMEJA, February 2022.

46. Camus, *supra* note 3, at 122.

47. Halim Barakat, *Days of Dust* (Three Continents, 1983).

48. For an excellent history of the civil and proxy wars in Lebanon, see Robert Fisk, *Pity the Nation: The Abduction of Lebanon* (Nation Books, 2002).

49. Camus, *supra* note 3, at 58.

50. *James Baldwin: The Last Interview and Other Conversations* (Melville House, 2014).

EPILOGUE

1. Jonathan Hoffman, "Why Do Some Muslim-Majority Countries Support China's Crackdown on Muslims?," *Washington Post*, May 4, 2021.

2. Frantz Fanon, "Algeria Unveiled," in *Decolonization: Perspectives from Now and Then*, ed. Prasenjit Duara (Routledge, 2003), 44.

3. Sigal Samuel, "China Is Treating Islam Like a Mental Illness," *The Atlantic*, August 28, 2018.

Bibliographic Essay

───────────────────────────────

This book aims to fill a critical void in academic and popular literature. It builds on an impressive corpus of books, both domestic and foreign, that interrogate the anatomy and effects of Islamophobia, a subject of considerable interest in academic literature for decades, and more recently in the political and popular spheres. This bibliographic review surveys the books that examine Islamophobia as a transnational and global form of (racial and religious) animus, which are currently few in number, in relation to an examination of Islamophobia as a system of interconnected projects, or "crusades," that find a common foundation in and are fueled by the American War on Terror.

A central text frequently cited in *The New Crusades* is *Islamophobia and the Politics of Empire,* by Deepa Kumar. Originally published by Haymarket Books in 2012 and republished by Verso in 2021 with a new preface, "20 Years after 9/11," the book frames Islamophobia as an imperial project spearheaded by the United States and its War on Terror. This thesis, which holds that the demonization of Muslim identity is a transnational tool wielded to facilitate American imperial aims, is echoed in my work and adapted in my framing of Islamophobia as deeply structural and pointedly "rational"—namely, an expedient to advance and entrench American political interests both at home, and as Kumar examines, in Muslim-majority nations. Kumar is not a Critical Race Theorist like myself, but race is central to her argument and analysis. She writes, "My key argument is that notions of race and Muslims as inferior beings could come to the fore in a context where European nations were in a position to actually challenge and eventually dominate once-powerful Muslim empires" (p. 20), evoking the modernity of Islamophobia and its roots in longstanding Crusades-era narratives (which in part inspired the title of my book). Kumar's book is a foundational interdisciplinary academic text, steeped in her area of research, media studies. It remains the most important text on Islamophobia as a transnational project, leveraged to advance American empire, today.

A series of texts examining Islamophobia beyond the United States and the American experience are organized as edited volumes. These, which feature academics and commentators, examine Islamophobia as *national case studies*. Often, these are case studies that examine Islamophobia within the narrow contours of national cultures, legal systems, and histories. A notable text, published in 2011 by Oxford University Press, is *Islamophobia: The Challenge of Pluralism in the 21st Century*, edited by John L. Esposito and Ibrahim Kalin. *Islamophobia* is a pointedly academic text, intended for scholars across academic disciplines, and offers both comparative analysis ("Islamophobia in the West: A Comparison between Europe and the United States," p. 21) and individual case studies. The case studies focus largely on Europe and the United States, which is understandable given that it was published before the modern emergence of violent Islamophobic movements in India and Myanmar, for example. The book examines "manifestations" of Islamophobia in the media, in art, in political rhetoric, and so forth, with only generalized attention to law.

Islam in Europe: Diversity, Identity and Influence, edited by Aziz Al-Azmeh and Effie Fokas, is another volume worth noting. The book, published in 2007 by Cambridge University Press, takes a deep dive into the roots and modern emergence of Islamophobia across Europe. It convenes an impressive roster of scholars and commentators, who provide trenchant and original analysis of anti-Muslim sentiment and systems across the continent, and of special interest, in contexts including Bosnia, Turkey, and Spain. While it is now somewhat dated and its scope is limited to Europe, I consider it a valuable text given its trailblazing analysis of Islamophobia in Europe, and more notably, of the European Union's role in "transcontinentalizing" Islamophobia and making it a central cog in the normative identity of modern Europe.

The Rise of Global Islamophobia in the War on Terror, published by Manchester University Press in 2022, builds on Kumar's work and echoes the thesis that Islamophobia is an imperial project. Edited by Naved Bakali and Farid Hafez, the book offers a timely treatment of Islamophobia from a collection of scholars and non-academics. Reflecting the international status of the editors and authors, the book expands the bounds of previous volumes geographically, examining Islamophobia as it has unfolded in countries including India and China and in Muslim-majority societies, primarily adopting the framing that Islamophobia is a political weapon employed by the United States—and its proxies—to access and maximize political gain. Like edited volumes that analyze international case studies or those that grapple with the distinct dimensions of Islamophobia on the American front (for example, *Islamophobia in America: The Anatomy of Intolerance,* published by Palgrave Macmillan in 2013 and edited by Carl W. Ernst, or *Islamophobia and the Law,* published by Oxford University Press in 2021 and edited by Cyra Choudhury and myself), *The Rise of Global Islamophobia in the War on Terror* is limited to academic and advocacy analyses. It does not integrate direct testimony, interviews, on-the-ground perspectives, and the legal analyses that I include in *The New Crusades.*

The development of Islamophobia, and its popular recognition, has spawned a series of newer books on the subject. Nazia Kazi's *Islamophobia, Race and Global Politics,* published in 2018 by Rowan and Littlefield, "connects Islamophobia to the [United States'] long history of racism." Rooted in anthropological analysis, the author's area of expertise, the "global" aspects of the book are tied to Islamophobia's expansion as an American imperial tool. In that vein, the book builds on the work of Kumar but offers less in terms of depth of analysis. Kazi analyzes the Islamophobia unfolding in Asian nations and beyond from the perspective of American policy, rather than as standalone subjects. Another recent book is *Fear of a Muslim Planet: Global Islamophobia in the New World Order,* published in 2021 by Skyhorse and written by Arsalan Iftikhar. Unlike the vast majority of texts within the (broader) field, *Fear of a Muslim Planet* is intended for a general audience. The author is a Muslim American pundit with ties to an academic think tank (Georgetown University's The Bridge Initiative). The book is written *very* accessibly, perhaps even excessively so, as some of its arguments would benefit from being tethered to legal, political, or anthropological analysis. In some regards, *Fear of a Muslim Planet* echoes Hamid Dabashi's masterful book *Brown Skin, White Masks,* published in 2011 by Pluto Press. Columbia professor and public intellectual Dabashi makes the case that American intellectuals and cultural gatekeepers functioned as global ambassadors and exporters of anti-Muslim views without explicitly calling it "Islamophobia" or "global Islamophobia." Iftikhar's book, published more than a decade later, is unique in that it directly takes on Islamophobia as a global phenomenon with the aim of reaching general audiences.

A number of other noteworthy books take on the subject of Islamophobia either collaterally or supplementarily. *The Racial Muslim: When Racism Quashes Religious Freedom,* authored by Sahar Aziz and published by the University of California Press in 2022, builds upon a growing roster of books that examine American Islamophobia. Aziz, a law professor and intellectual colleague, is primarily concerned with the law—and more specifically, American law's role in racially constructing Muslims as terrorists and liminals, others and pariahs. Much like my first book, *American Islamophobia: Understanding the Roots and Rise of Fear* (University of California Press, 2018), Erik Love's *Islamophobia and Racism in America* (NYU Press, 2017), Nazita Lavejardi's *Outsiders at Home: The Politics of American Islamophobia* (University of Cambridge Press, 2020), and others, Aziz's *The Racial Muslim* stands apart in terms of depth of analysis but is confined to an American scope. Islamophobia as a global phenomenon, a system or "interconnected network of systems," the contention made in *The New Crusades,* is not the focus of Aziz's book.

My aim with *The New Crusades* was to write a book unlike any of its predecessors. While I hoped to replicate the accessible tone and hybrid spirit of *American Islamophobia, The New Crusades* is far more aspirational in scope and methodology and includes the direct testimony of Muslims across countries and continents. It is unique in that regard, and it synthesizes academic rigor and expertise, my own deeply personal accounts, and original testimony and vignettes. I believe it will resonate with readers within and beyond Muslim communities and readers beyond the English-speaking world. *The New Crusades* stems from my unique position as a law professor, public intellectual with broad social media and global recognition, and activist with ties to the very communities I write about. It is my hope that it helps define how a new subfield is examined moving forward.

Index

Amazigh people (Berbers), 329n3

American imperialism: as advancing American political interests, 348; expansion of Islamophobia and, 349

American intellectuals, anti-Muslim views and, 350

American Islamophobia (Beydoun), 11–12, 298, 350

American political interests: domestic, 348; international, 348

Anand, Channi, 131

Anning, Fraser, 223–24

anti-imperialism, Ukrainian resistance as, 283

anti-Muslim animus/violence, infliction of, 315n117

anti-Muslim bigotry, policing and punishment influenced by, 18

anti-Muslim movement, liberal support for, 83–86

anti-Muslim sentiments/views: in Europe, 78, 348; exporters of, 350

anti-Muslim systems, in Europe, 348

Arab, as conflated with Muslim identity, 343n5

Arab, the (literary character), 281–82, 290

Arab and Middle Eastern Journalist Association, 291

Arab immigrants: naturalization claims of, 343n5; as nonwhite, 290, 343n5

Arab/Muslim/Middle Easterner conflation, 71–72, 282, 343n5

Arabs: Arab/Muslim/Middle Easterner conflation, 71–72, 282, 343n5; centrality of killing, 282; divide on immigration and, 288; as War on Terror threat, 287. *See also* nonwhite people

Ardern, Jacinda, 19, 215, 235–37, 242–43, 247, 247–53, 253

Armstrong, Linda, 240–42

Arnett, Chaz, 323n15

Asian nations, Islamophobia unfolding in, 349

atheism, in China, 147, 159

atheist liberals, as Islamophobes, 83–86

athletes against Islamophobia, 19

Atlas, Teddy, 260

Atran, Scott, 189

Atuahene, Bernadette, 113

Auschwitz concentration camps, 140–41, 157

Australia, 211–43

Ayoub, Abed, 166

Ayyub, Rana, 110, 112

Aziz, Sahar, 350

Azmeh, Aziz Al-, 348

Bahdi, Reem, 200

Baldwin, James, 27, 30, 49, 75, 95, 96, 190, 264, 271–72

Bangladesh, 112

banlieues, 39, 174, 177, 180, 181, 185–94, 329n3

Baquer, Syed Mohd Gulam, 105–6

Basha, Sabina, 116

Beaman, Jean, 189

Beauvoir, Simone de, 194

Belew, Kathleen, 224

Belgium, 18, 180, 202–3, 205–6

Benna, Zyed, 174–75, 179

Berbers (Amazigh people), 329n3

Bharat beliefs, 104

Bharatiya Janata Party (BJP), 102–8, 114, 123, 127

Biden administration, 82

Black, Jacob, 273–74

Black Lives Matter (BLM) Movement, 19–20, 267, 270, 272, 273, 275

Blackness, 59, 60, 267

Black people, treated as objects of property, 59, 60

Blacks, as refugees, 288–89

Black Skin, White Masks (Fanon), 86–87

Bolsonaro, Jair, 251

Bosnia, anti-Muslim sentiment and systems in, 349

Bourdain, Anthony, 99–102, 109–10

Brown Skin, White Masks (Dabashi), 350

Buddhism, 163–65, 167

Burmese Citizenship Law, 165, 166

Bush, George W., 37–38, 57–58, 62, 72, 76, 152–54

Bush administration: on civilizational divide, 62–63, 69, 79, 190; global War on Terror and, 130, 145; Iraq War and, xi, 79; on Islam and terror, 57, 59; Orientalism and, 71, 74–76; War on Terror, 85

Byler, Darren, 142

CAA (Citizenship Amendment Act), 109, 112–13, 114, 117

Cameroon, 179

Campaign for Uyghurs, 156–57, 298

Camus, Albert, 94, 110, 183, 281, 290, 293

Canada, Muslims in, 12

capitalism, whiteness and, 60

carceral humanism, outsourcing as, 323n15

Casbah, responses to resistance in, 292

caste system, 102, 103, 113

CBS News, 291

Chak, Farhan, 132

Charlie Hebdo attacks, 187

Cheney-Rice, Zak, 226

child soldiers, recruitment of, 34

Chimaev, Khamzat, 263

China, 349; Al-Qaeda and, 325n60; Belt and Road Initiative, 145; counterterrorism laws, 138; crises in, 12; elimination program in, 137–61; ethnic cleansing in, 18, 137–61; Han (ethnic group), 323n13; internments of Uyghur Muslims, 114, 137, 143–44, 156–58; Islamophobia in, 41; reeducation centers, 156; surveillance in Xinjiang, 298; as surveillance state, 137, 138–39, 142; Uyghur Muslim struggle, 297; War on Terror crusades in, 40, 78–79, 138, 145, 152–54, 160, 282, 325n60. *See also* Xinjiang

China Tribunal, 157

Chinese Islamophobia, 154–55, 158–59

Christchurch terror attacks: about, 211–14; Ardern after, 19, 247–53; fears after, 216–18; global Islamophobia after, 18–19, 211–43; white supremacy laws and, 222–26; white terrorist shooter of, 216–17, 218, 219–30, 234, 251

Christianity: Crusades (11th–13th century), 13–14; whiteness and, 60

Christians, in Rajasthan, 99, 101

Christian values, War on Terror view of Islam vs., 14

Citizen Outsider (Beaman), 189

Citizenship Amendment Act (CAA), 109, 112–13, 114, 117

citizenship issues: in India, 105, 109, 112–14, 117; in Myanmar, 165, 166; in Nazi Germany, 113; in US, 113

"Citizen and the Terrorist, The" (Volpp), 74–75

civilian deaths, framed as human shields, 286

France (continued)

    200; Islamophobia in Europe, 174–75; *laïcité* concept, 177, 180, 183; law on religious symbols, 175; origins/ modern emergence of Islamophobia in, 18; people of Amazigh origin in, 329n3; policing and punishment in, 18; racism in, 174–75; seizure of Algerian lands by, 342n4; War on Terror crusades in, 40, 78–79, 181, 186–87, 282

France 24 (news outlet), 289

Frazier, Joe, 255

freedom fights/fighter: public imagining of, 42, 287, 291; Ukrainians seen as, 283–84

Free Exercise Clause of First Amendment, 94–95

French Islamophobia, 42, 180–83, 206

French Intifada, The (Hussy), 187

fundamentalism, 93, 190

fundraising, for Uyghur Muslims, 297

gatekeepers: in government, 285; in media, 285; whiteness of Western, 290–91

Gaza: Israeli airstrikes in, 286; quest for dignity in, 42, 286

gendered theory of Islamophobia, 175–79, 306n9

Gendron, Peyton, 225

genocide: cultural genocide in Kashgar, 151–52, 154, 157; Rohingya genocide, 161–70, 328n112; of Uyghur Muslims, 146, 151–52; Uyghur Muslims against, 299–300

geopolitical issues: centrality of killing Arabs, 282; global support and divide on, 288; interests in, 287; race in, 287; religion in, 287; whiteness and, 292

Ghazali, Abu Hamid al-, 84

Giroux, Henry A., 51, 69, 312n56

global crusade, 68–71; struggles rooted in, 299; truth of terror and, 5

global issue(s): digital connections and, 3–4; good against evil narrative in Ukraine, 284; Indian annexation of Kashmir, 287; of Islamophobia, 350; Islamophobia as, 12; Saudi Arabian expansion, 286; self-determination in Muslim-majority nations, 285, 287, 288; solidarity for Ukraine, 284, 287, 288; vigilante violence as, 16; violence of Islamophobia, 14. *See also* American imperialism; Christchurch terror attacks

global support: geopolitical divide and, 288; racial divide and, 288; religious divide and, 288

God Is Not Great (Hitchens), 84–85

good-bad Muslim binary: after 9/11 attacks, 69, 70; Crusades (11th–13th century) and, 13–14, 60; global application of, 40–41; white supremacy laws and, 60–61

Gourevitch, Philip, 150

government, gatekeepers in, 285

Gujarat Files (Ayyub), 112

Gujarat massacres, 110, 115, 116

Gulbahar, Jelilova, 137–38

Hallaq, Eyad, 269–70, 276

Hamas, justification of civilians deaths by labeling as, 286

Hamid, Nafees, 189

Hamidi, Malika, 205, 207

Han (ethnic group), 323n13

Hansford, Justin, 267

Han supremacist campaign, 138, 144, 155, 157, 159, 160
Harris, Cheryl, 59
Harris, Sam, 83, 84, 85, 93
Hathaway, Donny, 44–45
Hayoun, Massoud, 232
headscarves (hijab). *See* hijab (headscarves)
hijab (headscarves), 205–8; banning of, 18, 42, 107, 175–77; in Belgium, 205–8; in China, 137; discourse on, 199–200; in France, 173–77, 200; stereotypes of Muslim women and, 330n7; as visible symbols of religious identity, 336n38; women attacked while wearing, 116
Hijab Ban of 2004, 18, 173–99, 180, 192, 194, 200, 250
Hinduism: as racialized identity, 104; as weaponized by Modi, 108
Hindu nationalism, 102–3
Hindus: as indigenous people, 105; in Rajasthan, 99, 101
Hindu supremacy, fueling imperialism in India, 286
Hindu supremacy (Hindutva), 99–133; Islamophobia of, 105–6, 108–9; loyalists portrayed as Pakistanis, 104; Modi and, 103–4, 108, 111–12; Muslim populations and, 17–18, 102–3; Nazi ideology and, 114; scapegoating of Muslims, 118–20
Hindutva (Savarkar), 104
Hitchens, Christopher, 84–85, 85
Hitler, Adolf, 113
Hosseini, Khalid, 26
humanity: dehumanization and denial through silence, 294; extending of, 285; humanizing of Ukrainian

refugees, 289; lack of humanizing Rohingya refugees, 290; lack of humanizing Syrian and Afghan refugees, 289, 290; media coverage on, 292; of victims of war, 293–94
human organ harvesting, 157
Human Rights Watch, 156
human shields, Israeli and Russian narrative on civilians as, 286
Huntington, Samuel P., 14, 63, 72, 73, 83
Husna (New Zealand Muslim woman), 211–16, 218
Hussein, Shoaib, 113, 114
Hussein (Shia Muslim refugee), 53–57
Hussy, Andrew, 187
Huxley, Aldous, 137

Ibrahim, Mucaad, 237
Ibtissam (French Muslim woman), 173–83, 195
Idris, Abdulhakim, 298
Iftikhar, Arsalan, 349–50
immigrants, stigma of terrorism: from Afghanistan, 291; from Iraq, 291
immigration: Arabs or Muslims and divide on, 288, 290; Citizenship Amendment Act (CAA) and, 112–13; leftist media on racism in, 290; *Trump v. Hawaii*, 311n41; Ukraine and traditional divides on, 288, 290
imperialism: Hindutva imperialism in Kashmir, 131, 298; imperial gaze, 34–35; Muslim inclusion and racism within systems of, 306n8; myths of, 294; Russian war on Ukraine as, 283, 288; US discourses of, 74

India: annexation of Kashmir, 124–25, 127–28, 130, 286–87, 298; anti-Muslim rhetoric in, 103–5; citizenship issues in, 105, 109; diversity of, 318n36; as global epicenter of Islamophobia, 17, 99–133; Gujarat massacres, 110, 115, 116; imperialism of, 286–87; Islamophobic violence in, 41, 108, 110–12, 119–20, 348; military takeover of Kashmir by, 286–87; Muslim Ban, 112–13; New Delhi massacre, 114–16; religious diversity in, 99, 101; remaking of Indian identity, 105; September 2019 rally, 111, 112; unfolding of Islamophobia in, 349; War on Terror crusades in, 40, 78–79, 282. *See also* Indian Islamophobia

Indian Islamophobia: fear of, 120; in Kashmir, 128; modern image of, 108; pervasiveness of, 106–7; in Rajasthan, 108; resurfacing of, 106; as rooted in Hindu supremacy, 105–6

indigenous peoples: in Chinese concentration camps, 40–41; experience of American, 59; in high-tech penal colonies, 40; as Muslim populations in China, 153

Indonesia, 108

Infidel (Ali), 83

Insh'Allah (God willing) (Arabic), use of, 310n17

interests: in relation to race, 287; in relation to religion, 287

International Court of Justice (ICJ), 164, 166, 167

international government action, inspiration for, 345n40

internationalism, decline in Western pundits and intellectuals, 288

International Union of East Turkistan Organizations, 143, 298

internments: in China, 114, 137, 143–44, 156–58; fear and, 40–41; in India, 114; Islam and, 40–41; of Japanese people in US, 61, 144, 311n40; of Uyghur Muslims children, 159–60

interviews, methodology of, 349

Iran, fighting terrorists in, 286

Iraq: comparisons to, 291; War on Terror and, 38, 78

Iraqi refugees, stigma of terrorism, 291

Iraq War: as illegal American crusade, 70; memories of, 49

ISIS terrorists, 88, 186, 188, 189, 190–93, 223

Islam: cast as unassimilable with societal values, 14; Chinese state's attack on, 145; criminalization of, 18, 142–43, 156, 161–70; Crusades (11th–13th century) and, 13–14; good-evil binary of Christianity and, 14; growth of, 38; Huntington on threat of, 14, 63; internments over, 40–41; Islamic proverb, 131; marked as enemy, 72, 81–82, 93, 299; as nonwhite, 343n5; racialization of, 288; radicalization theory and, 36–37; surveillance of, 156; War on Terror and, 37–39, 43

Islam in Europe (Al-Azmeh and Fokas), 348

Islamophobia: anti-Muslim animus/violence, 315n117; defined, 16; in Europe, 348; formation of, 38; fundamental trait of, 43; gendered theory of, 175–79, 306n9; India as global epicenter of, 17, 123; liberals on, 83–86; modern emergence in France, 173–94; modernity of, 348; Muslim

militarism, of India, 286–87

Mir, Ali Hussein, 130

modernity of Islamophobia, 348

modern state, warfare and creation of, 312n49

Modi, Narendra, 102–3, 115, 251, 286–87; Gujarat massacres, 110–12; New Delhi massacre and, 114–16; political narrative of, 105; populism of, 19; rise of Islamophobia and, 100–101; at Trump rally, 109, 111–12

Modi regime: anti-Muslim propaganda of, 101–3, 125–27; Hindu nationalism of, 102–3; Hindu supremacy (Hindutva) of, 127–28; ideology of, 104; Indian Islamophobia of, 105; Indian Muslim homes bulldozing by, 299; secularism and, 110

Mohamed (Somali Muslim boy), 25–28, 33–34, 35, 36, 38, 40, 43–45

Mohammed, Belal, 263

Morsi, Khalida, 232–34

mosques: in China, 41, 151–52, 154; in New Zealand, 212; in Wajir, Kenya, 31–32

Mrinal (Hindu activist student), 99–100, 102, 104, 108–9

Muslima (Uyghur Muslim student), 206, 297

Muslim Americans, citizenship of, 313n62

Muslim ban, 61

Muslim empires, European nations and, 13, 348

Muslim identity: Arab as conflated with, 343n5; Arab/Muslim/Middle Easterner conflation, 282, 343n5; demonization of, 347; expressions of, 38; as extremists, 287; as foreign caste in India, 99–133; gendered theory of Islamophobia and, 306n9; in India, 18, 108; as inferior, 348; as liminal, 350; in Myanmar, 165; 9/11 terrorist attacks and, 6–7, 344n31; objectification and, 281–82; Orientalism and, 73, 282; as others, 311n42, 350; outside US, 344n29; as pariahs, 350; policies of fear and, 307n31; as terrorists, 16, 38, 125–26, 129, 130, 165–66, 350; unseeing of true identity, 38–39, 43; in US, 344n29; visible symbols of religious identity, 330n7, 336n38; War on Terror and, 16–17, 38, 344n31. *See also* nonwhite people

Muslim immigrants: comparison of, 290; media outlets on, 289–90

Muslim-majority nations: denial of religious liberty in, 95; East Turkistan World Symposium, 297; political weaponization of Islamophobia by, 349; self-determination in, 42, 285, 287; solidarity for Uyghur Muslims, 297

Muslim men, ideas of violence and oppression of, 306n9

Muslim minority populations, global persecution of, 16

Muslim Registry, 113

Muslims: anti-Muslim rhetoric in India, 103–5; divide on immigration and, 288; experience of anti-Muslim sentiments, 11–12, 16; global response to disasters, 11; global systems of subordination against, 17, 77–78; inclusion and racism in imperial systems toward, 306n8; as inherently/exclusively terrorist, 94; Modi regime on, 102–3; Muslim Ban in India, 112–13;

199, 229; Muslim identity and, 73, 282; 9/11 terrorist attacks and, 74–76, 282, 306n6; origins in France, 68

Orientalism (Said), 69, 71, 74–76, 307n25

Orwell, George, 78, 83, 148, 312n55

otherization process, 311n42, 350

Our Dead behind Us (Lorde), 253

Out of Place (Said), 12, 68, 307n27

Outsiders at Home (Lavejardi), 350

Paddock, Stephen, 224

Pakistan, 112

Pal, Ramapada, 103

Palestine, self-determination in, 285

Palestinians: Darwish, 15; Hallaq, 269–70; Kanafani, 161; lack of global support for, 288; resistance in Sheikh Jarrah, 286; resistance from, 155

panopticon, 323n14

Parsees, in Rajasthan, 101

People of Color: as refugees, 288–89; as War on Terror threat, 287

persecution, US language for, 16

Peterson, Jordan, 84

phantasmic sites, 306n6

Plague, The (Camus), 183

policing: French systems of, 18; US template for, 16

political gain in US, access and maximizing of, 349

political weaponization of Islamophobia: as adopted by China, 349; as adopted by India, 349; as adopted by Muslim-majority societies, 349; by liberal atheists, 83–86; in New Zealand and Australia, 18; by US, 349

popular discourse, confined to US domestic racial issues, 288

postcolonial wars, Muslims enduring, 292

preventive repression, 158

Price of the Ticket, The (Baldwin), 49

prisons: e-carceration, 323n15; panopticon, 323n14

privacy, Giroux on, 312n55

profiling, US language for, 16

proxy war, struggles made by, 285

punishments, French systems of, 18

Quarry, Jerry, 255

Quebec, 18, 180, 200–206

race: double standards and, 292; faddish race consciousness, 290; global support and divide on, 288; Kumar on, 348; public imagining and, 287–88; racialization and, 336n42; in relation to interests, 287; in relation to religion, 287; Ukrainian support and, 284; US popular discourse on domestic issues of, 288

racialization: defined, 305n6, 336n42; of Islam, as enemy of Western civilization, 288; of Uyghur Muslims, 155

Racial Muslim, The (Aziz), 350

racial purity, political quests for, 14

racism: American racism, 59–61; anti-Black racism, 267; imperialism and, 306n8; Kazi on, 349; media coverage and, 291–92; Ukraine, 291; Ukrainian support as reflection of, 284; of Western media, 290–91

radicalization theory: effects of campaigns against, 35–37; Muslim focus of, 36–37; weaponizing of, 38, 40

Rajasthan, religious diversity in, 101–2

Rakhine State, 164, 165; Rohingya genocide in, 162, 328n112
Ramadan (Arabic), fast for, 307n33
Ramadan, fast for, 156
Rashid, Naeem, 237, 238–39, 243
Rashid, Talha, 239, 240
Rashtriya Swayamsevak Sangh (RSS), 104, 127
realpolitik: double standards and, 292; Muslim lives in, 290; Ukrainian support and, 284; Uyghur Muslim struggle and, 297
Reddy, Jaiwanth, 106
reeducation centers, 156
refugees: Arabs and Muslims as, 288; Blacks and People of Color as, 288–89; media coverage of Syrian, 289; media coverage of Ukrainian, 289; stigma of terrorism and nonwhite, 288–89; from Ukraine, 288, 289, 291
religion: double standards and, 292; free exercise of, 200; global support and divide on, 288; in relation to interests, 287; in relation to race, 287; as scapegoat, 141
religious diversity, in India, 99, 101–2
Representations of the Intellectual (Said), 72–73
resettlement of refugees, leftist media on racism in, 290
resistance: Fanon of organizing of, 299; media coverage on, 291; new forms of, 19; responses to Kashmiri resistance, 287; responses to Middle Eastern resistances, 42–43, 285; responses to Muslim-majority resistances, 42–43, 285; responses to Palestinian resist-ance, 287; responses to Ukrainian resistance, 42–43, 283–85, 287, 288; responses to Yemeni resistance, 287
Rise of Global Islamophobia in the War on Terror, The (Bakali and Hafez), 349
Roberts, John, 311n41
Robinson, Sugar Ray, 259
Rogan, Joe, 260–61
Rohingya genocide, 18, 161–70, 328n112
Rohingya Muslims, 18, 161–70, 168–69, 328n112
Rohingya refugees, 161–64, 168–69, 290
Roof, Dylann, 224, 227
Roosevelt, Franklin D., 61
Roy, Olivier, 190
Roya (Kashmiri Muslim activist), 128, 129, 130, 131
Rumi, 21
Rushdie, Salman, 99
Russell Tribunal, 132
Russia: Indian imperialism comparison to, 287; Ukraine's geography and, 288; war in Ukraine as imperialistic, 283, 288
Russian invasion of Ukraine, double standards in aftermath of, 289

Saadawi, Nawaal El, 29, 195
Sabi, Hamid, 157
Said, Edward: *Covering Islam*, 203; on exile, 163; on modern civilization, 229; on Occident/Orient discourse, 343n8; *Orientalism*, 69, 71, 74–76, 307n25; *Out of Place*, 12, 68, 307n27; political language of, 85; *Representations of the Intellectual*, 72–73; speech at UCLA, xi–xii, 68–69, 70–74, 82, 87
Salah, Mohamed, 19, 256–59
Salih, Tayeb, 199

Suu Kyi, Aung San, 164, 167

Syria: conflicts in, 345n40; refugees from, 87–92, 289

Syrian refugees, lack of humanizing media coverage on, 290

Tablighi Jamaat conference, 117–18

Tang Jiaxuan, 154

Tarrant, Brenton, 218, 219–30, 234, 251

Taseer, Aatish, 110

Taylor, Breonna, 266, 274

Taylor, Keeanga-Yamahtta, 268

terrorism: as inherent/exclusive to Islam, 93; linear lens of, 76; as preemptive tool against innocents, 35–37; reasons for consequences of, 5

terrorist identity: as inherent/exclusive to Muslims, 94; jihad (term) and, 307n1; Kashmiris and, 125–26, 129, 130; policies of fear and, 307n31; presumptions of, 35–37; public imagining of, 42, 287; War on Terror rendering, 16, 287

Traore, Bouna, 174–75, 179

Trump, Donald: anti-Muslim campaign of, 226–27; on Chinese genocide of Uyghur Muslims, 155; Islamophobia of, 81; MAGA slogan of, 318n46; Modi at rally for, 109, 111–12; Muslim Registry, 113; New Delhi massacre and, 114–16; populism of, 19; populist rhetoric of, 251; on racial shootings, 274; War of Terror and, 223

Trump administration: Muslim ban, 81; War on Terror and, 81–82

Trump v. Hawaii, 311n41

Truschke, Audrey, 103

Tunisia, 179

Turkey: anti-Muslim sentiment and systems in, 349; stateless Muslim populations in, 298

Tushnet, Mark, 311n42

Twain, Mark, 59

2020 Beirut explosion, 4–7, 10–11, 20

Ukraine: comparison of, 343n9; double standards and conflict in, 42, 292; geography of, 288; refugees from, 288, 291; responses to resistance in, 42–43, 283–85, 287, 292; struggle for self-determination of, 286; traditional divides on immigration and, 288

Ukrainian immigrants, comparison of, 290, 291

Ukrainians: as freedom fighters, 42; global support for, 288; as heroes, 287

UN Committee on the Elimination of Racial Discrimination, 143–44

underdog/imperial bully narratives: Muslim-majority nations and, 287; Ukraine and, 287, 288

UN High Commissioner for Human Rights (UNCHR), 167

UN Human Rights Council, 157

United Arab Emirates, Yemen and, 286

United Muslim Relief, 32

United States, 263–77; Afghanistan and, 291; expansion of War on Terror into China, 325n60; Iraq and, 291; Muslim identity inside the, 344n29; Muslim identity outside the, 344n29; news media outlets in, 345n38; PATRIOT Act, 16; political weaponization of Islamophobia by, 349; popular discourse on domestic racial issues, 288; proxies of, 349

Uttar Pradesh, 104–5, 119–20
Uyghur Muslims: Campaign for
    Uyghurs, 156–57, 298; in concentration
    camps, 143–44; diaspora of, 297; East
    Turkistan World Symposium, 297;
    ethnic cleansing of, 114, 137, 144–45,
    154, 299; human organ harvesting, 157;
    in Istanbul, 297; lack of global support
    for, 288; Olympic boycott campaign,
    145–46; persecution of, 18; self-deter-
    mination in, 140, 153, 154–55, 297, 298;
    struggles of, 297; surveillance of,
    137, 138–39, 142; War on Terror and,
    137–61

value: as assigned to Ukrainians, 284; as
    quantified by global support from
    governments, 284; as quantified by
    media, 284
Vedder, Eddie, 86–87
Veil and the Male Elite, The (Mernissi), 199
victim(s), 211–43; public imagining of, 234,
    235, 287; voices of, 14–15
View from Flyover Country, The (Kendzior),
    64
villain(s), 211–43; public imagining of, 234,
    235, 237, 287–88
violence of Islamophobia: Gujarat
    massacres, 110–12, 116; increase in, 44;
    in India, 107; New Delhi massacre,
    114–16; vigilantism, 16
Volpp, Leti, 14, 74–75, 78, 121, 305n6

Waheed, Nayyirah, 161
Wahhabi Islam, 58, 94
Wajir, Kenya, 17, 25–46; Al-Shabaab
    terrorist group and, 33–35; children
    and war in, 25–27

war: in Lebanon in 1980s, 292–93; media
    coverage on, 291; otherization process
    during, 311n42, 350
war crimes, against Algerians, 342n4
warfare, modern state creation and, 312n49
War on Terror: centrality of killing
    Arabs in, 282; crusades caused by, 5;
    crusades in China, 40, 78–79, 138, 145,
    152–54, 160, 282, 325n60; crusades in
    France, 40, 78–79, 181, 186–87, 282;
    crusades in India, 78–79, 104, 107, 282;
    crusades in Myanmar, 40, 78–79, 165,
    282; development of, 49–96; founda-
    tional myth of, 71; global expansion
    of, 37–38, 43, 76–77; global systems of
    subordination in, 17, 77; imperial gaze
    and, 34–35; Islamophobia and, 38–39,
    347; Kashmir and, 130–31; mandate of,
    282; Modi's BJP and, 107; Muslim
    identity and, 287, 344n31; Muslims as
    presumptive terrorist in, 35–37; news
    media outlets on, 5; 9/11 terrorist
    attacks and, 6–7; religious divide and,
    14; as rooted in Crusades-era narra-
    tives, 39–40; as seeking to divide,
    43–45; self-determination framed as
    terrorism by, 287, 288; struggles made
    by, 285, 292; surveillance of, 32–33; as
    unending, 66–68; Uyghur Muslims
    and, 18; in Wajir, Kenya, 17, 25–46
war victims, curating coverage of, 283
Werleman, CJ, 115
West, Cornel, 265
West Bank, quest for dignity in, 42, 286
Western civilization: Huntington on
    threat to, 14, 63; Islam as enemy of,
    37–38; racialization of Islam as enemy
    of, 13–14, 288, 291

Western interests, media serving interests of, 291–92

Western war, refugees from, 289

When We Were Arabs (Hayoun), 232

white: European as code for, 345n40; responses to killing of, 285

White, Dana, 261

whiteness: Americans privileged with, 20; of Arabs, 343n5; capitalism and, 60; Christianity and, 60; classification of, 59, 228; global impacts of, 292; media and power of, 290, 291; media serving interests of, 291–92; property value attached to, 59–60; public imaging and, 42–43

"Whiteness as Property" (Harris), 59

white race, belief in endangered status of, 335n27

white supremacist groups, slogan of, 335n27

white supremacy, 211–43; law and, 60–61; in New Zealand and Australia, 18, 222–26; racial order created by, 43; racism and, 271; in US, 103. *See also* Christchurch terror attacks

white victims, centering and seeing of, 285

woke, defined, 338n7

Xinjiang, 137–61; China's soft power campaign and, 145; digital surveillance of, 137, 138–39, 142, 147–48; as East Turkistan, 156; elimination program in, 18; mosques razed in, 151–52, 154; Uyghur Muslims persecution in, 18. *See also* China; East Turkistan

Yasin, Dar, 131

Yemen: media coverage on conflict in, 286; quest for dignity in, 42; Saudi Arabia and, 286; self-determination in, 285, 286; United Arab Emirates and, 286

Yemenis, lack of global support for, 288

Yu, Miles Maochun, 153

Yusef (Chinese university student), 146–47

Zahr, Amer, 270–71

Zeinab (Uyghur Muslim refugee), 151–52, 156–57, 158, 159, 160, 205

Zemmour, Eric, 289–90

Zinn, Howard, 57, 276

Zuboff, Shoshana, 169

Founded in 1893,
UNIVERSITY OF CALIFORNIA PRESS
publishes bold, progressive books and journals
on topics in the arts, humanities, social sciences,
and natural sciences—with a focus on social
justice issues—that inspire thought and action
among readers worldwide.

The UC PRESS FOUNDATION
raises funds to uphold the press's vital role
as an independent, nonprofit publisher, and
receives philanthropic support from a wide
range of individuals and institutions—and from
committed readers like you. To learn more, visit
ucpress.edu/supportus.